T0210570

Cloud Defense Strategies with Azure Sentinel

Hands-on Threat Hunting in Cloud Logs and Services

Marshall Copeland

Apress®

Cloud Defense Strategies with Azure Sentinel: Hands-on Threat Hunting in Cloud Logs and Services

Marshall Copeland
New Braunfels, TX, USA

ISBN-13 (pbk): 978-1-4842-7131-5   ISBN-13 (electronic): 978-1-4842-7132-2
https://doi.org/10.1007/978-1-4842-7132-2

Managing Director, Apress Media LLC: Welmoed Spahr
Acquisitions Editor: Smriti Srivastava
Development Editor: Laura Berendson
Coordinating Editor: Shrikant Vishwakarma

Cover designed by eStudioCalamar

Cover image designed by Pexels

Distributed to the book trade worldwide by Springer Science+Business Media LLC, 1 New York Plaza, Suite 4600, New York, NY 10004. Phone 1-800-SPRINGER, fax (201) 348-4505, e-mail orders-ny@springer-sbm.com, or visit www.springeronline.com. Apress Media, LLC is a California LLC and the sole member (owner) is Springer Science + Business Media Finance Inc (SSBM Finance Inc). SSBM Finance Inc is a **Delaware** corporation.

For information on translations, please e-mail booktranslations@springernature.com; for reprint, paperback, or audio rights, please email bookpermissions@springernature.com.

Apress titles may be purchased in bulk for academic, corporate, or promotional use. eBook versions and licenses are also available for most titles. For more information, reference our Print and eBook Bulk Sales web page at http://www.apress.com/bulk-sales.

Any source code or other supplementary material referenced by the author in this book is available to readers on GitHub via the book's product page, located at www.apress.com/978-1-4842-7131-5. For more detailed information, please visit http://www.apress.com/source-code.

Printed on acid-free paper

Dedicated to the memory of Marshal (Mark) Edwin Hilley.
"Mark was my brother in every way."
His family, friends, and extended family of first responders are
mourning his passing after a battle with COVID-19.
Mark Hilley was a Gulfport firefighter and Harrison
County Fire Rescue Battalion Chief.
District Chief Mark Hilley served more than
20 years and was also a veteran of
the U.S. Marine Corps. "Mark Hilley is the epitome of a
firefighter's firefighter. He devoted his life to public service."
Please keep Mark's family, wife Carla, children Natalie
and Cade, and Mark's mother Bonnie in your prayers.

—Marshall

Table of Contents

About the Author ix

About the Technical Reviewer xi

Acknowledgments xiii

Introduction xv

Part I 1

Chapter 1: Azure Sentinel Overview 3

    Azure Sentinel Platform Benefits 4

    Azure Deployment Recommendations 7

    Global Design and Cost Preparation 8

    Azure Sentinel Enablement 14

    Azure Logs 17

    Azure Metrics 19

    Data Ingestion 27

    Summary 38

Chapter 2: Other Azure Security Services 39

    Azure Log Analytics 39

    Azure Monitor 42

    Azure Security Center 55

    Enable Security 57

        Microsoft Defender for Endpoint 61

        Microsoft Defender for Identity 71

    Summary 75

Chapter 3: Getting Started with Azure Sentinel and XDR Capabilities............77

Security Operations Center with Azure Sentinel and XDR..........................78

Azure Sentinel SIEM and Azure Security...79

Azure Sentinel Prioritization...83

Microsoft 365 Defender, XDR 90

Security Road Map...101

Summary..103

Part II..105

Chapter 4: Sentinel Data Connection 107

Azure Control Plane and Data Plane 107

Native Data Connectors 111

Log Analytics Storage Options 123

Industry Leaders' Third-Party Data 125

Kusto Query Language..126

Threat Intelligence – TAXII Integration 136

Summary..143

Chapter 5: Threat Intelligence 145

Threat Intelligence 145

Communicating Using STIX and TAXII 150

Options for Threat Intelligence...154

Implementing Microsoft Threat Intelligence 155

Other Considerations for Threat Intelligence 157

Summary..161

Chapter 6: Multi-tenant Architecture 163

Azure Design: Single and Multi-tenant...164

Single-Workspace Considerations 172

Multi-workspace Considerations 174

Azure Security Platform 176

Summary... 182

Part III 183

Chapter 7: Kusto Query Language and Threat Hunting 185

Where Does Azure Data Reside.. 185

Kusto Query Language Training 189

Introduction to the Kusto Query Language 192

Threat Hunting with Azure Sentinel 205

Summary... 211

Chapter 8: Introduction to the MITRE Matrix 213

MITRE ATT&CK 214

CISO Summary... 231

Cybersecurity Threats 235

Current Security Facts 237

Microsoft Security Intelligence Report (SIR)... 238

2021 Verizon Data Breach Investigations Report (DBIR) Update 240

Ponemon Institute: IBM Sponsored 244

Secure Cloud Steps... 247

Azure Cloud Networking, Encryption, and Data Storage.................................... 248

Identity Multi-factor Authentication (MFA).. 248

Software Is a Key Vulnerability 249

OWASP, Security Development Lifecycle (SDLC).. 249

Finding Cloud Blind Spots Improves Your Network Security Knowledge............. 250

NVD Use with ITIL/Change Management Patching 251

Security Responsibility Model 252

Summary... 254

Chapter 9: Azure Sentinel Operations...**255**

Modern Security Operations Center Structure 255

Workbooks 263

Playbooks.. 267

Notebooks 272

Log Management 273

Summary.. 279

Index...**281**

About the Author

Marshall Copeland is a senior consultant focused on cybersecurity in Azure public cloud. Marshall Copeland currently works at Microsoft Corporation supporting enterprise customers' security teams using Azure security services, Azure Sentinel, Azure Security Center, and Azure Defender for hybrid network security management and data protection. He previously worked in cloud security roles at Optiv Security and Salesforce.

About the Technical Reviewer

 **Brian O'Hara** is an information security professional who has been supporting the cyber defense efforts of small businesses and large enterprises for more than 12 years. He has held a variety of Security Operations Center roles with responsibilities including security architecture, threat hunting, detection engineering, digital forensics, and incident response. He maintains multiple industry certifications and participates regularly in local cyber community events and conferences. He currently works as a consultant performing incident response and improving Security Operations Center efficiency through SIEM configuration auditing, alert tuning, and detection engineering.

Acknowledgments

Marshall Copeland would like to dedicate this book to the memory of Marshal (Mark) Edwin Hilley. His family, friends, and extended family of first responders are mourning his passing after a battle with COVID-19. Mark Hilley was a Gulfport firefighter and Harrison County Fire Rescue Battalion Chief. District Chief Mark Hilley served more than 20 years and was also a veteran of the U.S. Marine Corps. "Mark Hilley is the epitome of a firefighter's firefighter. He devoted his life to public service." Please keep Mark's family in your prayers. Special acknowledgment to Brian O'Hara, a true security professional with great cyber defense insight. Thank you, Brian. Thank you to Shrikant Vishwakarma, Smriti Srivastava, and the Apress team for your dedication to this publication.

Introduction

The Microsoft Azure Sentinel engineering team has brought their best security work in Azure Sentinel, the cloud-native SIEM (Security Information and Event Management). The need for the next-generation defense is to combat cybercriminals and nation states that continue to threaten human health, steal intellectual property, and terrorize businesses. Plain but certainly not simple, this is cyber war. Global cybercrime events continue to publicly remind governments, businesses, and security leaders that digital criminal efforts are ever-evolving, complex, and never-ending. Criminals in foreign countries are protected. Cyberwarfare from nation states is supported by an endless supply of resources and time.

This hands-on guidance in this book will provide you with a comprehensive understanding, enabling you, in minutes, to save money by integrating with data you already have and start defending your business today.

Target Audience

The following security roles will benefit from this book:

- Security Operations Center (SOC) team members
- Blue and red team members
- Cloud security analysts
- Network and server administrators
- IT professionals

This book provides excellent guidance for security and IT team members who are responsible for security attack mitigation and respond to cybercriminal attacks.

Summary of Contents

A brief description of subject matter in each chapter:

Part I

Includes Chapters 1, 2, and 3. You enable Azure Sentinel and begin allowing security data into your services, integrate other Azure security services with Azure Sentinel and each other, and learn how these services extend the layered data security.

Part II

Includes Chapters 4, 5, and 6. You are provided guidance that includes security metrics, logs, and events based on limited data and not duplicate storage cost. Details about security threat intelligence (TI) providers and ingestion into Azure Sentinel and consideration for supporting Azure Sentinel for a global business using global Azure regions are also discussed.

Part III

Includes Chapters 7, 8, and 9. Threat hunters with Azure built-in templates, automation (SOAR), and customized Kusto Query Language (KQL) queries for new threats, custom watch lists, and security defenses are discussed. There is an introduction to the MITRE organization and how it is supported in Azure Sentinel and daily, weekly, and monthly best practices for successful operations with Azure Sentinel.

PART I

CHAPTER 1

Azure Sentinel Overview

This chapter provides an accelerated review of Azure Sentinel from an insider's perspective and guidance on how to install it after a quick overview of features. Some of the security features include AI (Artificial Intelligence) security and Security Orchestration, Automation, and Response (SOAR) capabilities. Necessary prerequisite recommendations are discussed, and then we proceed to the onboarding guide to adopt Azure Sentinel as "cloud native." Cloud-native services, such as Azure Sentinel, are native to the cloud and are enabled as a security service using a Platform as a Service (PaaS).

In this chapter you learn

- Azure Sentinel platform benefits

- Global design and cost considerations

- Azure Sentinel enablement

- Data ingestion

Throughout this book, topics and guidance include alignment with your business security team's cybersecurity framework and other security references to align where necessary to support the business.

A challenge in adopting the cloud is changing foundational adoption of cloud-native services first. Adoption of cloud services challenges the "status quo" of current IT operations. With your current on-premises infrastructure, either your business or IT has specific software dedicated to support security workloads for the traditional data center. Moving to the cloud includes using cloud servers to support this new software-defined network (SDN) and cloud infrastructure.

3

© Marshall Copeland 2021
M. Copeland, *Cloud Defense Strategies with Azure Sentinel*, https://doi.org/10.1007/978-1-4842-7132-2_1

Azure Sentinel Platform Benefits

You should begin the discovery of features that benefit the business using a well-defined foundation of Azure Sentinel. The first concept to learn is the level of functionality that helps position the security team and the dexterity of the service provided. Azure Sentinel is a cloud service that supports security teams' requirements for the enterprise Security Information and Event Management (SIEM) platform. Azure Sentinel accumulates many different streams of data (i.e., metrics and logs) from Azure services like activities from users, computers, applications, virtual machines (VMs), and other devices. The data can be correlated from Azure cloud, another cloud (i.e., AWS, Google, IBM, etc.), and an on-premises data center. It includes software-enabled connectors to onboard many third-party security solutions like Amazon Web Services, Barracuda Web Application Firewall, Palo Alto Networks, and VMware ESXi. Additionally, there are SOAR and Artificial Intelligence (AI) to help analyze large volumes of data across an enterprise deployment.

Now that you have a definition of Azure Sentinel, the business benefits gained from security features included that focus on SIEM services can be summarized as follows:

- Collect data.

- Detect anomalies.

- Investigate events.

- Respond appropriately.

With the Azure Sentinel definition in place, you will continue to learn about the benefits for the business. The next few topics help the business understand the industry benefits of Azure Sentinel.

Azure Sentinel is a cloud service. One of the major business benefits of Azure Sentinel is the solution is an Azure cloud service and, being cloud native, supports the reduction of resources to update software and hardware. Many current solutions in the market support the adoption of the cloud from a traditional dedicated hardware or virtual machine (VM) deployment model.

Cloud services remove the requirement to consider hardware component repairs or hardware version updates, which always take up a large part of the line item budget. In addition to the license for the operating system (OS) hosting dedicated hardware, other resources include people and time to patch and update the underlying OS. Azure Sentinel is always up to date and does not require patching, and new features are added without taking the system off-line. This is a major cost benefit that allows subject matter experts (SMEs) to focus on learning Azure Sentinel, detecting anomalies, and leveraging all the security features to protect the business.

Integration with other platforms is a great business benefit. The integration of data from other services is clearly defined and discussed, and you are guided through the implementation of both third-party programs and Microsoft services. Microsoft and Azure cloud services that are easily integrated include

- Microsoft 365 sources like Office 365

- Microsoft 365 Defender (rebranded Microsoft Threat Protection)

- Microsoft Defender for Endpoint (rebranded Microsoft Defender Advanced Threat Protection)

- Microsoft Defender for Office 365 (rebranded Office 365 Advanced Threat Protection)

- Microsoft Defender for Identity (rebranded Azure Advanced Threat Protection)

- Azure Security Center (ASC)

Integrated data include Azure events, logs, diagnostics, and performance metrics (i.e., identity, network, virtual machines, Azure host, etc.).

You will complete exercises to enable many of the Azure cloud services and also learn about integration of many of the third-party data sources.

Note   You can learn more and read about updated information at `https://azure.microsoft.com/en-us/services/azure-sentinel/`.

The benefit of this SIEM solution as a security service should not be overlooked. It allows team members to refocus on deployment in one or more geographical Azure regions and becoming a Sentinel subject matter expert (SME). The integration of AI and automation improves the effectiveness in reduction of security alerts. To be really effective requires sufficient compute core resources (CPU and memory) with large amounts of data for analysis. Azure Sentinel accelerates by scaling up the core resources as the ingestion of data is increased to best support the velocity of data provided from Azure and on-premises services.

Ease of deployment for a single tenant does require planning considerations that affect the metric and log collection process. The process often may begin with the collection from VMs in an Infrastructure as a Service (IaaS) design. Data is written to an Azure Log Analytics workspace that is used by Azure Monitor, Azure Security Center, and Azure Sentinel. Additional Azure services are discussed in Chapter 2. Once the enterprise deployment expands to multiple geographical regions and on-premises, then the design considerations require more planning time. However, the Sentinel service provides an easier process to connect data from many other products through proxy or directly. You can review a simplified architecture in Figure 1-1.

Microsoft Azure Security Reference

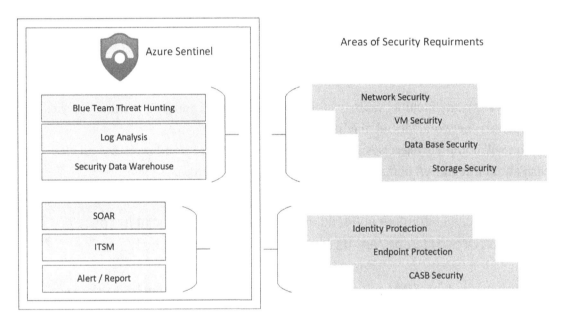

Figure 1-1. *Microsoft Azure security reference with Azure Sentinel*

The next section provides discussion and guidance to prepare for Azure Sentinel service implementation with a few recommendations to prevent missteps that require architecting.

Azure Deployment Recommendations

Connection to the same Log Analytics workspace used by Azure Monitor is very often a first step. The guidance for Monitor and Security Center to share the same workspace is detailed in Chapter 2. An additional consideration would be proximity to the Azure region that hosts most of your business data. If the business is in one of the US regions or in the United Kingdom, the selection is less complex. Sentinel supports connection to many additional Microsoft solutions that may be used by the business today.

Additional Microsoft solutions include

- Azure Active Directory (ADD) Premium

- Azure Defender for Identity

- Azure Defender alerts from Azure Security Center

- Microsoft Cloud App Security

This is a list to help you plan for additional collections for data analytics including Microsoft 365 Defender and other Microsoft 365 sources. In addition, most Common Event Format (CEF) log collection is supported, as well as other industry standards like syslog collections.

Azure Sentinel does not recreate alerts that are created in other Microsoft solutions, such as Azure Defender, but does present the information. Sentinel is a single view used to correlate all data shared across the enterprise.

Requirements include access to a dev/test environment for testing and creation. All production is deployed using the CI/CD pipeline. Requirements include

- Compliance standards for administrators

  - Separation of duties

  - Least privilege

- Network isolation

  - Limited public IP address

- Audit of Azure resources

Deploy using "cloud-native" applications first, like Azure Sentinel. Then decide to use Azure services that provide "like" services that were used on-premises. Often, in the adoption of cloud-native services, like Azure Monitor, Azure Security Center, and

Azure Sentinel, you do not have to manage the infrastructure. The need for updates for software and hardware is removed, and the SME can focus on security for business applications and data.

Companies adopting Microsoft Azure cloud solutions are often following an Agile deployment model. The best way to incorporate Azure Sentinel as a deployment iteration is as a pipeline "module." To help with the Agile deployment, a visual guide on adoption with a timeline, in Figure 1-2, is provided with Agile deployment support.

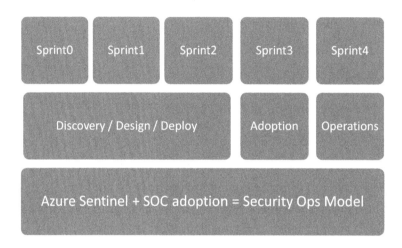

Figure 1-2. *Azure Sentinel Agile deployment example supporting the security operations model*

Global Design and Cost Preparation

Select an Azure region that is the same as that of the majority of the Azure IaaS and PaaS services used for the business. Azure Sentinel can be run in most (but not all) regions that support the Log Analytics workspace. The few exceptions are China, Germany, and other countries with strict sovereign data requirements. This is an important factor because the work performed by Azure Sentinel includes analysis and interaction with the Log Analytics workspace. Data generated includes

- Analytics rules
- Incidents/customer data
- Bookmarks
- Other data

Note   The current list of Azure regions that support Log Analytics can be found at `https://azure.microsoft.com/global-infrastructure/services/?products=monitor`.

Often the cost of a solution is not clearly defined because the total cost of ownership includes hard cost and soft cost. A hard cost example would be the cost of data storage, in US dollars per gigabyte. A soft cost does include many current processes and choices. An example of a soft cost is the cost to ramp up on Azure Sentinel skills for the security team. Additional soft cost areas include

- Incident management (within Sentinel or integration in the current ITSM)

- Redundant third-party services

- Time to transfer security skills

- Cybersecurity Kill Chain

- Other security knowledge

Often a seasoned security team is aware of additional resources needed to maintain and improve cyber knowledge. However, if this is the first SIEM cloud service design, an additional consideration using Azure Sentinel is the need to understand the industry-standard Lockheed Martin Cyber Kill Chain and the MITRE Adversarial Tactics, Techniques, and Common Knowledge (ATT&CK) framework. First, you need to understand Cyber Kill Chain as shown in Figure 1-3.

The first introduction to the criminal activity stages during an attack was provided by Lockheed Martin. The stages—from left to right, reconnaissance, weaponization, all the way through command and control (C2)—are used by security researchers as a method to reference actions that constitute a cyber-attack attempt. Detection of a cyber-attack and then deterring it from being successful is the main goal of the security team. The different Security Operations Centers (SOCs) work together and continue to stop cyber-attacks by breaking the kill chain earlier in the model, closer to stage 1 or 2 in the kill chain model.

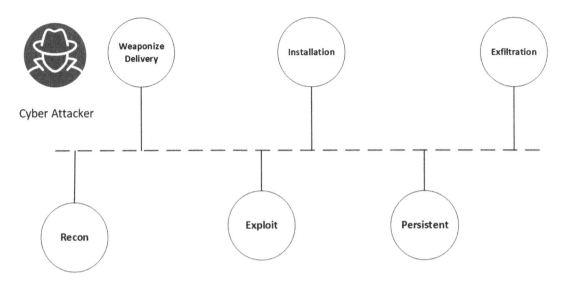

Figure 1-3. *Cyber Kill Chain stages for reference*

Note   The updated information on the kill chain and persistent threats from data collected by Lockheed Martin can be found at `www.lockheedmartin.com/en-us/capabilities/cyber/cyber-kill-chain.html#`.

The next discussions include a way to better prepare for attackers, the tools used to attack, and what businesses they attack that lead to the MITRE ATT&CK framework.

The framework is a global knowledge-based reference on cybersecurity adversary tactics that is always updated as a community effort. It provides specific threat models and methodologies across government and private sectors. This type of reference is invaluable that your security blue team hunters should leverage. The ATT&CK matrix (Figure 1-4) provides information that follows the kill chain. The matrix shows documented patterns of how known attackers have used cyber-attack methods and tools to complete a successful cyber breach. Both the kill chain and ATT&CK matrix are merely starting points to understand how bad actors and cyber hackers attack your business. Azure Sentinel uses the data collected and leverages the ATT&CK matrix data along with other technical threat indicators (TTIs).

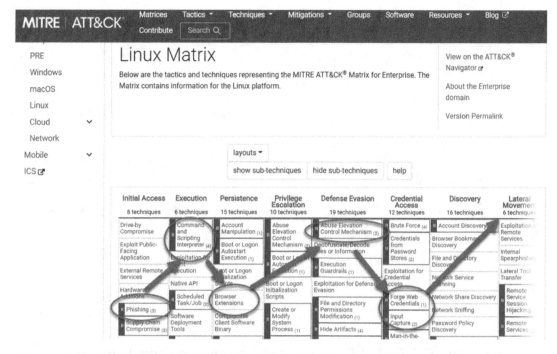

Figure 1-4. *MITRE ATT&CK framework example using the Linux OS*

Throughout this book, you will be reunited with the MITRE ATT&CK framework as you learn about the Azure Sentinel hunting performed. The data covered by the framework can be customized for the type of platform your business has in place, as shown in Figure 1-5. The ATT&CK matrix supports data gathered from previous cybersecurity attacks depending on the operating system (OS) and based on the public cloud.

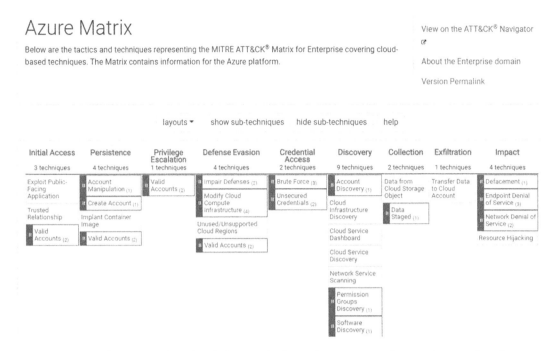

Figure 1-5. *The MITRE ATT&CK matrix focusing on attacks on Azure cloud*

Azure Sentinel data storage cost: The use of Azure Sentinel does not have a direct monthly fee to draw down Azure credits. The cost begins when you ingest data feeds to leverage Microsoft cybersecurity AI and automation. If you created a new (empty) Analytics workspace and want to keep the cost to a minimum, then select a few data connectors to reduce the data storage cost.

You should be aware that Microsoft allows the use of some data connectors that have low cost, and I've read documentation that leads you to believe it has no cost, but that is not entirely true. Fist, all logs that are ingested by Sentinel and go through the workflow are adding to the cost of traffic ingestion. Second, some of the cost is included in many of the premium SKUs (like Azure Active Directory P2/E5) that you have already purchased. The data from the following connectors listed has minimum storage cost:

- Azure Activity (Azure platform logs)

- Azure Active Directory Identity Protection (AAD P2)

- Azure Information Protection

- Azure Advanced Threat Protection (only alerts)

- Azure Security Center (only alerts)

- Microsoft Cloud App Security (only alerts)

- Microsoft Defender Advanced Threat Protection (monitoring agent alerts)

- Office 365 (logs)

You need to consider the cost of data connectors and cost of storage into the Log Analytics workspace. A free or low-cost option is good. However, for any SIEM solution to be successful, many other Sentinel data connectors are needed. Data streaming, processing, and storing charges are incurred for other connectors, for example:

- Ingesting data into Log Analytics

- Sending data through Azure Sentinel

- Optional use of Logic Apps for automation

- Optional running of your own machine learning models

- Optional running of any VMs as data collectors

If your Azure subscription uses pay-as-you-go (PAYG), shown in Figure 1-6, you pay a fixed price per gigabyte (GB) consumed, and it is charged on a per-day basis. Microsoft has provided the option to use discounts based on larger volumes of data. Choosing a different pricing tier to save money is a manual process.

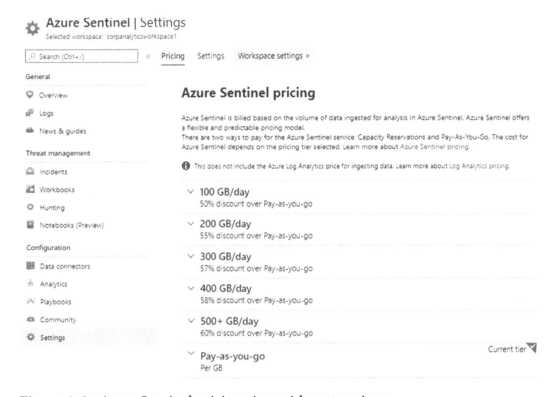

Figure 1-6. *Azure Sentinel pricing view with cost savings*

Azure Sentinel Enablement

With all the prerequisites in place that you have learned so far in this chapter, it is now the appropriate time, and a little anti-climactic, to enable Microsoft Azure Sentinel as your new cloud Security Incident and Event Management (SIEM) solution. In fact, there should be no events or data to review until you follow the guide to enable specific Sentinel data connectors.

It is always a best recommendation to have a business driver with specific success criteria rather than simply creating an instance and reviewing the features. If you are new to Azure Sentinel or to a SIEM solution, then a valid proof of concept (POC) may be the next step. Please use the following POC success criteria to enable Sentinel, data connection, and security features to validate Azure Sentinel security benefits.

The Azure Sentinel proof of concept (POC) includes the following areas for data connection and business security benefits as shown in Table 1-1. Note the remainder of this chapter is used to enable data collection and prepare for additional security workflows to provide best recommendations and guidance.

Table 1-1. *Azure Sentinel POC testing criteria example*

Sentinel Feature	Included	Additional License	Business Benefit
Data connectors	Yes	No Azure/yes third party	Data and KQL
--	Yes	No	
Azure host logs	Yes	No	
Azure IaaS/PaaS	Yes	Depends	

The following exercise enables the Log Analytics workspace in the Azure region for the business and then enables the Azure Sentinel cloud solution. Select an Azure region that supports the Log Analytics workspace, ideally located where the main servers and data reside. You can review the Azure regions at `https://azure.microsoft.com/en-us/global-infrastructure/services/?products=monitor&regions=all`.

Collecting data from the Azure platform, Azure Active Directory, and business applications running 24/7 does suggest the need to analyze issues faster and create alerts that are actionable for the Security Operations Center (SOC) teams. Logging of hardware-specific data and hypervisor information and alerts is managed by Microsoft, and everything else is up to the Azure subscription owner.

To better understand how the data is categorized in the data platform, which is included as part of your Azure services, you need to learn where data is collected and how it is aggregated. The more challenging requirement for the security team is the understanding of where, inside Azure, do data streams come from. More importantly, you need to know the costs associated with analyzing and storing the data. The virtual machine in the cloud still has a financial cost when running. The VM has virtual CPU, memory, network, and data storage requirements, just like a VM running in your on-premises data center. Other on-premises monitoring includes applications for application analysis, visualization of user connections, dashboard views, and log monitoring and security alerting.

There are two major categories of data described from the Azure Monitor data platform:

- Logs
- Metrics

These two types are used as labels or descriptors for the types of information that are collected and aggregated from a variety of sources inside Azure. Both logs and metrics are collected for utilization through Azure Monitor. Refer to Table 1-2 to review a few characteristic differences between logs and metrics.

Table 1-2. *Characteristics to identify metric data and log data*

Logs	Metrics	Characteristic
Numeric and text	Numeric	Data type
Service workload driven	Regular intervals	Collection times
Log Analytics/Monitor	Metrics Explorer	Where to review in Azure Portal

As your cloud network team members add more VNets and IP subnets, traffic flow needs to be measured and alerted as the cloud network expands. When projects are created to include virtual machines and applications, the insight for server and application health should be analyzed, and alerts need to be enabled. You need to consider the maturity of application services in the cloud. Please review the information in Figure 1-7 for a visual representation of the Azure Monitor services. This diagram is used to demonstrate information aggregation as part of the Azure data platform.

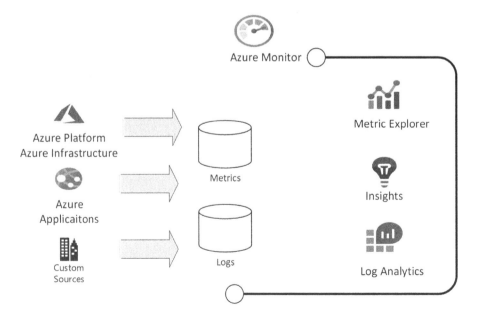

Figure 1-7. *Azure data platform visual representation*

More Azure IaaS and PaaS service metrics and logs are added for analysis. These are services that are requested using the Azure Portal journey (part of the deployment wizard) that collects input and makes the services available. As the Azure architect or operations team, you did not build the VMs, network, and applications for any of these services. However, the Security Operations Center (SOC) is still required to monitor and secure the services. When any of the services are not performing optimally or unauthorized data access is being attempted, alerts are required to inform the responsible team. The SOC team should be informed of changes affecting networking, systems, and applications to account for anomaly data. Now you have been provided some of the best methods to leverage Azure Monitor.

Note   Azure Functions is marketed as a serverless service, which means the service runs on a VM core that you do not manage but that VM writes log and metric data in Azure you must use.

You learned that the Azure platform sends logs and metrics to Azure Log Analytics workspaces (one or more) and manages archives or storage and Azure event hubs. Now you continue to gain insight into the platform logs and metrics and its sources of data.

Azure Logs

Azure Monitor is an up-to-date cloud-native service and has the advantage of being the single cloud solution that your Azure operations team can utilize for analysis and alerting on the correlated data derived from the many cloud data sources. Data that are classified in Azure as logs are numeric or text (or both) with information like a time stamp and label. You may read online documentation that refers to diagnostic logs, but the name has changed to resource logs. However, there may still be a little confusion because the configuration label is "Diagnostic Settings" in Azure, as used to enable the collection of resource logs.

Most operational data are stored to a resource log and can be used by Azure Monitor to perform data analysis. As a single example of the complexity log data, let us review platform logs. An updated Azure Monitor Agent (AMA) consolidates agents and writes to logs in Azure Monitor stored in a Logs Analytics workspace, and data is written in a time that matches the system load. Read more about the AMA agent at the URL: `https://docs.microsoft.com/en-us/azure/azure-monitor/agents/azure-monitor-agent-overview?tabs=PowerShellWindows`. A busy workload with many clients connected or reports being created generates a large volume of data, for storage in the workspace. Please review the information in Table 1-3 to gain a better understanding of the Azure Monitor log sources.

Table 1-3. *Azure data metrics, logs, and sources*

Source	Data	Description (Log Analytics)
Tenant and subscription	Azure Active Directory audit logs, diagnostics, management groups, and subscriptions	Integrated AAD logs with Azure Monitor for each directory.
	Activity logs	Install Log Analytics (AMA updated agent); to be written automatically in a native store.
Azure resources (cloud only)	Resource diagnostics including resource logs	Configure diagnostic settings for data diagnostics to be written.
	Monitoring solutions	Writes data collected to workspace.
	Metrics (logs)	Platform metrics for Azure Monitor; can connect to Azure Sentinel.
	Azure table storage	Azure storage resources (blob).
Virtual machines	Agent data	Linux and Windows OSs (with Azure agent installed), events, performance data and logs.
	Monitoring solutions	Various solutions' data written for log collection.
	System Center Operations Manager (SCOM)	Connect ops manager management group to Azure Monitor.
Applications	Requests and exceptions	Requests, page views, exceptions.
	Usage and performance	Requests, browserTimings, performanceCounters.
	Trace data	Distributed tracing tables.
	Availability test	Summary data of availabilityResults table.

A cloud operations team member can create a diagnostic setting to allow platform logs and metrics to different locations. Please review the following note.

Note   The security team should be aware that each Azure resource can support a separate diagnostic setting, one per Azure service, and each Azure service has different options for log destinations.

Azure Metrics

Data that are classified in Azure as metrics will always be numeric. All metric data collected at a point in time includes needed information including a time stamp, name, or other identifications. Metrics are most effective for correlating data and finding trends in data over a span of time and used to create a baseline. Metrics are critical for quick alerting on issues detected as a deviation of the baseline or an anomaly when compared to that baseline. You should become familiar with the level classification of data and metrics. Please refer to Table 1-4 for Azure data classification.

Table 1-4. *Sources of Azure Monitor metrics*

Source	Data	Description (Log Analytics)
Platform metrics	Azure resources for health and performance: every 60 seconds	Distinct metric set per resource (auto-configuration for VM host)
Guest OS metrics	VM OS: Windows/Linux	VM metrics must be enabled by VM agent extension: Windows Diagnostics Extension (WAD)/InFlux Data Telegraf Agent (Linux)
Application metrics	Enable Application Insights for data	Detects application performance, issues, and trending usage including server response time and browser exceptions
Custom metrics	Enabled in custom applications (Application Insights custom data)	API usage (auto-configuration)

Metric resources are stored for 90 days for most sources but not all metric sources. That is true for guest OS metrics created when you enable them for the Azure Resource Manager (ARM) Windows OS and Linux OS VM, so the monitored metrics are in this 90-day timeline. Diagnostic data is collected in Azure storage divided into tables and blobs through a "data sync" process. If data is needed for a longer time because of regulatory compliance, additional data sync processes are needed to move the necessary metrics.

The Log Analytics agent collects some of the guest OS metrics, like performance counters, and sends them to a Microsoft Azure Log Analytics workspace for only 31 days. You can extend the time to 2 years, but beyond that timeline, you need to select a long-term storage option using automation scripts that move metrics into Azure Blob Storage. Application Insights log-based metrics for event logs are stored for 90 days. You can refer to Azure Monitor service limits – Azure Monitor | Microsoft Docs for the Log Analytics storage limits.

Next, you learn to use Azure Monitor as a single view to correlate all the individual services available and performance data. As you enable an Azure service, Monitor is automatically enabled to provide a view of data for analysis using both metrics and logs specific to the service you just enabled. Azure data foundation includes the workflow for logs, metrics, and their data sources that are collected. The service can write to a Log Analytics workspace (logs) or a metrics database. Depending on the Azure service, Azure Monitor writes to both Log Analytics logs and metrics database.

Note   If you would like an extensive documentation on Azure Log Analytics and VM metrics and logs, please enjoy a free preview of another of my books, *Cyber Security on Azure: An IT Professional's Guide to Microsoft Azure Security Center*, ISBN 978-1-4842-6531-4, at `https://apress.com`.

ENABLE AZURE SENTINEL

This exercise guides you through the creation of a Log Analytics workspace in an Azure region and then enablement of Azure Sentinel in an Azure subscription. Once Sentinel is enabled, continue to other exercises for data connection.

1. Log in to Azure Portal using one of your subscriptions. If you have multiple subscriptions, select the one that is used to support Azure Sentinel. You need the Azure Contributor role according to Role-Based Access Control.

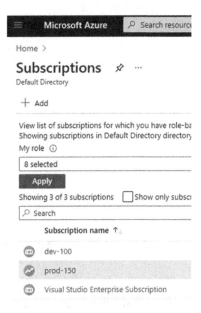

2. Select the subscription; in this example, the prod-150 subscription is selected. Search for Log Analytics workspace. If this is your first workspace, you should see an option to create a Log Analytics workspace. Select that option.

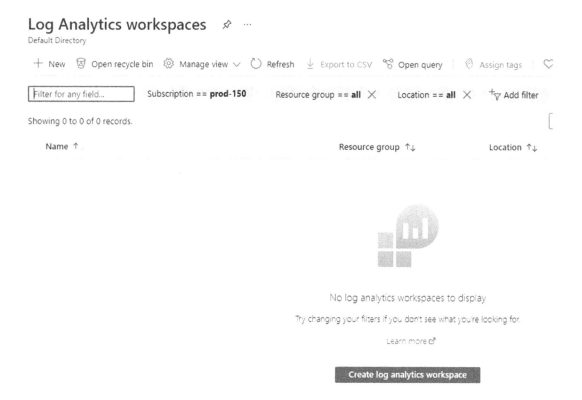

3. Enter the resource group name that follows your Azure naming convention. Enter the instance details of the Log Analytics workspace. The name is the name that is used by Azure Sentinel in this exercise. Select the Pricing Tier button to move to the next journey screen.

Create Log Analytics workspace   ...

Basics   Pricing tier   Tags   Review + Create

> ⓘ A Log Analytics workspace is the basic management unit of Azure Monitor Logs. There are specific considerations
> should take when creating a new Log Analytics workspace. Learn more

With Azure Monitor Logs you can easily store, retain, and query data collected from your monitored resources ir
and other environments for valuable insights. A Log Analytics workspace is the logical storage unit where your lc
is collected and stored.

Project details

Select the subscription to manage deployed resources and costs. Use resource groups like folders to organize ar
manage all your resources.

Subscription * ⓘ

    prod-150

└──── Resource group * ⓘ

    (New) prod-security-siem-rg
    Create new

Instance details

Name * ⓘ

    securityprod150

Region * ⓘ

    West US

Note   *The same Log Analytics workspace should be used for Azure Monitor and
Azure Security Center as discussed in Chapter 2.*

---

4. From this screen, select the small down arrow to the right of the Pricing tier field to reveal the pricing tier options. For this exercise, we select the **Pay-as-you-go** model from 2018. Select the Tag button to move to the next journey screen.

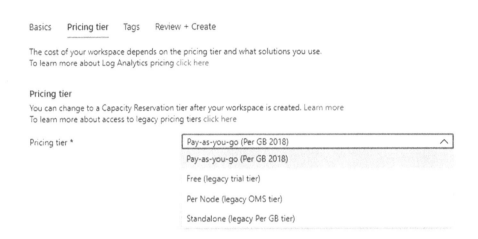

5. Enter the appropriate Azure tags to identify this resource for billing and troubleshooting. You have the option to enter multiple tags for more efficient billing and troubleshooting. Select the Review and Create button to create the Log Analytics workspace.

6. Once the workspace is created, you can search for it from the Azure Portal view. You may have more than one Log Analytics workspace displayed. Note: If you have enabled Azure Security Center previously, a Default-Workspace-123... name may be displayed. *In Chapter 2, you learn how to enable Azure Security Center to use the same Log Analytics workspace for Azure Sentinel.*

7. In Azure Portal, search for Azure Sentinel and select the icon.

8. To enable Azure Sentinel for the first time, select the correct Log Analytics workspace.

Azure Sentinel 🖈 ⋯
Default Directory

+ New   ⊙ Open classic view   ⚙ Manage view ⌄   ↻ Refresh   ↓ Export to CSV   ⅋ Open query

| Filter for any field... | Subscription == **2 of 3 selected**   Resource group == **all** ✕   Location =

Showing 1 to 1 of 1 records.

☐ Name ↑↓	Resource group ↑↓
☐ 🛡 prod-loganalytics-wrksp	prod-security-logs-rg

9. You should see a screen that displays the Azure Sentinel Overview landing
    page. If this is the first time you enable Sentinel, there should not be any events
    or alerts.

Note   *You may need to use multiple Log Analytics workspaces to support the
European General Data Protection Regulation (GDPR) and other compliance
standards. Data remains in the Azure regions to support privacy laws.*

Now that you have completed this exercise, you have enabled the Azure Sentinel service in
your Azure subscription. Continue through this chapter to enable Sentinel data connectors and
follow the guides to ingest Azure data for cybersecurity threats and anomalies.

The next section provides guidance and considerations that support the connection to both
Azure and Azure services. The final set of exercises in this chapter show you how to connect
the data sources.

Data Ingestion

You can use Azure Portal anytime and search for Azure Sentinel and select it to reveal the Sentinel Overview page. Before you begin to see events, alerts, and incidents, you need to go through the steps to connect the log and metric sources provided by Azure from the Data connectors pane.

Once you have connected some of the data sources provided by Microsoft Azure in the next exercise, you will take a tour through the Azure Sentinel information summary to become familiar with the interface.

You can also configure Azure Sentinel to work directly with all the data sources from the Azure framework and IaaS and PaaS services that include logs and metric data in the Log Analytics workspace. You also configure Azure Sentinel data connectors to consume data from

- Microsoft security events

- Azure Security Center

- Azure Active Directory

- Comment Event Format

These are the Sentinel data connectors you will use in the configuration of data feeds. However, there are more than 100 (and counting) data connectors you will be aware of for Azure deployment. This exercise walks you through the most common data connectors, and then you can use the same processes to connect to other data.

ENABLE AZURE SENTINEL DATA CONNECTORS

The prerequisites require "Contributor" permissions to the Log Analytics workspace and "Reader" permissions to any subscription logs that stream into Azure Sentinel.

1. From Azure Portal, search for Azure Sentinel and select the icon to open the Overview page. On the left menu, scroll down and select Data connectors.

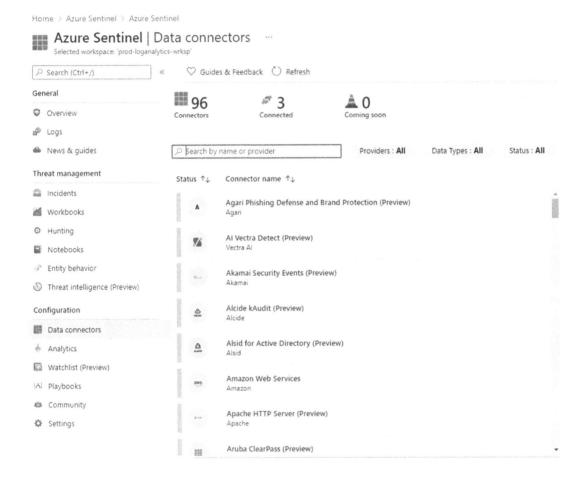

2. Your screen should have no data connectors active (this example displays three connected). Search for or scroll down to find and select Azure Activity. On the far-right pane, select Open connector page.

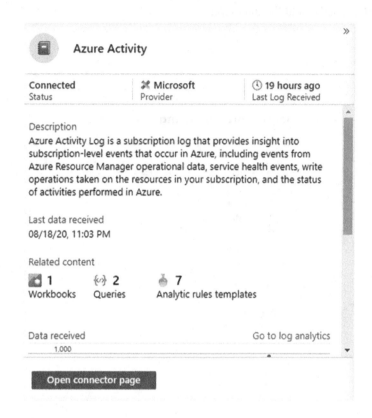

3. From the Data connectors Azure Activity window, look at the far right and select the Connect option. The status will change from Disconnected to Connected. Data from the Azure Activity log is now connected for near-real-time streaming into Azure Sentinel.

4. You need to confirm the event data collected from the Windows servers. This is accomplished from the Log Analytics workspace. However, you can navigate to the data location by selecting Settings on the bottom-left menu. Then select Workspace settings at the top menu.

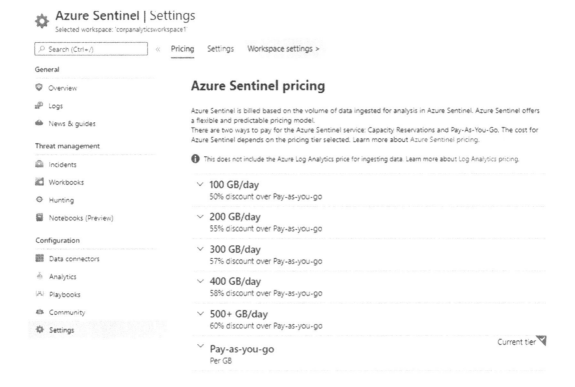

5. This selection takes you to the Log Analytics workspace. Scroll down the menu to Settings and select Advanced settings.

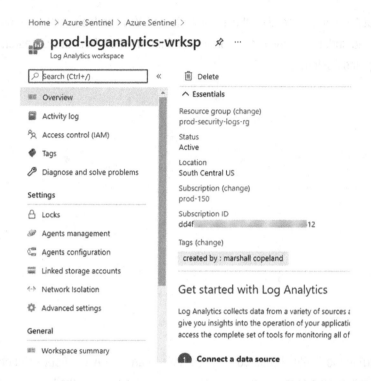

6. Once the Advanced settings pane opens, click Data, and it defaults to Windows Event Logs. From the search bar, start typing the word "Application" and select it from the results displayed.

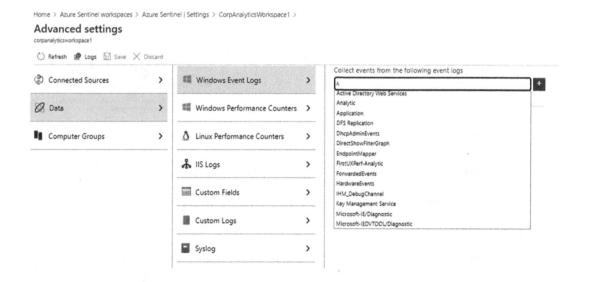

7. Select Application and click the + button to add. You can leave all the defaults checked under columns Error, Warning, and Information. Repeat the search for Setup and System.

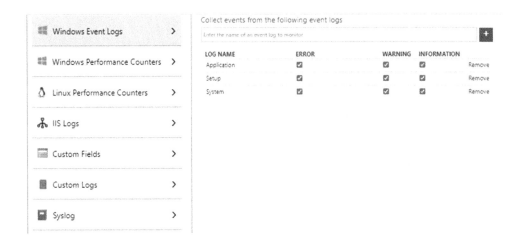

8. Return to the Sentinel Data connectors view. Search for Azure Active Directory or scroll down on the menu. Select Open connector page on the bottom right.

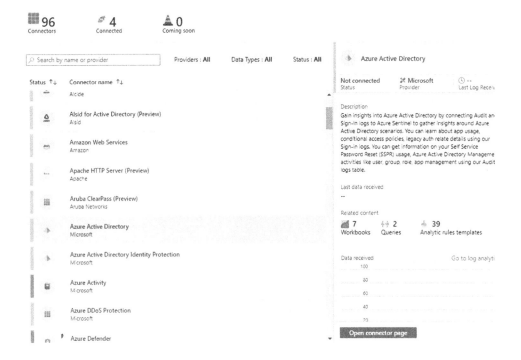

9. Validate the prerequisites have been met. Notice the check marks beside the top right items. Under Configuration, select all of the Azure Active Directory log types (even those in preview).

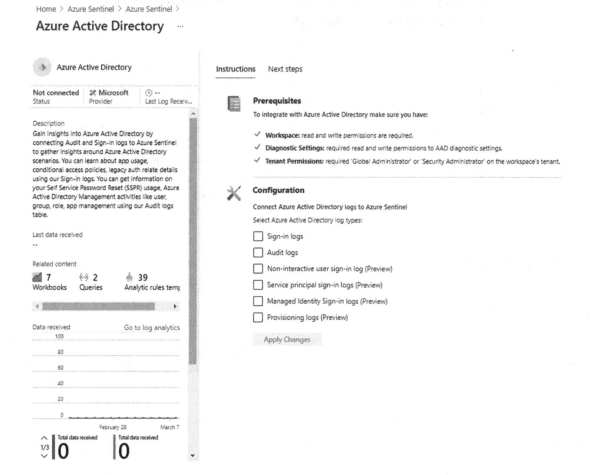

10. When you select at least one configuration, the Apply Changes button is enabled. Click to save the selections.

11. Return to the Sentinel Data connectors view. Enable the data connector for Azure DNS by searching for DNS, or scroll down and select DNS and then click Open connector page on the bottom right.

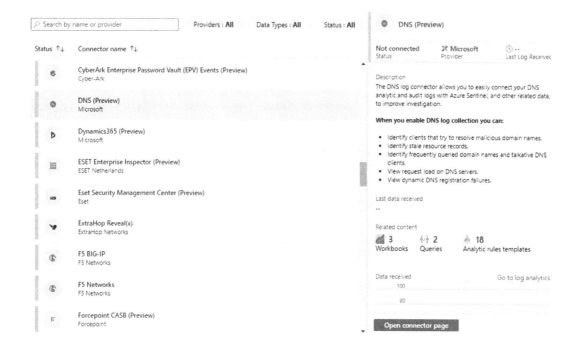

12. Notice the prerequisites (top right), and you need to install the Azure agent on Windows VMs. (DNS logs are collected from Windows VMs currently.) After validating, click the Install solution button.

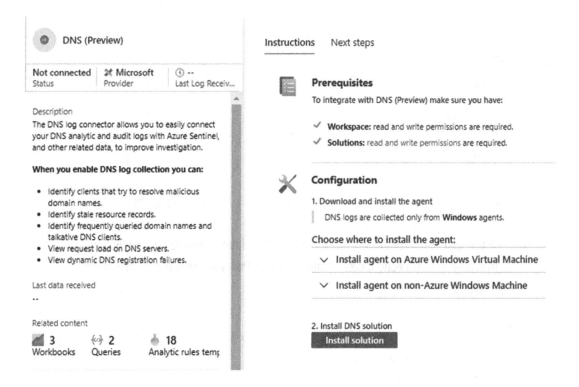

13. Return to the Sentinel Data connectors view. Scroll down or search for Azure Key Vault. Select Open connector page on the bottom-right screen.

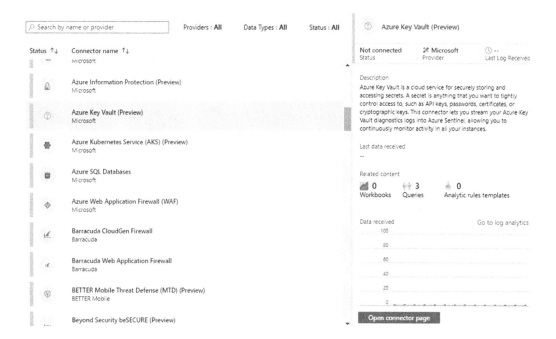

14. Notice that the prerequisites include a "role" addition to enable data collection. To enable data collection, click Configure Azure Policy Assignment wizard at the bottom of the screen.

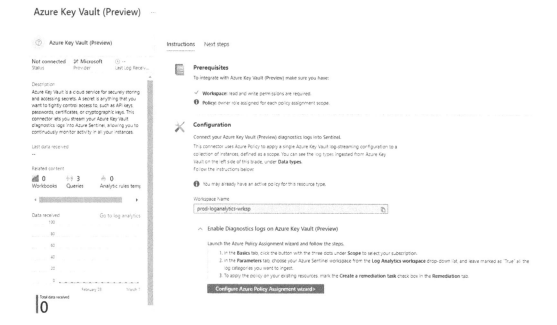

15.   The options for deployment start with the Azure subscription configuration.

16.   Because this deployment journey includes an Azure policy, you may choose to exclude a specific resource group. Select Next.

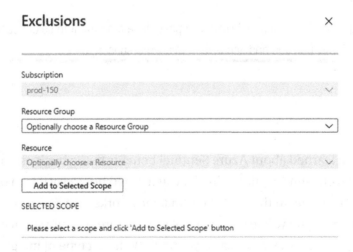

17. Use the drop-down arrow to select the same Azure Sentinel Log Analytics workspace. Select Next to support Remediation steps.

Deploy - Configure diagnostic settings for Azure Key Vault to Log Analytics workspace

Assign policy

Basics   **Parameters**   Remediation   Non-compliance messages   Review + create

Specify parameters for this policy assignment.

Effect *

| DeployIfNotExists | ∨ |

Setting name *

| AzureKeyVaultDiagnosticsLogsToWorkspace |

Log Analytics workspace *

| prod-loganalytics-wrksp | ∨ | ... |

AuditEvent - Enabled *

| True | ∨ |

AllMetrics - Enabled *

| True | ∨ |

18. You can leave the additional options at the default settings and click the Review + create button without creating a remediation task. Click Create at the end of the journey screens to enable data collection.

This completes the guided steps to enable data collection. If you have specific third-party virtual appliances, like Barracuda, Palo Alto, Cisco, or others, follow the guidance integrated in the connector page.

Before returning to the Azure Sentinel Overview page, take a moment to select each of the other options that may be used and licensed in the Azure subscription.

Summary

In this chapter, you learned about Azure Sentinel benefits to the business and how to enable Sentinel in your subscription. Finally, you learned how easy it is to enable data connections and store data in the same Log Analytics workspace as Azure Monitor.

In the next chapter, you will learn details of other Azure security services and how to integrate the major features with Azure Sentinel. With that type of integration, the security team has a view across the entire Azure and on-premises enterprise.

CHAPTER 2

Other Azure Security Services

You will continue to learn about other Azure security services that not only are stand-alone but support Azure Sentinel. You should be aware that these solutions can work together to support the overall Azure security layers to protect the business and customer data. These security services are all cloud native, so there is no need to update hardware or software. However, each of these services requires a dedicated book to help explore the benefits, and we are limited to an overview of each in this chapter.

In later chapters, the key features of these additional services needed for integration with Azure Sentinel from this chapter are revisited. These individual services extend functionality for an overall enterprise view using Azure Sentinel.

In this chapter you learn about

- Azure Log Analytics

- Azure Monitor

- Azure Security Center

- Microsoft Defender for Endpoint

- Microsoft Defender for Identity

Azure Log Analytics

You should begin the discovery of features that benefit the business. You will complete exercises to enable many of the Azure cloud services and also learn about integration of many of the third-party data sources.

© Marshall Copeland 2021
M. Copeland, *Cloud Defense Strategies with Azure Sentinel*, https://doi.org/10.1007/978-1-4842-7132-2_2

Note   You can find updates on Azure Sentinel features that benefit your security posture at `https://azure.microsoft.com/en-us/services/azure-sentinel/`.

Some Azure customers find the documentations for Azure Monitor and Log Analytics confusing; the documentations to use and deploy the services are similar but not the same. Not to oversimplify the powerful Azure Monitor service but the relationship can be visualized this way: Log Analytics is a component service within the Azure Monitor solution.

Azure Monitor is the current service to receive, store, and display Azure data. The consolidation supports a more consistent approach to collect metrics in a single view for both Azure IaaS and PaaS deployments. Azure Monitor log data is stored in a Log Analytics workspace. The Log Analytics service supports editing and running queries to analyze the log data. The actual work of the queries is the "analytics" just like the work of the Azure Application Insights service, which is another component of Azure Monitor. There may be a little confusion because the term Log Analytics has changed to Azure Monitor Logs and the updated agent Azure Monitor Agent (AMA) consolidates the different agents. This was done to support a consistency with identification of metrics consumed by the Azure Monitor service.

Before the adoption of cloud services, data was collected from hardware, operating systems (OSs), and software applications. Information included servers, desktops, laptops, and mobile devices. Subject matter experts (SMEs) knew the exact data center rack of servers that provided detailed log information for identity platform, application health, and encrypted file storage. When you move applications into the Azure public cloud, you need to learn new methods to validate applications are performing as expected and be alerted if an admin change made your data vulnerable to attacks. The integrity and availability of applications and the Azure data platform are identified using Azure logs and metrics.

Figure 2-1 is a visual representation of the Azure Monitor service. This diagram is used to demonstrate information aggregation as part of the Azure data platform.

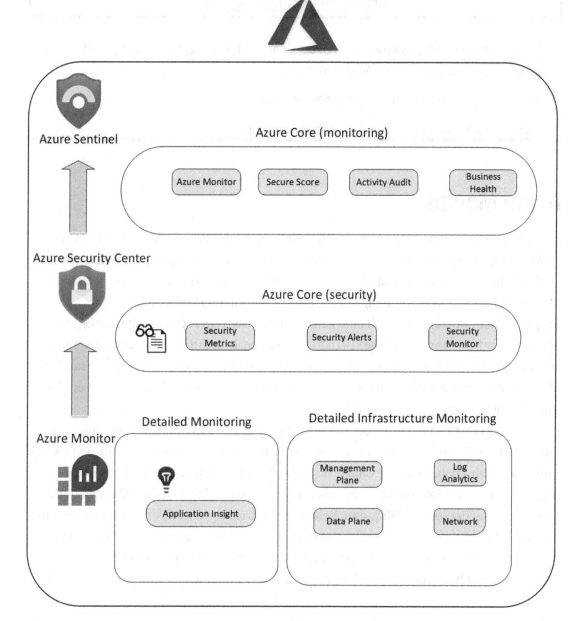

Figure 2-1. *Visual representation of Azure core security and monitoring services*

EMERGENCY ACCOUNT SIDE BAR

A break glass account is an Azure Active Directory account only if replication is disabled between on-premises and Azure Active Directory.

@customer.com is replicated to Azure Active Directory.

@on-microsoft.com is an Azure Active Directory account.

Azure Monitor

Another source of data is supported with the addition of Windows Azure Diagnostics (WAD) in Azure Monitor that collects metrics and logs from the guest operating system, which is the OS from the virtual machine. You should plan to migrate to the Azure Monitor Agent and take advantage of the consolidation. Read more at the URL: `https://docs.microsoft.com/enus/azure/azure-monitor/agents/azure-monitor-agent-overview?tabs=PowerShellWindows`. You may be a little confused by the term guest OS, but this is not the Azure hypervisor but the VM running on the host. Standard platform metrics for the host are already collected, so you need to know how to enable the diagnostics extensions for your VM.

Guest OS Data: The Azure security operations (SecOps) team can enable metrics and logs from the guest operating system. This data can be written directly into the Azure Monitor metrics database. The data is not available by default and can be validated from Azure Portal. Open Azure Portal and select any virtual machine and scroll down to the Monitoring section on the left menu. Select the Metrics view, and you notice without the agent installed, there is only data for the hyper-V host, identified as the virtual machine host. Please refer to Figure 2-2. Notice the Metric drop-down defaults to CPU Credits Consumed, aka how much in US dollars this VM costs to date.

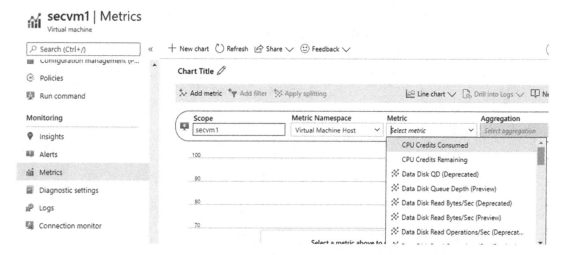

Figure 2-2. *Metrics for virtual machine host without guest OS diagnostics*

When you create a virtual machine, you should enable guest OS diagnostics during VM creation, as shown in Figure 2-3. You can see the option to enable metrics and logs on the VM.

Create a virtual machine

Learn more

✅ Your subscription is protected by Azure Security Center basic plan.

Monitoring

Boot diagnostics ⓘ   ◉ On ○ Off

OS guest diagnostics ⓘ   ◉ On ○ Off

Diagnostics storage account * ⓘ | webtierrgdiagall ▾ |
Create new

Figure 2-3. *Guest OS diagnostics enabled during the VM creation*

Once the agent is installed, the metrics can be shared. Using the portal to view VM settings to share, open the landing page and scroll down the left-side menu and select Diagnostic settings. You should have a similar view as shown in Figure 2-4 to gain an understanding of the metrics, logs, and syslogs that are collected. Select the individual configuration options, make any changes, and then click the Save option. The diagnostic settings need to send to the Azure Log Analytics workspace using the example later in this chapter.

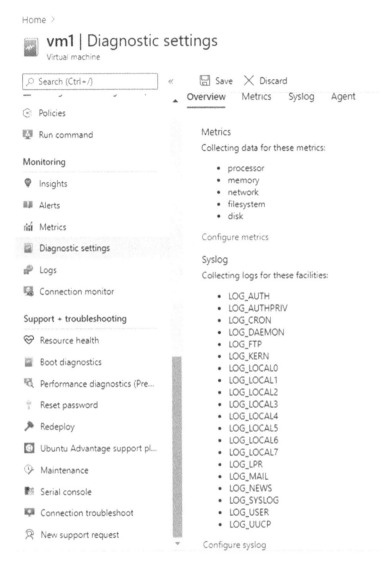

Figure 2-4. *VM metrics and diagnostics collected*

Note   The only prerequisite to follow the exercise to enable guest OS metrics is to have Windows VMs deployed and **Contributor** access on the VM and the resource group of the Log Analytics workspace.

ENABLE GUEST OS METRICS AND SEND THEM TO AZURE MONITOR

1. Open Azure Portal and select the Windows VM to enable. Scroll down the menu on the left-hand side and select Diagnostic settings under the Monitoring section. The Overview **blade** will display. If you have not enabled a diagnostics storage account for this VM, you can enable it now before you continue.

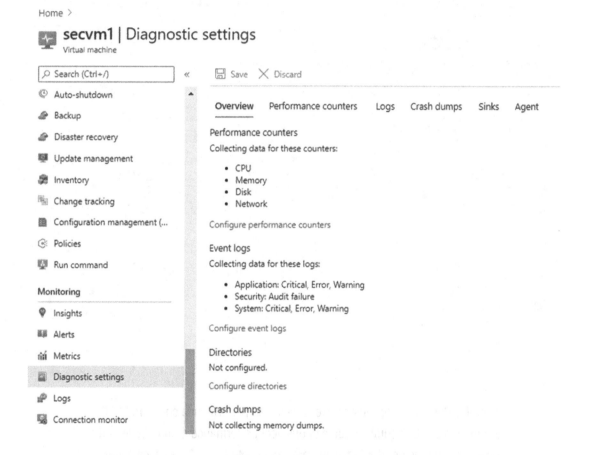

2. Select Performance counters at the top menu to the right of the Overview blade. Once the Performance counters blade is displayed, select the Custom counter view.

💾 Save   ✕ Discard

Overview   **Performance counters**   Logs   Crash dumps   Sinks   Agent

Choose **Basic** to enable the collection of performance counters. Choose **Custom** if you want more control over which performance counters are collected.

(None   Basic   **Custom**)

Configure the performance counters to collect, and how often they should be sampled:

Performance counter	Sample rate (seconds)	Unit
☑ \Processor Information(_Total)\% Processor Time	60	Percent
☑ \Processor Information(_Total)\% Privileged Time	60	Percent
☑ \Processor Information(_Total)\% User Time	60	Percent
☑ \Processor Information(_Total)\Processor Frequency	60	Count
☑ \System\Processes	60	Count
☑ \Process(_Total)\Thread Count	60	Count
☑ \Process(_Total)\Handle Count	60	Count
☑ \System\System Up Time	60	Count
☑ \System\Context Switches/sec	60	CountPerSecond
☑ \System\Processor Queue Length	60	Count

1   2   3   4   5   ＞

3. From this Custom view, you can use all selected performance counters (3 GB storage/VM per 24 hours), or you can unselect performance metrics to limit the amount of storage per VM. Once you have completed any changes, click the Save option on the top left.

4. Select the menu item **Sinks**. From this menu, you can enable diagnostics to be sent to Azure Application Insights. You can also choose to send VM metrics to Azure Monitor for comparison of Azure resource metrics and these VM metrics.

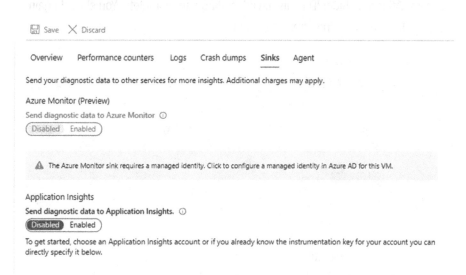

5. Use your mouse to select the option to create a managed identity in Azure AD for this VM to share data with Azure Monitor. Set Status to On and click Save.

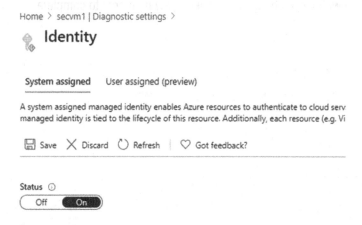

6. You will see a pop-up window that requires your consent to register the selected VM with Azure Active Directory. By selecting to save this setting, you are allowing the VM to be granted access to Azure AD. Select Yes to enable the access. After the object ID is displayed, settings are complete. You should again select Diagnostic settings from the menu.

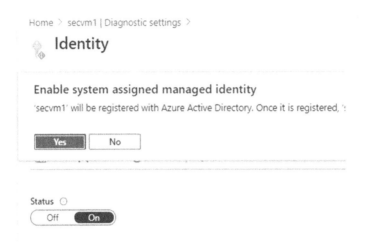

7. From the Sinks blade, under Diagnostics settings, you should choose the option Enabled, to send diagnostic data to Azure Monitor. Click Save on the top left. Updating with these changes may take a few moments to complete.

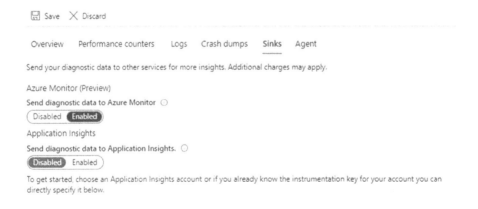

Collection time of all selected performance counters begins once you click Save from this moment in time moving forward.

Monitoring the health, metrics, and performance of the Azure platform and the Azure resources in use allows a single view of all the correlated data. This collection of data from a variety of Azure resources allows us to leverage the power of Microsoft Kusto Query Language (KQL) in a single window.

You can, of course, enable the collection of metrics and data from an individual resource to be shared with Log Analytics. This next exercise enables data (logs and metrics) from multiple resources to be shared with the Log Analytics workspace without the need to enable at each resource.

ENABLE INDIVIDUAL DATA SOURCES FOR THE LOG ANALYTICS WORKSPACE

1. From Azure Portal, search for Log Analytics workspace. Click the workspace icon and scroll down to the Workspace Data Sources menu on the left-hand side.

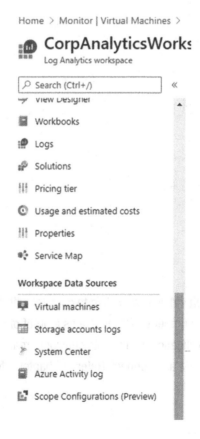

2. This example demonstrates connecting virtual machines, including diagnostic
    data and storage account logs. Select Virtual machines to display the VMs.

3. Click the text **Not connected** to present the view of the status. Select the
    option Connect on the top left of the menu. The update shows **Connecting** after
    about 60 seconds.

4. Repeat step 3 for each VM you would like to connect with the workspace. You
    may want to limit the number of VMs to five as a proof of concept. (Once you
    have completed the validation, you should consider creating an Azure policy to
    deploy agents on the VM and connect. Refer to Chapter 7 for guidance on Azure
    policy creation.)

5. Return to the Monitor pane and select the Virtual Machines view from under the Insights menu. Choose the option to enable the virtual machine. In this exercise, there are three VMs not monitored by Azure Monitor services.

6. In the Azure Monitor Insights Onboarding pop-up window, choose Enable to allow the data collection validation to begin. This step takes over 60 seconds to complete.

Azure Monitor   ✕
Insights Onboarding

Get more visibility into the health and performance of your virtual machine

With an Azure virtual machine you get host CPU, disk and up/down state of your VMs out of the box. Enabling additional monitoring capabilities provides insights into the performance and dependencies for your virtual machines.

You will be billed based on the amount of data ingested and your data retention settings. It can take between 5-10 minutes to configure the virtual machine and the monitoring data to appear.

ⓘ The map data set collected with Azure Monitor for VMs is intended to be infrastructure data about the resources being deployed and monitored. For details on data collected please click here.

Enable

Have more questions?
Learn more about virtual machine monitoring ☐
Learn more about pricing ☐
Support Matrix ☐
FAQ ☐

7. If you close the pop-up window, the VM you just enabled may display
    Enabling – Waiting for data. Click the Why? to get details about collecting data
    to Azure "Insights."

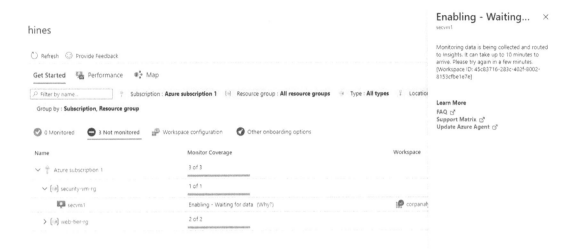

8. Close the Enabling – Waiting… pop-up window and repeat step 5 for each VM
    you would like to monitor.

9. Next, this exercise connects a single Azure storage account to the Azure Log
    Analytics workspace. From the left menu, select Storage accounts logs.
    Select + Add.

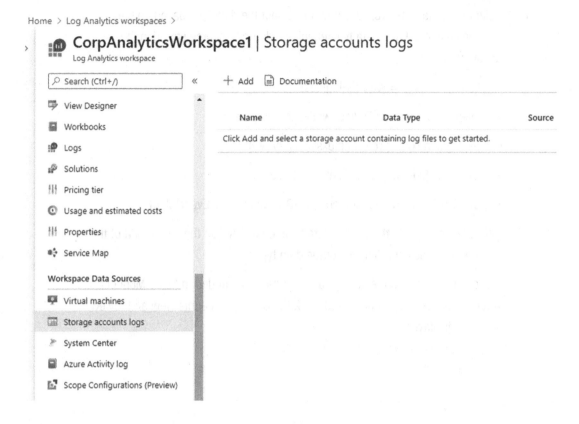

10. Use the drop-down menu to select the storage account; in this example, we select PROD-150.

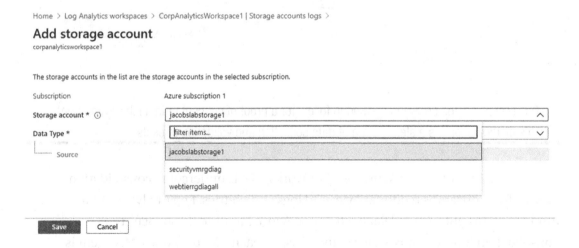

11. Select the Data Type drop-down menu. Select the data type based on the storage contents. Each data type enables a different source stored in the account:

  - IIS logs [source = wad-iis-logfiles]

  - Events [source = WADWindowsEventLogsTable]

  - Syslog (Linux) [source = LinuxsyslogVer1v0]

  - ETW logs [source = WADETWEventTable]

  - Service Fabric events [source = WADServiceFabric*EventTable]

12. This exercise selects the Events data type. Click Save on the bottom left of the pane. You can select multiple storage data types.

13. You can now validate the storage account has been added to Azure Monitor. After the connection is configured, click the Storage accounts view and review the data displayed.

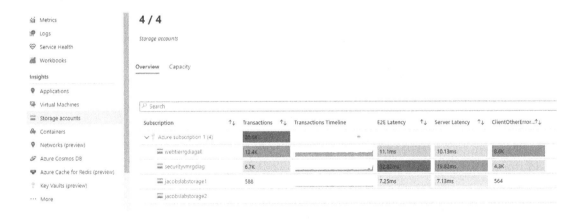

This exercise is the preferred method to follow for a proof of concept or in a lab environment. This method supports a steady state of data collection and validation of costs.

You now know that the Azure Monitor workspace is undergoing consolidation of what first appears as redundant views of logs and metrics. Log Analytics, Azure Application Insights, Azure Diagnostics, and Azure Monitor. If you focus the consolidation topic on support for Azure VMs, on each VM, only one AMA agent is required, the same agent for Windows and Linux OS. Older installations show one of the agents you will see running on your VM, the Microsoft Monitoring Agent (MMA), which is installed when you enable Azure Security Center to manage VMs and collect data.

Note   There are multiple Azure Monitor agents. Consolidation information can be found at the URL: `https://docs.microsoft.com/en-us/azure/azure-monitor/agents/azure-monitoragent-overview?tabs=PowerShellWindows`.

Azure Security Center

This is another cloud service that leverages a client installation to receive data on a virtual machine (VM), physical system, or another cloud service. You can configure Azure Security Center to collect data from your Azure VMs, VM scale sets, IaaS containers, and non-Azure computers that may still be on-premises. The information collected is used to monitor and then alert on security vulnerabilities and threats. At the beginning of this chapter, you learned about the Log Analytics agent with Azure Monitor and the Log Analytics workspace. It is this agent with the Azure extensions that reads various security-related configurations, metrics, and event logs from the machine and copies them for data ingestion into your configured Log Analytics workspace for analysis. Installation of AMA agent replaces the older Log Analytics agent and this has been discussed, and you may recall the agent installed collects both metrics and logs.

Note   Azure Security Center is often referred to by the abbreviation ASC.

Azure Security Center depends on an agent being installed. It uses the same Log Analytics agent, now the AMA agent, and the same agent edition installed for use with Azure Monitor. The agent is referred to in some documentation as the "AMA," so just know it is the same one. NOTE: The older agent is referred to as the MMA agent and can still be used because of the current GAPS on the coverage. In the future, Microsoft continues to invest in a single agent.

The agent has a list of Azure VMs, both Windows and Linux, supported to provide the security extensions needed for Azure Security Center. The security logs and events are read to provide security actions based on the extension capabilities. The extensions and resources continue to be enhanced as shown in Figure 2-5. The agent can be configured differently for Windows OS to include metrics, performance counters, and logs. These are configured from the console, but for most deployments supporting Infrastructure as Code (IaC), configurations are included in an ARM template. Azure Security Center provides another method to install the Azure extensions to enable logging and monitoring.

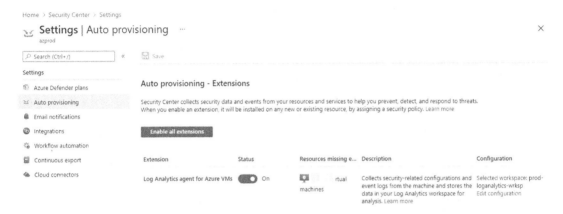

Figure 2-5. *Azure Security Center auto-provision and extensions*

The pre-configuration recommendation is to create a Log Analytics workspace that would support Azure Monitor and Azure Security Center. You can use the same Log Analytics workspace for Azure Security Center and reduce the cost of redundant storage. This recommendation was defined earlier in this chapter in the "Azure Log Analytics" section. If you skipped that previous step, you can change the Log Analytics workspace with the exercise in this section. Azure Security Center cannot use the default Log Analytics workspace that was created when Azure Security Center was enabled.

Note   When changing to the shared Log Analytics workspace, do not delete the original until all the MMAs have changed to report to the new Log Analytics workspace.

Enable Security

The services supported by Azure Security Center are constantly changing at the pace of cloud innovation, so even though you are reviewing virtual networks, virtual machines, and database services in the exercises, additional preview features on the road map include additional Azure cloud services, third-party services, and integration with cloud-native services like Azure Firewall Manager.

This first exercise is to enable Azure Security Center, install agents, and allow the collection of data to begin. It may take up to 24 hours to start collecting baseline information and making recommendations.

ENABLE SECURITY CENTER STANDARD TIER

You gain the benefit of additional security features when upgrading to the standard tier, and the first 30 days are part of a free trial. This provides the best opportunity to evaluate the Security Center functionality for your subscription.

1. From Azure Portal, search for Security Center, and click the icon to take you to the landing page.

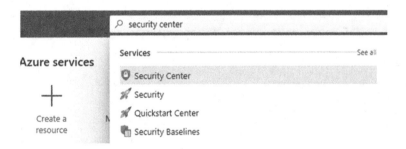

2. The interface has changed over the years. However, the strength and integration in the API configuration is where the improved feature set is appreciated.

3.   From the left menu, click the Getting started pane.

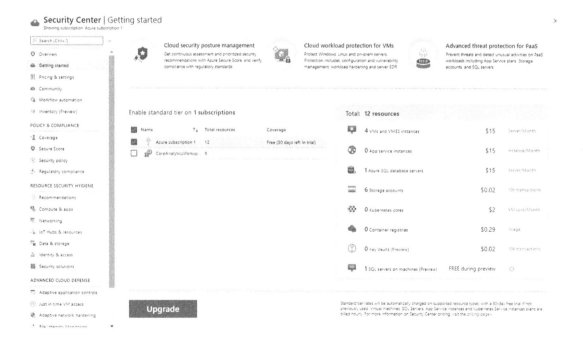

4. There is a preliminary review of the cost based on the current Azure deployment services. Select the entire subscription. Note you can be selective if you have many subscriptions. Click the Upgrade option to begin your 30-day free evaluation.

5. You will gain information by choosing the option Install agents. The Azure tenant is part of a trial subscription. Click Install agents. (Note you do have options to install manually and to test without installing agents.)

6. Return to the Getting started pane and select the production Log Analytics workspace (or your equivalent) and click Upgrade to share the Security Center data collected with the Azure Monitor service.

The Upgrade option has configured the connection to the Log Analytics workspace and all current and future VMs. Virtual machines provisioned in your Azure subscription automatically receive the Microsoft Monitoring Agent (MMA). This is called auto-provisioning, and it should be your default method to configure Security Center.

Azure Identity: Security Center leverages Role-Based Access Control (RBAC) provided by Azure Active Directory (AAD). There are two roles you should use with Azure Security Center:

- Security Reader

- Security Admin

The Security Reader role should be assigned to all users who only need read access to the dashboard. The Security Admin role should be protected as are other sensitive administrative credentials.

As for storage, the agent collects information and sends it to the Log Analytics workspace. Another great point about using the standard tier is you have up to 500 MB per day. If data exceeds 500 MB per day, additional charges will apply, like the data storage charges provided in Chapter 1. Security Center adoption considerations should include the length of time for data retained beyond 30 days. With the Log Analytics workspace, you have the option to send to Blob Storage for a portion of the data storage requirements.

Microsoft Defender for Endpoint

Additional security options are available for your business using Microsoft Defender for Endpoint, which you learn about now. Then you will learn about Microsoft Defender for Identity next in this chapter. You may have one or both of the two security products deployed in your enterprise. The alerts, metrics, and logs from these products (and Microsoft 365 Defender) should be enabled to allow Azure Sentinel data ingestion. You should follow the exercises outlined in Chapter 1 to enable data connection with Azure Sentinel.

Microsoft Defender for Endpoint has two prerequisites to consider that are needed to deploy this layer of security services successfully. They are

- Definitions

- Licenses

Definitions are a good starting place as the less complicated of the two prerequisites. Definitions help you understand how both Microsoft Defender for Endpoint and Microsoft Defender for Identity work separately and then work together with Azure Sentinel. In addition, you gain more insight into the differences in security features between the products. You learn how to better leverage Azure Sentinel as a Security Information and Event Management (SIEM) cloud service.

There are several threat protection security features available to strengthen a layered security model. The Microsoft security products you may or may not be aware of include

- Microsoft Defender for Microsoft 365 (Office 365)
- Microsoft Application Guard for Microsoft 365
- Microsoft Defender Antimalware
- Microsoft Defender Firewall
- Microsoft Defender Exploit Guard
- Microsoft BitLocker
- Microsoft Windows Information Protection
- Microsoft Defender for Endpoint
- Microsoft Defender for Identity

This list of security products available continues to be improved and expanded. However, this discussion only focuses on Microsoft Defender for Endpoint and later Microsoft Defender for Identity. Many security features are included with Defender for Endpoint, and you may see information as shown in Figure 2-6 that is used to define the utilization of Defender.

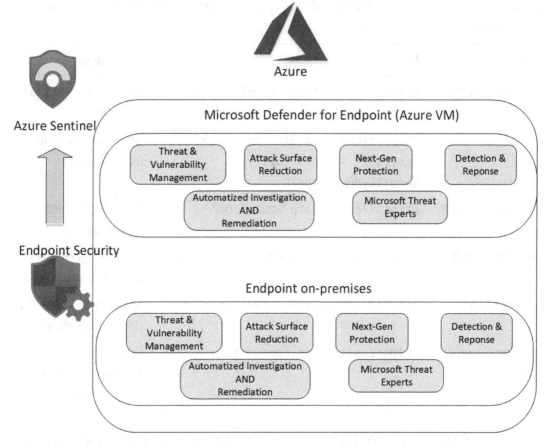

Figure 2-6. *Microsoft Defender for Endpoint Azure VMs and on-premises and integration with Azure Sentinel*

This is a technical guide and not intended to support sales or as marketing guidance. However, there are many next-generation security features supported by Microsoft Defender for Endpoint. You may be aware that Microsoft has a few security portals, and Table 2-1 may help guide you into the correct portal based on your subscription and license model.

Table 2-1. *Microsoft security portals for operation and administration (Note consolidation of portals should be expected)*

Portal	Link	Description
Defender Security Center	`https://securitycenter.microsoft.com/`	Microsoft Defender for Endpoint
Azure Portal	`https://portal.azure.com/#blade/ Microsoft_Azure_Security/ SecurityMenuBlade/0`	Azure Security Center (directed blade)
Defender for Identity	`https://portal.atp.azure.com/`	Defender for Identity (previously ATP)
Cloud App Security	`https://portal.cloudappsecurity.com/`	Microsoft Cloud Access Security Broker (CASB)
Microsoft 365	`https://security.microsoft.com/`	Microsoft 365 Defender (Office 365 Defender)
Defender Security Intelligence	`https://microsoft.com/wdsi`	Updates on Defender for Endpoint, submission of samples, more

Microsoft Defender for Endpoint is an inclusive license to provide included services such as threat and vulnerability management. You expect endpoint management to help remediate vulnerabilities and misconfigurations. Additionally, there is reduction of the attack surface including network access regulation to protect the endpoint and to regulate access to domains and URLs with web protection.

Emerging threats are difficult to prevent, so Defender for Endpoint extends the security layers in what is categorized as next generation. Detection and response suggest the need for a blue team to hunt for advanced threats. Automatic investigation and remediation can reduce the volume of alerts to allow resources to focus on advanced threat intelligence.

Microsoft provides a way for customers to improve their security by using a dynamic metric titled "secure score." You see this in Azure Security Center and in Defender for Endpoint. The Microsoft security products identify unprotected computers and prioritize the recommended actions.

ENABLE MICROSOFT DEFENDER FOR ENDPOINT FREE TRIAL

This process guides you though the steps to enable a free trial of Defender for Endpoint for testing. It can be used as stand-alone security for business systems, and in later chapters, the data connector allows Microsoft Azure Sentinel to leverage the intelligence data.

1. Open your Edge browser and start by opening the page of the URL
   `www.microsoft.com/en-us/microsoft-365/security/`
   `endpoint-defender?ocid=docs-wdatp-portaloverview-`
   `abovefoldlink&rtc=1`. Click the Start free trial button on the screen.

2. Review the Trial Online Service Terms, and please read the Acceptable use section. You may also notice that the new branding changes Microsoft Defender ATP to Defender for Endpoint. This has not been updated on all the guidance. After reading the terms of use, select the I accept these terms and conditions, and click the Next button to continue.

Please read the Trial Online Service Terms for Microsoft Defender Advanced Threat Protection; when you accept these, we can finish up your registration.

3. To continue, enter the details about the trial subscription. Validation is completed through the email address and phone number you enter. Enter the correct code to prove you are human. Click Submit to continue.

Microsoft Defender ATP

Please enter your details

First name*

Marshall

Last name*

Copeland

Work email*

Marshall.Copeland@austincyber.com

Phone*

512-555-1212

Company name*

Austin Cyber

Job title*

Systems / Solution Architect ⌄

Country*

United States ⌄

Number of devices in your organization

Select number of PCs ⌄

What other security solutions are you
using/evaluating? (optional)

Azure Sentinel

Microsoft may use your contact information to provide updates and special offers about Microsoft
Windows and other Microsoft products and services. You can unsubscribe at any time. To learn more
you can read the privacy statement.

Enter the characters you see

New | Audio

HD3LVLSSDX

Submit

4. There will be a notice that the application is being reviewed. An email will be sent to the work address once a decision is made.

> **Microsoft Defender ATP**
>
> We're now reviewing your application...
>
> Thank you for completing the Microsoft Defender ATP trial application. We'll review your application and contact you via email within the next 7 business days.
>
> Once your application is approved. you'll receive an invitation email with on-boarding instructions.
>
> Questions, issues? We're just a click away on the Microsoft Defender ATP tech community.
>
> Thank you for your interest in evaluating this new service,
> Microsoft Defender Advanced Threat Protection Team

5. When approved, an email with onboarding instructions that you must follow is sent.

With this Azure Defender for Endpoint cloud service enabled, the integration with Azure Sentinel, completed in a later chapter, with other metrics and logs, provides a holistic security profile view from Azure Sentinel.

With Defender for Endpoint deployed, there is an additional add-on service that can be used for your team to gain expert advice. Microsoft Threat Experts is a managed service that enables you to receive proactive "targeted attack notifications" on demand.

Note   A 90-day free trial of Experts on Demand can be applied for by navigating on the Defender menu: Settings ➤ General ➤ Advanced features ➤ Microsoft Threat Experts. Once accepted, you will get the benefits of targeted attack notifications and start the free 90 days.

Finally, you should be aware that Microsoft Defender integrates with many Microsoft security and management products. The list includes

- Azure Sentinel
- Azure Security Center

- Defender for Identity

- Defender for Microsoft 365 (Office 365)

- Microsoft Cloud App Security

- Microsoft Intune

MICROSOFT 365 DEFENDER SIDEBAR

There is a single security portal that provides administration for many of the Defender products. The consumer version, Microsoft 365 Home, is not discussed. If you have a small business and would like Advanced Threat Protection, it is not included in Office 365 for Business Premium. You will need to update to license version for the enterprise, discussed in this chapter.

The Office 365 Defender portal URL is https://security.microsoft.com/. A view of the Office 365 Defender portal is displayed.

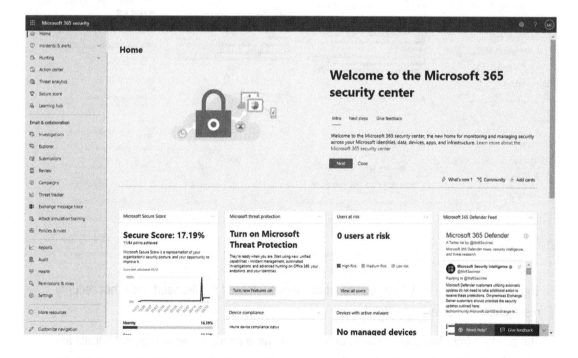

The Microsoft 365 Defender portal view shows the administration menu and secure score percentage.

The Microsoft Defender portal was designed with a focus on larger businesses and enterprise businesses by combining Microsoft Defender for Endpoint, Microsoft Defender for Office 365, Microsoft Defender for Identity, and Microsoft Cloud App Security. The security value for an enterprise customer increases as the many security products correlate data from security alerts. The alerts are grouped into prioritized incidents to help focus on what is most important. The incident is a potential cybersecurity attack event on the business. The first time you select Incidents & alerts, the incidents from the menu on the left, there may be a delay, to create a cloud resource for the Azure tenant. The delay can take several minutes, so please plan.

Once the Azure configuration is finished, you can start to explore incidents, hunting, and threat analytics.

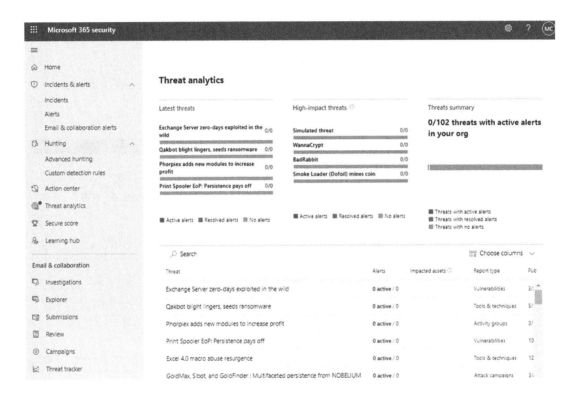

The Threat analytics view includes the latest threats released by Microsoft and other security researchers and other impactful threats.

The changes from Microsoft Security Consolidation have created several different portals as cloud development decreases the update times. A security setting you should be aware of to help with the consolidation is the option to redirect the old portal, `https://protection.office.com`, to the current portal, security.microsoft.com. Refer to the following figure depicting the screen after selecting the Microsoft 365 security Settings view\Email settings\ Portal redirection.

Portal redirection

Automatically redirect all accounts in your organization from **protection.office.com** to **security.microsoft.com**, the new home of Microsoft Defender for Office 365.
Learn more about portal redirection

Automatic redirection
 Off

ⓘ This change will take effect upon signing out of the portal and signing back in again.

This Microsoft 365 security setting redirects old office portals to the new security portal.

You can use the data provided by Azure Defender for Office 365 by enabling the Azure Sentinel data connector.

Licenses as a prerequisite may not be an issue for many enterprises since they may include Defender for Endpoint in their Enterprise Agreement (EA). Microsoft Defender services contain many capabilities including uncovering vulnerabilities and misconfigurations in real time.

Note   Download a very complete comparison table of Microsoft 365 licenses from https://go.microsoft.com/fwlink/?linkid=2139145.

Microsoft Defender for Identity

Microsoft Defender for Identity (formerly Azure Advanced Threat Protection, also known as Azure ATP) is a cloud-based security solution that leverages your on-premises Active Directory signals to identify, detect, and investigate advanced threats, compromised identities, and malicious insider actions directed at your organization.

Finally in this chapter, you need to learn about Microsoft Defender for Identity (rebranded Azure Advanced Threat Protection), which you enable in a trial subscription.

ENABLE MICROSOFT DEFENDER FOR IDENTITY

This process guides you though the steps to enable a free trial of Defender for Identity for testing. It is included in the Enterprise Mobility + Security E5 license. You can refer back to the preceding note to download the 365 license comparison.

It can be used as stand-alone security for business systems, and in later chapters, the data connector allows Microsoft Azure Sentinel to leverage the intelligence data.

1. Open your Edge browser and start by opening the page Try Microsoft Defender for Identity on Microsoft Evaluation Center. Please Click the button Continue to walk through the wizard for the trial.

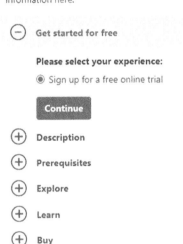

2. This process begins differently with a business email address. Enter the email and click Next to continue.

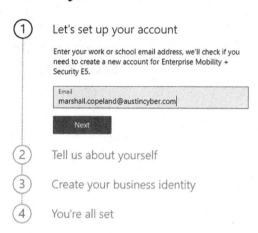

3. Once you click Next, the process validates your user information and asks
    you to sign into your Azure tenant. Optionally, if this is a dev/test, you have the
    option to create a new account.

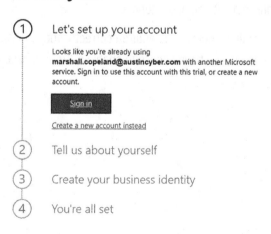

4. You can sign in to associate the trial of the E5 license with your cloud tenant. If you optionally choose to create a new account that is separate from your production, you need to enter data in the fields to continue.

5. Click Next. Then enter business identity so Microsoft can validate and associate your trial with an Azure tenant.

6. Once all of your data is entered correctly and your Azure tenant has been validated, you have access to enable a 3-month trial for 250 users.

7.   Select the Try now button to continue.

With the Microsoft Defender for Identity cloud service enabled, the integration with Azure Sentinel in a later chapter, with other metrics and logs, provides a holistic security profile view from Azure Sentinel.

Summary

In this chapter, you have enabled many of the foundational collection points to be used with Azure Sentinel. You learned that metrics and logs from both the Azure platform and Azure IaaS and PaaS services are collected in the Log Analytics workspace.

Finally, you were guided through exercises that enabled trials for both Microsoft Defender for Endpoint and Microsoft Defender for Identity. With all of this data collection and analytics being performed at the individual cloud service levels, you begin to gain an insight into how Azure Sentinel provides an entire cybersecurity health view of your enterprise.

CHAPTER 3

Getting Started with Azure Sentinel and XDR Capabilities

Security teams have varied backgrounds and may be continuing their security journey that originated from a traditional on-premises environment or from other cloud service providers. Now they are asking for guidance to secure their business using Azure services and gain knowledge of how to best use Azure Sentinel.

Follow this guide to provide answers to best proceed and use this cloud-native Security Information and Event Management (SIEM) service. If on-premises SIEM is part of your career, then shifting work based on recovered hours in a day is part of what you need to prepare. Traditional work processes that no longer require a team effort include selecting a new SIEM solution, purchasing servers, and updating hardware over the years.

You will recover time that used to entail every three years a new project to identify the best new SIEM solution to purchase. Another company process no longer required is SIEM server's hardware updates. Microsoft Azure Sentinel features are added at cloud speed, and hardware updates are provided by the cloud service providers (CSPs) as standard provisioning. (Note: Microsoft updates server hardware as needed, at a two- or three-year cycle.)

Chapter 2 provided processes to have many data connectors enabled, and you may have enabled other connectors. Now you need to organize the information the security data provides and make Sentinel work for the company.

© Marshall Copeland 2021
M. Copeland, *Cloud Defense Strategies with Azure Sentinel*, https://doi.org/10.1007/978-1-4842-7132-2_3

In this chapter you learn and gain insight about

- Security Operations Center with Azure Sentinel

- How Sentinel leverages Azure security

- Security data prioritization

- Extended Detection and Response (XDR)

- Security Road Map

Security Operations Center with Azure Sentinel and XDR

The Azure services supported by Azure Sentinel are constantly being updated at a faster pace than traditional release cycles for on-premises software. The updates do appear in the console overnight, and because of this innovation, staying up to date is challenging. Even with the extensions of Azure Sentinel benefits to the business, the complexity and level of sophistication of attacks require the integration of other Microsoft security solutions for Extended Detection and Response (XDR).

This section is the foundation for current Azure security services. You should understand the basic functionality of the different services before you continue to learn about the "Extended" Detection and Response features with the integration of the Azure services. Extended Detection and Response is not surprising when solutions like Azure Security Center and Microsoft Defender for Servers and SQL and other security services integrate easily with each other and with Azure Sentinel.

Now that you have the basic appreciation of the benefits of a cloud-native SIEM, you need to enable features used by Azure Sentinel data connectors. Your Security Operations Center (SOC) requires a functional Azure Sentinel configuration that is a major extension of incident management. With this solution, you begin customization for your Security Operations Center. Also, you continue to learn and tailor Azure Sentinel for more security benefits supporting your company.

In Chapter 2 you completed the basic onboarding process. You followed many individual connector exercises to enable data collection from different Azure services. As you begin to customize the alerting and data available from third-party integration products, you need to also begin minor efficiency modifications to leverage Azure Sentinel insight.

You begin by understanding how to

- Enable rules from templates or create new rules.

- Investigate an incident to validate the anomaly.

- Respond to true positives.

- Tune noise of false positives.

First, the high-level view of the Azure Sentinel console provides an outline of the data ingestion based on the connectors enabled.

Some of the areas you need to enable include

- Reviewing the data available

- Alert Rule Templates

- Actions

- Bookmarks

- Incidents

- Incident comments

Democratization is a method of delegation of the cloud, to manage the Azure cloud at different levels including tenant, subscription, and resource group. An automation account may be used to create a subscription, not a manual process. This follows the goal to support an ITSM (like ServiceNow)-managed service.

Azure Sentinel SIEM and Azure Security

As you build the next Security Operations Center (SOC) around Azure Sentinel as the Security Information and Event Management (SIEM) service, you begin to realize that the SIEM solution provides visibility into all corners of the network. With additional Azure security services like Azure Defender for Endpoint, Identity, and Servers, Azure Sentinel taps into the data and alerts they create. These additional platform building blocks along with other Azure security services, some discussed in earlier chapters, provide a holistic security platform for the SOC analyst.

The Azure Sentinel cloud SIEM leverages other security services including

- Log Analytics workspace

- Azure Monitor

- Azure Defender services

- Azure Logic Apps

The **Azure Log Analytics workspace** (LAW) is comprised of two components, a database for "metrics" and flat file storage for "raw log data." This is the main reason the Azure service is not titled the Log Analytics Database. Additional data can be stored in the Log Analytics workspace from other Azure services.

Azure "activity logs" is data stored in a LAW providing resources about the Azure infrastructure. You learned earlier about the data plane and management plane, so the artifact examples include administration, service health, alerts, auto-scale activity, security, and policy.

Metrics include data from the Azure guest virtual machine (VM) operating system (OS) and the hyper-V host operating system the guest VM is running on. You gain telemetry to track Windows OS performance counters and Linux OS counter data, get notification of issues, configure action data, and preform advanced analytics.

Diagnostic logs from the guest OS and applications have artifacts like performance counters, app logs, Windows event logs, IIS logs, crash dumps, and other error logs.

Azure Diagnostics is another service that writes to the LAW about the health of the application. Data collected includes performance counters, application logs, and Azure diagnostic logs.

Application Insights writes metrics and emits alerts based on web tests and proactive diagnostics. Once enabled from the Azure Monitor workspace landing page, Application Insights provides details for the overall performance of applications in Azure and dependencies from other services.

Log Analytics is a data repository for Azure infrastructure logs and events from the Log Analytics agent. The Windows and Linux agents with the Log Analytics extensions write logs and events. Azure Monitor, Azure Diagnostics and if System Center Operations Manager (SCOM) from on premises.

The **Azure Monitor** service can be described as a landing page for all metrics and data that can be stored in the Log Analytics workspace. If you want to learn how to better use Azure Sentinel and the Kusto Query Language (KQL), then spend time leaning Azure Monitor.

The automation included with Azure Monitor acts on the telemetry collected from all the Azure cloud and on-premises services. This provides real-time metrics on the guest VM and containers, and this data allows the analyst to drill into logs for troubleshooting and security diagnostics. If you enable Application Insights from Azure Monitor, it can detect issues across one or multiple applications.

You collect a lot of monitored resources in the LA workspace, and this data can be used to create alerts based on a single metric or multidimensional metrics. The alerts can support configuration of automated actions and notifications to alert service owners. Information can be viewed in customized dashboards and workbooks. Workbooks in Azure Monitor can visually display the data from varied sources with actionable links to provide more data points. Workbooks are working dashboards that support actions from the data being displayed.

Azure Defender services include the services that provide insight into their function by their individual product names. Microsoft Defender for Endpoint (MDE) is a cloud-based service that connects to the agent already installed on Microsoft Windows and Windows Server operating systems. Additionally, you can install agents for Linux, MacOS, and others. Microsoft Defender for Endpoint supports advanced security investigations on the network and endpoints. One of the features supports leveraging threat intelligence (TI) created by Microsoft security teams.

Microsoft Defender for Identity (MDI) is a cloud-based service that supports security on Microsoft Active Directory Domain Services (AD DS) on-premises. It has an agent that when installed with a read-only account detects and prevents credential theft. This security solution monitors user and system behavior and their activities to build a baseline. Microsoft Defender for Identity is used by the SOC analysts to detect attacks in the cloud hybrid environment.

Azure Security Center is constantly being updated, and the security service is engineered to support two main security areas. **Area 1**: The cloud security posture management (CSPM) includes features to identify a secure score and detect misconfigurations from the company standards in Azure. It leverages Azure policy to provide auditing on correctly configured services running in Infrastructure as a Service (IaaS), Platform as a Service (PaaS), and anywhere data is stored like Blob Storage. Many customers struggle with the free Azure Security Center vs. the Azure Defender cost as shown in Figure 3-1.

Area 2: The cloud workload protection (CWP) allows Azure Defender to integrate directly with the cloud services. The many services that it integrates with include Azure App Service, Azure Storage, SQL, Kubernetes, container registries, Key Vault, Azure Resource Manager, Azure DNS, and open source relational databases.

Azure Defender for	Resource Quantity	Pricing	Plan
Servers	0 servers	$15/Server/Month	On / Off
App Service	0 instances	$15/Instance/Month	On / Off
Azure SQL Databases	0 servers	$15/Server/Month	On / Off
SQL servers on machines	0 servers	$15/Server/Month $0.015/Core/Hour	On / Off
Open-source relational databases	0 servers	$15/Server/Month	On / Off
Storage	1 storage accounts	$0.02/10k transactions	On / Off
Kubernetes	0 kubernetes cores	$2/VM core/Month	On / Off
Container registries	0 container registries	$0.29/Image	On / Off
Key Vault	0 key vaults	$0.02/10k transactions	On / Off
Resource Manager		$4/1M resource management operati...	On / Off
DNS		$0.7/1M DNS queries	On / Off

By clicking Save, Azure Defender will be enabled on selected resource types. The first 30 days are free.
For more information on Security Center pricing, visit the pricing page.

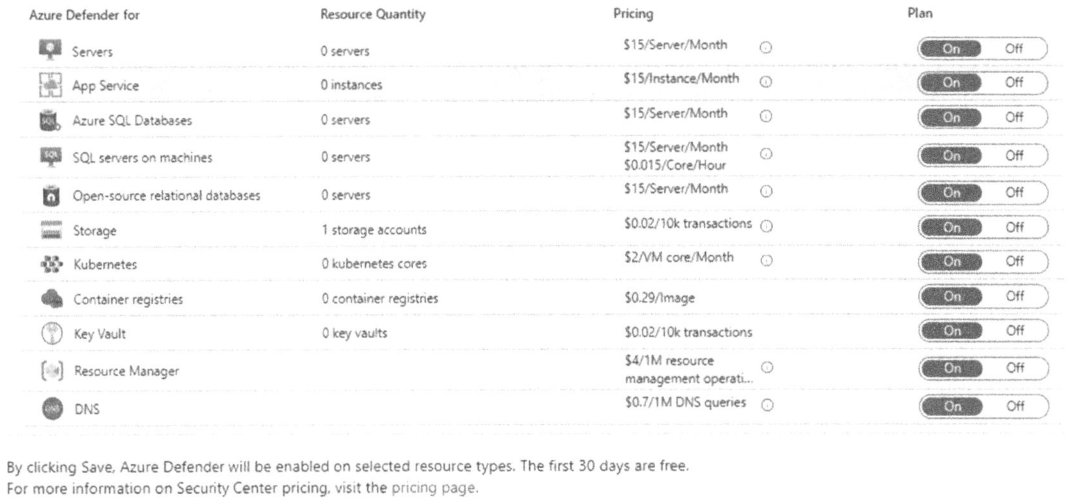

Figure 3-1. *Azure Security Center Defender pricing displayed in the console*

Azure Logic Apps is a cloud platform that is used to automate workflow. The workflow, for our focus, supports integration directly with Azure Sentinel and Azure Security Center. This cloud service is under the covers in Azure Sentinel to support the Security Orchestration, Automation, and Response (SOAR) capabilities. However, Logic Apps allows integration from Azure with almost any other type of applications. The Logic Apps platform supports using your own code and a low-code and/or no-code way to integrate cloud and on-premises applications in your hybrid network. Using the designer console, as seen in Figure 3-2, you communicate with other services like opening a ServiceNow incident from inside Azure Sentinel or other Defender solutions.

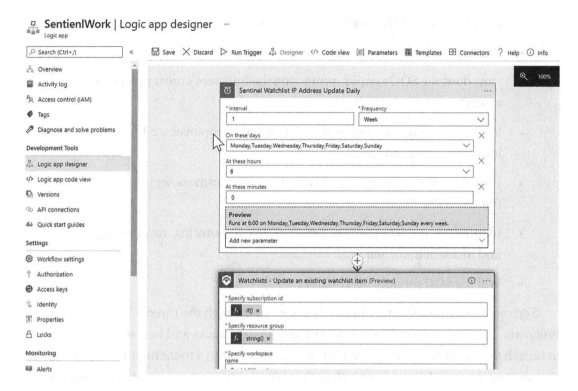

Figure 3-2. *Azure Logic Apps designer console*

Microsoft provides customers Azure Sentinel commitment tier options:

1 TB/day

2 TB/day

5 TB/day

Azure Sentinel Prioritization

In Chapter 1 you gained an overview of Azure Sentinel and how the cloud-native SIEM allows current SOC resources to eliminate laborious tasks of hardware upgrades and software updates. In Chapter 2 you followed exercises to connect data streams like logs, metrics, and threat intelligence data. Azure Sentinel is your company's SIEM solution, data is flowing, and now you need to prioritize the customization. So this SIEM supports the mission of your Security Operations Center. The mission is not a mission statement. However, the mission of the security team is the purpose and scope to support the security for the Security Operations Center business.

Some examples of the SOC business questions may be

- What is the SOC purpose and security mission?

- How does the SOC support protecting the business's most precious assets?

- Identify the SOC customers, like all company employees, all locations, or any partners.

- How does SOC security aligns with the CISO/business security framework?

- Identify the services the SOC provides, like monitoring, responding, and incident management.

- Will the SOC services be available 24/7?

Security Operations Center efficacy is achieved through the three pillars of People, Processes, and Technology. The process of identifying attacks and bad actors attempting to breach the business security and correlating all data into a meaningful event story line best defines the use of Azure Sentinel. A visual representation can be seen in Figure 3-3.

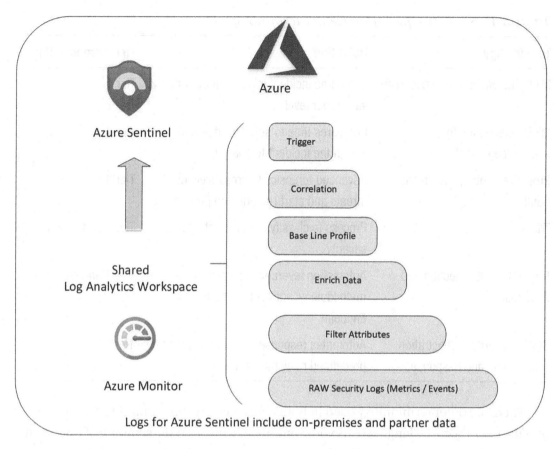

Figure 3-3. *Azure Sentinel ingestion, filtering, and enriching of data flow*

One area that should be reviewed is the terminology that is used by the SOC team to understand some of the ways to measure the effectiveness of the team to improve with training and time. In Table 3-1, the terminology used by the Security Operations Center is shared based on the level of expertise that follows Figure 3-3, and Tier 0 in this example is the automation level.

Table 3-1. *Security Operations Center terminology*

Terminology	Definition	Tier Responsibility
MTTR, mean time to remediation	Compares incident investigations with the same peer level	Tier 1 Tier 2
MTTA, mean time to acknowledgement	Compares time to acknowledge and assign the incident to analyst	Tier 1
Proactive hunting, blue team hunting	Advanced forensics to proactively detect threats and start remediation procedures	Tier 3
Triage	Process to classify the incident and its severity	Tier 1 and higher
EDR, Endpoint Detection and Response	Automation leveraging existing methodology: antivirus, Defender for Endpoint	Tier 1 and higher
SOAR, Security Orchestration, Automation, and Response	Automates response to incident types with predefined response procedures	Tier 0

There are other terminology used in both cybersecurity threat hunting, in Chapter 7, and the cloud security language. As you continue to gain an understanding of Microsoft Azure Sentinel, the connectivity between people, processes, and technology becomes more apparent. Additional levels of knowledge often follow the terminology used in the Security Operations Center conversations, as displayed in Figure 3-4. As the security subject matter experts (SMEs) increate their knowledge, the security incidents that they are assigned become more difficult. The security of the business follows this type of assignment of security incidents/anomalies across the cybersecurity industry.

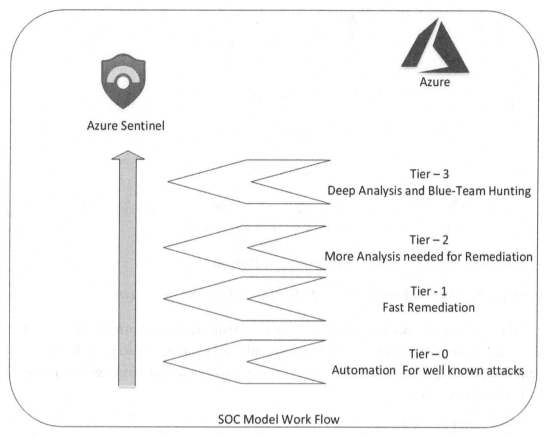

Figure 3-4. *SOC Model used for workflow and skill levels*

The creation of processes is easier to outline through planning sessions and use of whiteboard simulations.

By now you may have become aware of the integration between the Microsoft Defender solutions that together create an Extended Detection and Response (XDR) unified platform as seen in Figure 3-5. Azure Defender security support is the next topic.

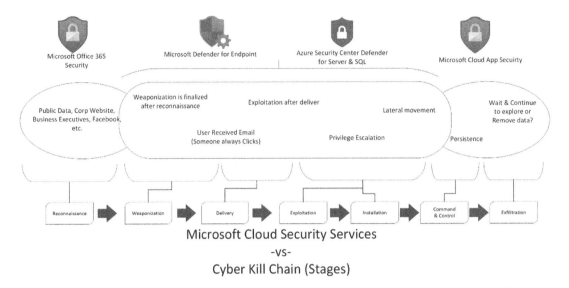

Figure 3-5. *Microsoft unified threat identity and protection design*

The Log Analytics workspace (LAW) is used in Azure Monitor, Azure Security Center, and Azure Sentinel, so it is a challenge to bring all the data into LAW so it can be used in Sentinel. Selecting data that matters is important, and from a high-level view, there are two categories of data:

- Forensic-value logs

- High-value logs

Learning to use the structure of the data is foundational, so it may help to think of LAW from the analogy of the Azure Windows log structure. The value of information is sometimes only appreciated once seen from Azure Sentinel because it brings all the logs into a central location: LAW. We have data coming in. All the Microsoft-provided logs are brought in, and custom logs are brought in. Custom logs can also be created and then brought into LAW.

Log Analytics workspaces have agents running on systems and bringing log data and metrics into them. Examples are event logs, "Windows event logs."

Syslog proxy is a Linux-based agent and can forward logs from appliances. We gather data from agents and proxy logs from on-premises systems. From Azure, we pull the logs from API systems.

If we use the example of Microsoft Defender for Endpoint (MDE), which has a native agent that is built into Windows 10 and Server 2019 and is managed from the MDE portal, it is pulling data into the data store. Now that we have agents collecting proxy data or other data into LAW, Sentinel provides the view and automation that allows visibility into normalizing traffic, data, and network patterns.

In Defender for Endpoint, we pull data from advanced hunting tables and start to query information for insights into criminal activity. This data is anomaly based and what you are looking for in blue team hunting, the SOC Tier 3 requiring SOC analysts with a high skill set.

The mindset of the analysts is to think "What would cause an anomaly?"

Other SIEM solutions would collect data and then rely heavily on the SOC to query the data and use skills to find the bad activity.

Consider the value of the data being collected. Look over the last 90 days and summarize by the eventID. How much data are you collecting? The point is the data collected from down-level systems rely on the policy of data being collected at the device.

Example:

Domain controller logs and events, both success and failure, need to be collected by Microsoft Defender for Identity.

We filter the data and bring it into the Log Analytics workspace so it can become more valuable in an "Alert Rule."

Alert monitoring is used in reporting because of the SIZE. Forensic-value logs create a lot of security noise. This is threat intelligence that can be collaborated with known indicators of compromise (IOC). We do not need an alert that someone logged into a system, but we do need to collect the data for forensic value and create a timeline. What is the value of an event where an entity opened a file or document? You may not care about the alert, but it is needed for forensic value if the file or document is altered to cause harm. Events have no clear forensic value by themselves. Think about all the events that take place when a user logs onto an OS. Many events are triggered, but not all of them are alerts.

Microsoft is one of the best threat intelligence (TI) providers, with Bug Bounty programs and strong relationships with research and government partners. Microsoft has a TI database, and value for customers is to tap into TI.

Note   Threat intelligence is covered in Chapter 5.

Additional Windows Security Events (preview) to limit the Create Data Collection Rules select the Custom collet option. Security eventid=4688) or

Microsoft 365 Defender, XDR

Azure Defender solutions also add to the Security Operations Center (SOC) building block components that are used for SOC analytics. The Azure services supported by Azure Sentinel are constantly being updated at a faster pace than traditional release cycles for on-premises software. The updates do appear in the console sometimes what seems like overnight, and because of this innovation, staying up to date is challenging. Even with the extension of Azure Sentinel benefits to your business, the complexity and level of sophistication of attacks require the integration of other Microsoft security solutions for Extended Detection and Response (XDR).

The inclusion of data collection from other systems is a new approach to collect and qualify data from system endpoints and email systems. Extended Detection and Response is defined by cyber-industry security analysts as designed to provide additional benefits like

- Integrated security across domains

- Endpoint intelligence that is actionable

- Automated integration benefits

You have learned about the individual Microsoft security stand-alone services so far. Now you begin to see their ability to connect seemingly disparate alerts to continue to shift security left in the kill chain. The end-to-end threat visibility across all company resources can be correlated and prioritized based on the resource type and Artificial Intelligence (AI) that is applied to the data. Microsoft made a marketing decision to change the names of many of their security products to help align with customers' security needs. However, the two different realms of IT need to be supported, in the Microsoft Azure cloud and on-premises. The two focus areas are

- Microsoft 365 Defender (end user based)

- Azure Defender (cloud and hybrid based)

Microsoft 365 Defender has four major security services that help provide the capabilities for XDR. Security requires data for identity, the user endpoint, the application in the cloud, email, and the files and documents used in business. Collecting more data is not the answer to the question, "Am I being hacked?" Artificial Intelligence is used to reduce the individual work items so the Security Operations Center can reduce the alerts that require human intervention. Raw data is collected by different individual Microsoft security services, as seen in Figure 3-6, and shared instantly to other services for a collective analysis.

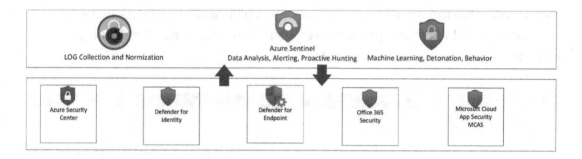

Microsoft Azure Sentinel and XDR Integration

Figure 3-6. *Defender XDR integration of security services*

The reduction of alerts so they are manageable for a business is critical, and Microsoft 365 Defender technologies together help the security analyst.

Microsoft 365 Defender provides Extended Detection and Response (XDR) by combining four technologies:

- Microsoft 365 Defender (previously Microsoft Threat Protection)

- Microsoft Defender for Endpoint (MDE, previously Microsoft Defender Advanced Threat Protection (ATP))

- Microsoft Defender for Office 365 (previously Office 365 Advanced Threat Protection)

- Microsoft Defender for Identity (MDI, previously Azure Advanced Threat Protection)

If you have been a Microsoft customer, you have, no doubt, heard the phrase "better together." The recent license changes allow the use of these security products together and provide a more holistic view of your hybrid enterprise. Microsoft Defender for Endpoint supports iOS and Android to extend the protection across all major operating system platforms including MacOS.

There are consolidation actions that continue to combine the (too many) Microsoft security access portals, so eventually you do not need to use the individual product security portals. The most current view of consolidated services includes Microsoft Defender for 365 (`https://security.microsoft.com`) as shown in Figure 3-7. You should notice that this console view includes email (Office 365 Defender), endpoint (Defender for Endpoint), and product investigations to support combining three individual consoles into a unified portal.

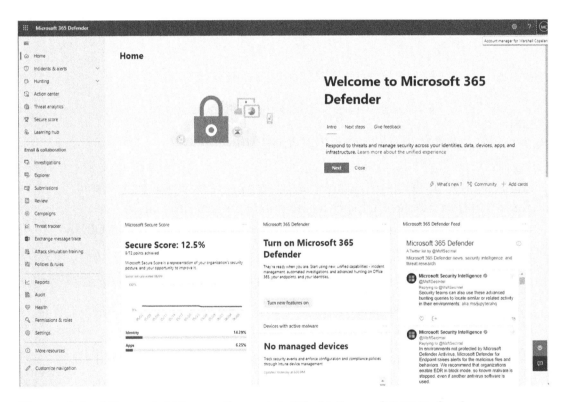

Figure 3-7. *Microsoft 365 security portal, titled Microsoft 365 Defender*

If this is the first time you have logged into the Microsoft 365 Defender portal, you need to create the Defender for Office 365 email portal in the following exercise. The Microsoft Security Center console consolidates these Microsoft 365 Defender services:

- Microsoft Defender for Endpoint

- Microsoft Defender for Office 365

- Microsoft Defender for Identity

- Microsoft Cloud App Security

The security console brings together previous individual security portals, to provide a full story of the attacks, product alerts, and attack behaviors. This one portal supports different security teams to perform effective threat analysis and blue team hunting across all endpoints and Office data.

Note   Follow your change management process to enable the XDR capabilities provided in this exercise. The critical change requires preparation and discussion with your security team. All the organization accounts will be redirected, so please do not make this one-way change without considerable team discussions.

ENABLE MICROSOFT 365 XDR INTEGRATION

The security features are available if you have the correct prerequisites enabled with these few steps. The license is validated once you connect from your browser to security.microsoft. com . The Azure role based on Role-Based Access Control (RBAC) needed to be assigned at the Azure tenant or Azure subscription is **Security Administrator** or **Global Administrator**.

- Microsoft 365 E5 or A5

- Microsoft 365 E3 with the Microsoft 365 E5 security add-on

- Microsoft 365 A3 with the Microsoft 365 A5 security add-on

- Windows 10 Enterprise E5 or A5

- Enterprise Mobility + Security (EMS) E5 or A5

- Office 365 E5 or A5

- Microsoft Defender for Endpoint

- Microsoft Defender for Identity

- Microsoft Cloud App Security

- Defender for Office 365 (Plan 2)

If you are not sure of the license and need to validate, go to the Microsoft 365 admin center to view the current company license at `https://admin.microsoft.com`. Select the Billing menu and then the Licenses tab to validate the eligibility.

1. Once your browser is open and connected to security.microsoft.com, select from the left-hand menu Settings (gear icon). The view provides settings for integration.

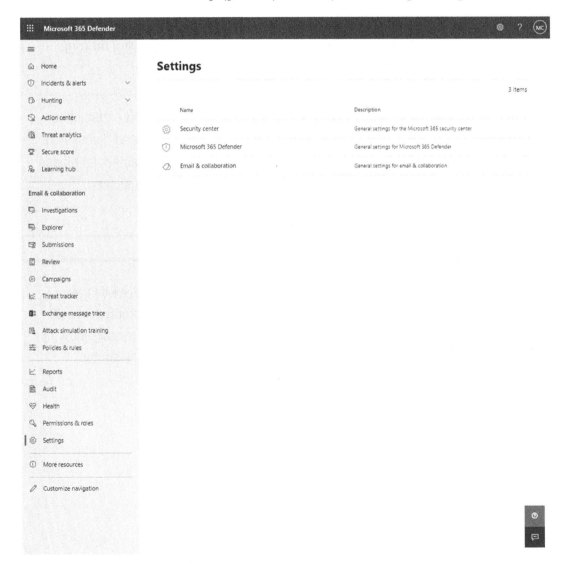

2. Select the Microsoft 365 Defender name with the description General settings
   for Microsoft 365 Defender. It may take a few minutes for the security
   workspace to be created.

3. Refresh the console if necessary, and once the screen displays the three
    options again, you can validate your account connectivity by selecting Microsoft
    365 Defender.

4. Return to the previous screen and select Email & collaboration to review
    the necessary change. Select the option to have the older portal, `https://
    protection.office.com`, to be redirected to this portal you are using,
    `https://security.microsoft.com`.

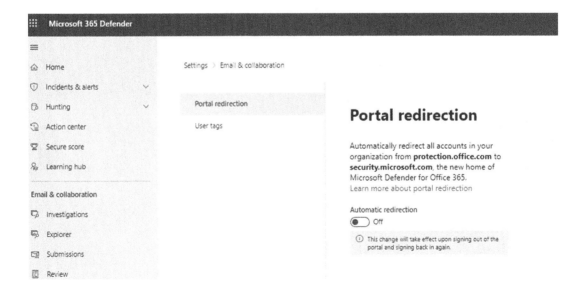

5. If you have followed the Azure cloud change process of your company and are ready to proceed, select the toggle switch and notice the pop-up warning.

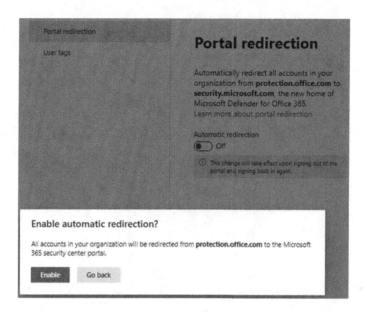

6. The change will take effect once you sign out of the portal and then sign back in. Once signed back in, the security portal integration is complete, and you can begin to use the XDR capabilities. Notice the integration of email and collaboration added for this exercise.

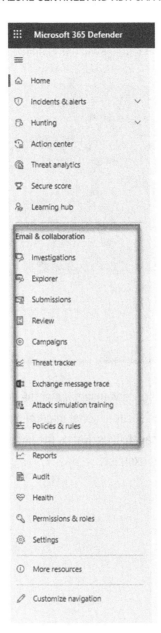

The new Azure Sentinel Extended Detection and Response (XDR) integration adds currently available metrics and logs.

As you begin to spend time in the Azure Defender security console, the XDR integration can be seen immediately throughout the portal. All alerts come from each of the Microsoft 365 security products. Additional security exercises in this book are used to help provide context to one of the many Microsoft Defender security benefits and to help with security training to become more efficient. The exercises provided support cyber-attack simulations to help build confidence as you begin to integrate Azure Defender security to provide more current defense strategies with the security incident response process.

If you are new to Microsoft security services, there are many training features that are integrated into them. You need to evaluate the training options that best support your time and resources. With that in mind, you should review the new integration and consolidation of security features to minimize the learning curve. Microsoft has invested in educating you from inside the security console and reducing the need for some instructor-led classes. Select the Learning hub option from the left-hand menu, as shown in Figure 3-8.

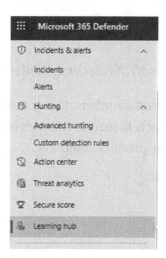

Figure 3-8. *Microsoft 365 Defender learning hub*

The learning hub is the best place to come up to speed on all of the integration for security using Microsoft 365 Defender. As you can see in Figure 3-9, the topics include Microsoft Defender basics to start and help build expertise and dexterity in this security solution.

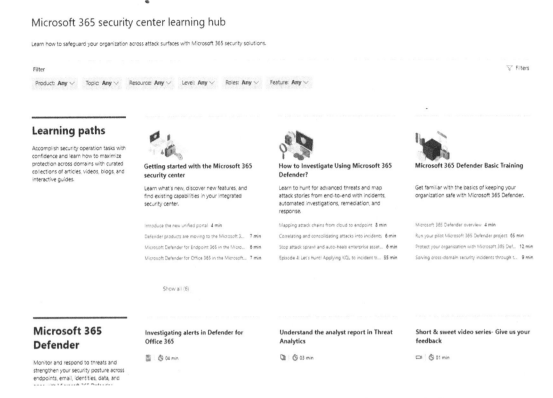

Figure 3-9. *Overview of Microsoft 365 security center learning hub*

If there are several security team members, it may be easier to divide the learning paths by selecting different products to learn. As shown in Figure 3-10, select the drop-down menu just to the right of the product label.

Microsoft 365 security center learning hub

Learn how to safeguard your organization across attack surfaces with Microsoft 365 security solutions.

Filter

| Product: Any ∨ | Topic: Any ∨ | Resource: Any ∨ | Level: Any ∨ | Roles: Any ∨ | Feature: Any ∨ |

🔍 Search by product

☐ Microsoft 365 Defender   49

☐ Microsoft Defender for Office 365 30

☐ Microsoft Defender for Endpoint   29

☐ Microsoft Defender for Identity   2

☐ Microsoft Cloud App Security   1

interactive guides.

Getting started with the Microsoft 365 security center

How to Investiga Defender?

Figure 3-10. *Product filtering view in the learning hub*

When you have different team members assigned to different products, the sharing of alerts, tracking, and reporting can be consumed more quickly. This effort may take some coordination on when each product is tested using the built-in attack simulation as shown in Figure 3-11.

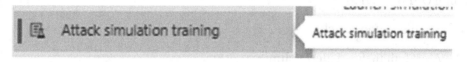

Figure 3-11. *Attack simulation training*

Select this option to view the types of attack simulation to learn the benefits of Microsoft 365 Defender and improve the overall security posture.

Security Road Map

Once you have started to configure the components for the Security Operations Center discussed in this chapter, there may be a need to pull data from logs that currently do not have a built-in data connector. Over 100 connectors pulling metrics and logs from Azure services and partner solutions are necessary to help as many customers ingest logs from security solutions they have invested in. Some larger customers may have custom-built, in-house solutions they would like to include and pull data from to be used in hunting queries.

The need to poll for data is with the Application Programing Interface (API) for the applications. If this in custom or a third part security solution that currently does not have a built-in data connector. Currently ingest is supported using the Common Event Format (CEF) format, Syslog, and Logic Apps.

A feature that should be enabled in your production Azure Sentinel deployment is User and Entity Behavior Analytics (UEBA). The process of User and Entity Behavior Analytics is to build a baseline of activity starting with the raw data from logs and metrics. An example would be triggering an alert rule from an event ID on a specific server with a date and time stamp. Then contextual information is added based on insight into the user, work title, and sensitivity of the server, whether or not the server is a high-value asset. UEBA then analyzes if this is the first time the server has been accessed by this user account and the geolocation the request was seen in. Was it from a known "botnet network"? All data is aligned with the MITRE framework to help provide information on this alert.

This Azure Sentinel feature can support better SOC metrics including "time to acknowledge and alert" and "time to remediation" once an adversary is discovered. One of the critical considerations for enabling UEBA is for the security team to realize what problems it will solve. Specifically having a use case is important to appreciate the value of enabling UEBA, such as

- Sophisticated attacks

- Alert fatigue from alert volume

- Tuning rules

- Insider threats

You read the current information from threat reports like Microsoft Security Intelligence Report (SIR), Verizon Data Breach investigations Report (DBIR), IBM Phenome, and others so you know attackers are clever and well-funded and have sophisticated malware. Create a baseline of user traffic patterns by enabling User and Entity Behavior Analytics (UEBA), which can help security teams to focus on high intrinsic value targets and gain quick awareness of sensitive system accounts and users.

Azure Sentinel rules often lack context regarding type of incident if no baseline is created. Rules need to exclude artifacts like an IP address and include other information like a machine name, so the alert is customized for your network. Many SOC analysts are challenged by the security noise that alerts create, and these alerts are classified as false negatives or false positives. UEBA is designed to help remove as much of the noise once an automated baseline is created. Baseline creation requires time and validation and does not account for exceptions. (Exceptions like temporary role changes that mandate different behavior for administrators on vacation skew the baseline. You should expect additional tuning because of this security noise.) The expectation is the UEBA continues to have engineering hours invested to provide better security protection.

Data is pulled from a watch list for custom entities, Azure Active Directory logs, Microsoft security events, and sign-in logs. Future access points will be added to support security from different repositories and other third-party security solutions.

Summary

In this chapter, you learned how Microsoft supports XDR with additional security solutions like Defender for Endpoint and Defender for Identity. You learned that the integration between the solutions MDI and MDE is easily enabled and provides the extended reach to provide more security for your company. Next you begin to use the integration of XDR and Azure Sentinel with other industry standards for Threat Intelligence.

PART II

CHAPTER 4

Sentinel Data Connection

In Chapter 1 you learned about a few of the Azure Sentinel data connectors to bring data into the Sentinel AI and automation for analysis. Now you expand on the process of RBAC security to connected data from Azure, resources, and virtual appliances for applying "hunting" to discover anomalies in your network.

A deeper dive is provided to help you gain insight into the differences between the data plane and control plane. Then you continue to learn about where specific Azure native data is being provided and how to validate the data is flowing from that data source. Validation of flow includes learning more about the Kusto Query Language (KQL) and greater information on the following topics.

In this chapter you learn about

- Azure control plane and data plane

- Native data connectors

- KQL queries and validation of data flow

- Log Analytics storage options

- Industry leaders' third-party data

Azure Control Plane and Data Plane

Begin your learning in this chapter with the clarification of a few key terms to help you identify the data that comes from Azure, namely, the control plane and data plane. This may be clear for many of the IT teams. However, if you're new to Azure or if the definitions are not crystal clear, then identifying the differences now helps to level set your foundational knowledge. Azure Sentinel is useful to better identify when there are changes to the data plane even with resource locks in place.

© Marshall Copeland 2021
M. Copeland, *Cloud Defense Strategies with Azure Sentinel*, https://doi.org/10.1007/978-1-4842-7132-2_4

Managing resources in your Azure subscription using Azure Portal, the CLI, PowerShell, or the Azure published REST APIs uses the **control plane**. The key term is the **management** of resources in your Azure subscription. Requests, however they are created, using the control plane operations are sent to Azure Resource Manager (ARM). Two of the examples of using the control plane would be to create a virtual network (VNet) and then add virtual machines (VMs) that will be used to host a database service. This database service would be placed into the virtual network by the control plane. There are many components that are enabled though the use of the control plane. During your previous Azure architecture work, you create a resource group. You then apply Role-Based Access Control (RBAC) to the VM such as the storage accounts for the virtual disks. This high-level creation of the virtual machine is an example of where Azure Resource Manager uses Role-Based Access Control (RBAC). Azure Resource Manager handles all the control plane requests and applies features automatically to the resource, which also uses the control plane.

Note   The control plane manages requests based on green field (aka new resource) and brown field (aka existing resource). Keep these use cases in mind as you read this chapter.

The data plane operations are sent to an endpoint that pinpoints the resource instance, making a configuration change to the data that is part of the database server, from the previous example. The best way to think of this is operations sent to a single database server out of the many VMs that are a database server in the same virtual network. This is where the security controls must be considered to support the data plane security gaps.

Authenticated and authorized users interact with resources using the data plane. This interaction should be a serious consideration for the security team, governance team, auditing team, and Security Operations Center (SOC) team that are proactively hunting alerts from Azure Sentinel. Team members need to be alerted when data is edited (an anomaly) or something occurs that's not part of normal application or data processes.

If we continue using our database sever example, an Azure resource lock could be put in place to prevent malware from deleting the database. If the malware has successfully accomplished credential theft as an authorized user, then business integrity becomes more challenging to be maintained. The Azure lock does not prevent the deletion or altering of data through user database queries. The security team needs to take into consideration the different methods users use to interact with data maintained in the Azure resource.

As a reminder, earlier you learned that the control plane is used for the management of resources, additions (green field), and updates (brown filed). Azure provides several security services that should be put in place to help you manage the control plane. The best practice security recommendations include

- Least privilege restrictions

- Use of scoped Azure RBAC

- Preventing deletion of resources

- Preventing modification of resources

The use of Azure locks also causes different security protection effects based on the Azure service. Azure locks applied to services are different based on the Azure service. Azure provides two management locks that are applied to resources and support the security triad—Confidentiality, Integrity, and Availability (CIA)—differently. The two different locks are

- Read Only

- Do Not Delete

If we use an Azure storage account example and apply the Azure management lock Read Only to the storage account, then data requests are managed to a specific level of security.

Read Only locks prevent users from deleting or manipulating an Azure resource, like the storage account. Read Only locks applied to a storage account prevent assignment of RBAC roles at the scope of the storage account but not the data in the container. Read Only locks on a storage account, or a database, do not prevent data from being deleted or modified. A Read Only lock prevents the Azure storage account (container) from being deleted. Refer to Figure 4-1 to gain a visual understanding of Azure Services that have different lock attributes.

The effects of Read Only locks and Do Not Delete locks are different across Azure resources. Locks are assigned to the resource and not the data in the resource. However, not all Azure resources support locks.

Note   Read more details about locks and some of the effects at Lock resources to prevent changes – Azure Resource Manager I Microsoft Docs.

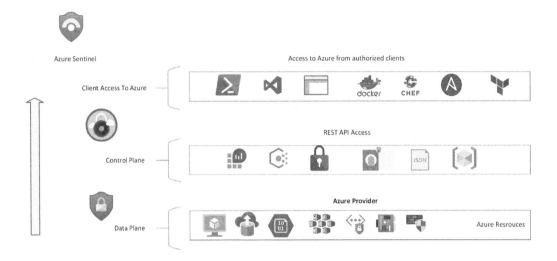

Microsoft Azure Sentinel + Data Plane + Control Plane + Client access to Azure

Figure 4-1. *A visual separation of the Azure data plane and control plane*

You have a better understanding of some of the management abilities of the control plane and the data plane. Now you need to gain deeper insight with guidance into specific log files. With the security focus, you need to learn and train the Azure security teams about activity in logs to better determine

- Actions taken at the subscription level

- What account or user started or stopped an operation

- Date and time of the operation

- What are the related attributes to the operation

Note   The operation can be part of normal change management or could be an attack from a criminal.

A consideration when deciding to use a resource lock on Azure resources is to focus on the resource group. Consider the data plane and the type of information to which the resource has access. The three main categories would be an Azure storage account that has data in Blob, files, etc., Azure SQL Database, and, an odd exception, Azure storage account "list keys" operation. Both options from the portal, Do Not Delete and Read Only, prevent the resource from being accidently deleted. However, the rule of thumb is as follows:

- If the resource focus is on data manipulation for normal operation, then use the Do Not Delete lock.

- If the resource focus in not on the data, which in this definition is focused on "no changes allowed," then use a Read Only lock.

- Exceptions for Read Only locks include any time there is an HTTP POST request, as in the list of keys from an Azure storage account, or when an unrealized "list" command is needed to read data.

The next topic is saving data from Azure data plane services, and just a little reminder, the standard data activity logs are kept for 90 days, so providing ranges of dates beyond the 90 days is sometimes required for security operations. You learn how to save security-related activity and logs beyond 90 days in the "Log Analytics Storage Options" section in this chapter.

Native Data Connectors

Azure Sentinel requires more data to provide the Security Operations Center (SOC) team the best actionable data. Now you walk through many of the standard data collection processes in additional exercises. Remember, in Chapter 1, you learned how easy it is to enable Azure Sentinel. If you skipped that exercise, please return to that chapter and complete it before attempting the exercises in this chapter.

You have the production Log Analytics workspace identified (from Chapter 1), and now as you go through the data connection process, the data is written once to the workspace to save on cost by preventing duplicate data repositories.

You should always attempt to improve the quality of data, from both the management plane and data plane, for SIEM analysis. There is a balance needed because if there is too much data, the signal-to-noise ratio will increase and so will the false negatives. There are over 100 data connection options, especially if you enable data collection using different third-party systems. Refer to Figure 4-2 for a visual understanding of the log categories. More data collected may not increase the efficiency of the SOC team because of the amount of noise ingested by Azure Sentinel. The foundational data collection should include

- Azure resource logs (data fidelity increases with premium license)

- Azure platform logs (host logs)

- Azure network data

- Azure Active Directory data

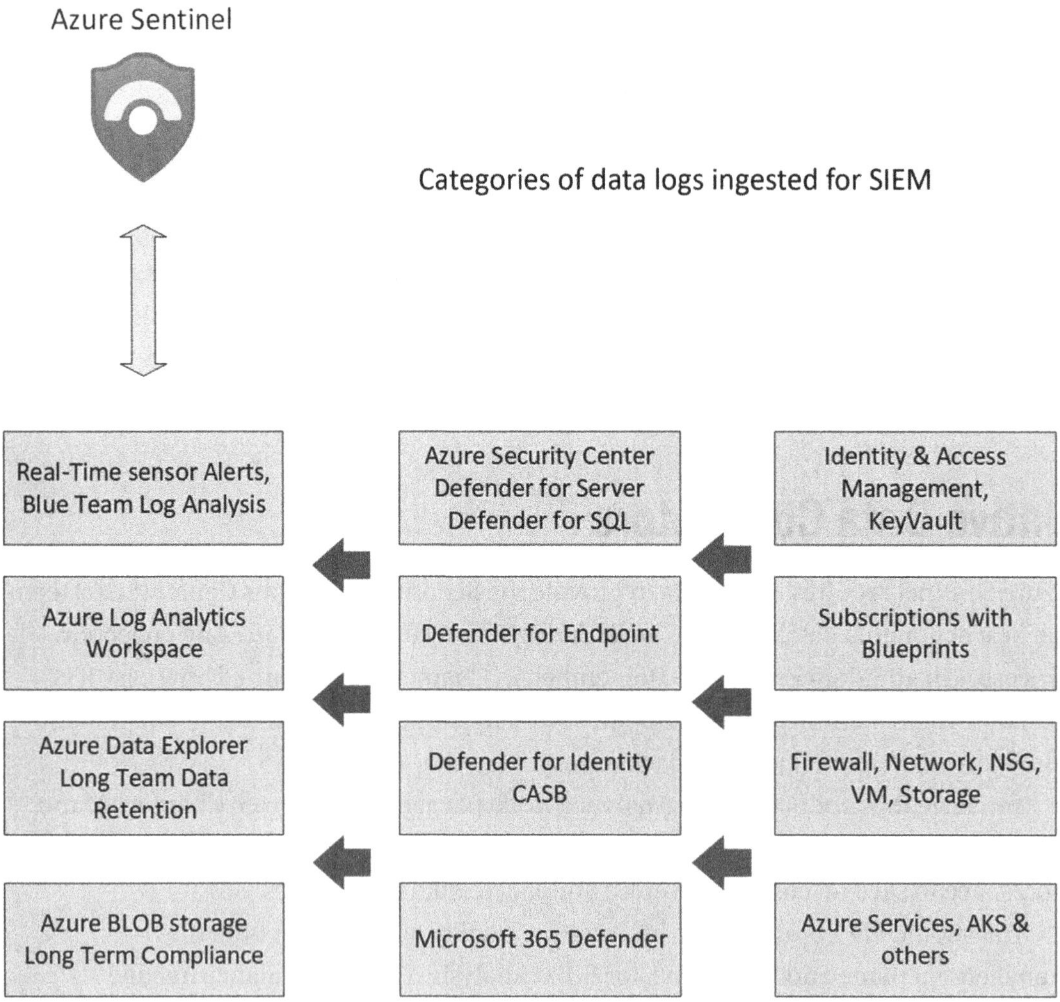

Azure Sentinel

Categories of data logs ingested for SIEM

Real-Time sensor Alerts, Blue Team Log Analysis	Azure Security Center Defender for Server Defender for SQL	Identity & Access Management, KeyVault
Azure Log Analytics Workspace	Defender for Endpoint	Subscriptions with Blueprints
Azure Data Explorer Long Team Data Retention	Defender for Identity CASB	Firewall, Network, NSG, VM, Storage
Azure BLOB storage Long Term Compliance	Microsoft 365 Defender	Azure Services, AKS & others

Figure 4-2. *Categories of different types of data logs ingested for a SIEM solution and used to stop attacks earlier in the kill chain*

Collecting data has similar challenges as projects that encompass "big data" and no-SQL databases. The process includes: velocity, volume, and value of the data. Table 4-1 provides some of the challenges for SIEM solutions as they causally relate to challenges of big data projects. Some tables and images include more categories than the main ones listed here.

Table 4-1. *Data veracity for data science and big data projects*

Category	Definition
Volume	Throughput of data for continuous monitoring
Variety	Unstructured data, different taxonomies
Value	How relevant is the data
Velocity	Speed of processing for faster data generation rates (i.e., more connectors increase ingestion)
Variable	Non-deterministic data point velocity increasing (i.e., attack increase from nation states)

Next in the process you need to continue to configure additional Azure Sentinel connectors for data analysis, and this next exercise could be used as a template in your deployment. This exercise does not repeat the foundational data connectors from Chapter 1 and does expect all data connectors to remain enabled for all future exercises in the book.

ENABLE AZURE FOUNDATIONAL DATA CONNECTORS

1. First, log into Azure Portal, with the RBAC privileges recommended for access to Sentinel, Azure Contributor and Security Administrator roles. Search for Azure Sentinel and go to the Azure Sentinel service.

Note   Additional privileges may be required based on the Azure service or third-party service Sentinel is connecting. ·

---

2.   Select Azure Sentinel ➤ Data connectors.

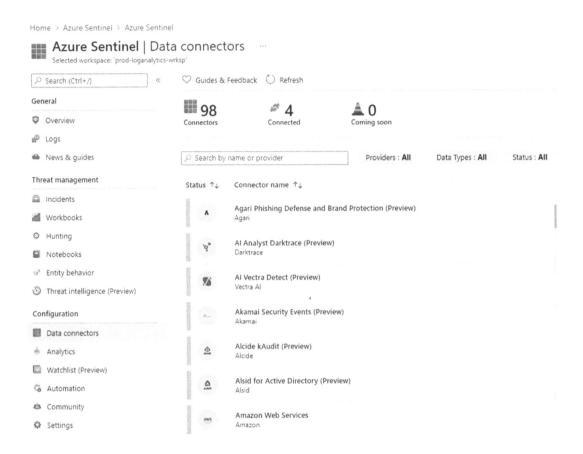

3.   This exercise guides you to enable a few of the Microsoft provider connectors
     that are licensed for Azure and Microsoft products. The easiest method is to
     deselect the All option and scroll down and check the box by Microsoft and then
     click OK.

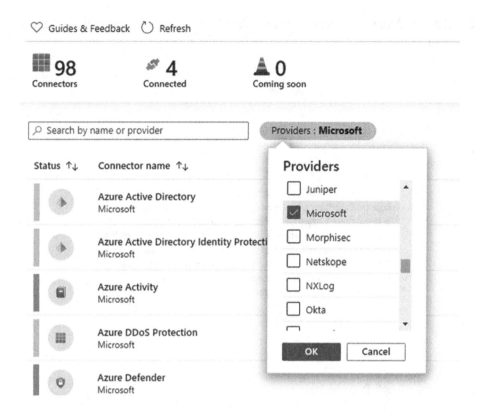

4. Also, you can simply search for each individual connector starting with DDoS from the filter view.

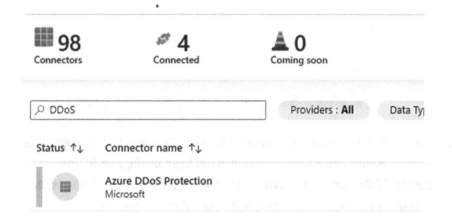

5. Highlight Azure DDoS Protection and select Open connector page on the bottom right.

6. Notice the prerequisites (in the window text) and then select Open Diagnostics settings. **If your Azure subscription has not been configured for the standard DDoS protection plan and you want the enhanced features, then follow the instructions and enable it now before continuing**.

Instructions   Next steps

Prerequisites

To integrate with Azure DDoS Protection make sure you have:

✓ **Workspace:** read and write permissions are required.

ⓘ **Azure DDoS protection plan:** Requires a configured Azure DDoS Standard protection plan read more about Azure DDoS protection plans.

ⓘ **Enabled Azure DDoS for virtual network:** Requires a configured virtual network with Azure DDoS Standard enabled read more about configuring virtual network with Azure DDoS.

Configuration

Connect Azure DDoS Protection to Azure Sentinel

Enable Diagnostic Logs on All Public IP Addresses.

Open Diagnostics settings >

Inside your Diagnostics settings portal, select your Public IP Address resource:

Inside your Public IP Address resource:

1. Select + **Add diagnostic setting.**
2. In the **Diagnostic setting** blade:
    ○ Type a **Name**, within the **Diagnostics settings** name field.
    ○ Select **Send to Log Analytics.**
    ○ Choose the log destination workspace.
    ○ Select the categories that you want to analyze (recommended: DDoSProtectionNotifications, DDoSMitigationFlowLogs, DDoSMitigationReports)
    ○ Click **Save.**

7. Select Open Diagnostics settings, select Send to Log Analytics, and choose the same Log Analytics workspace that is used with Azure Sentinel. In this Azure environment, it is the production Log Analytics workspace.

Home > Azure Sentinel > Azure DDoS Protection >

Diagnostic settings ⚲ ⋯

○ Refresh   ♡ Feedback

Subscription * ⓘ	Resource group ⓘ	Resource type ⓘ
prod-150 ⌄	Prod-Security-Logs-RG ⌄	Log Analytics workspaces ⌄

prod-150 > Prod-Security-Logs-RG

ⓘ **Select any of the resources to view diagnostic settings.**

Name	Resource type	Resource group	Diagnostics status
🖥 prod-loganalytics-wrksp	Log Analytics workspace	Prod-Security-Logs-RG	✔ Enabled

8. Select the correct Log Analytics workspace and select the + Add diagnostics setting.

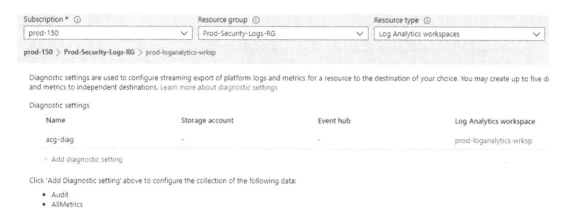

9. From the Diagnostic setting view, check the boxes to the left of Audit and AllMetrics.

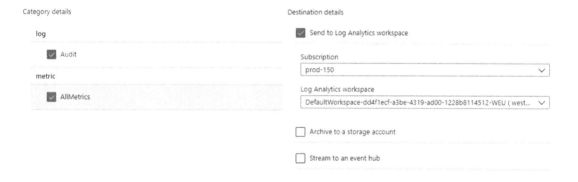

10. Use your mouse to select the down error on the right of the Log Analytics workspace (default) field and select the same production Log Analytics workspace as with Azure Sentinel.

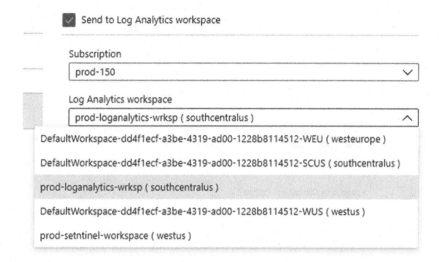

11. Finally you can name the diagnostic setting, and the Save option becomes enabled, so you can save the data and return to the Sentinel view.

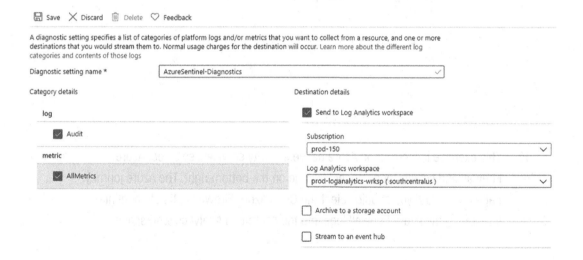

12. From the Sentinel search screen, type the word **firewall**. Notice the number of Microsoft Azure native connections and third-party firewall appliances. Notice there are several, and if you have one of these virtual appliances installed, you should configure it.

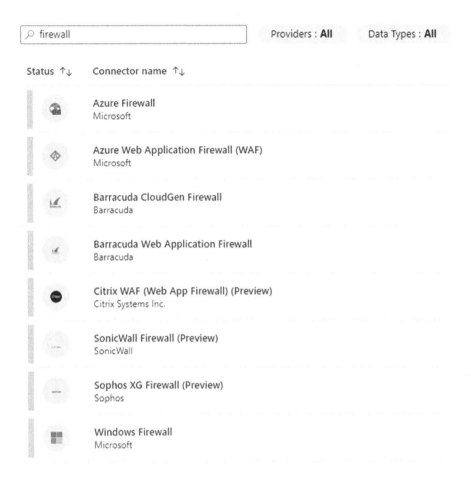

13. This exercise is focused on Azure native security services, so select Azure Firewall and select Open connector page on the bottom right. The Azure journey page opens, and you should select the Open Azure Firewall option to continue integrating the Azure Firewall logs into the Azure Log Analytics workspace.

Instructions   Next steps

Prerequisites

To integrate with Azure Firewall make sure you have:

✓ **Workspace:** read and write permissions are required.

Configuration

Connect Azure Firewall to Azure Sentinel

Enable Diagnostic Logs on All Firewalls.

Open Azure Firewall >

Inside your Firewall resource:

1. Select **Diagnostic logs.**
2. Select + **Add diagnostic setting.**
3. In the **Diagnostic setting** blade:
   - Type a **Name.**
   - Select **Send to Log Analytics.**
   - Choose the log destination workspace.
   - Select the categories that you want to analyze (recommended: AzureFirewallApplicationRule, AzureFirewallNetworkRule)
   - Click **Save.**

14. Select the Enable option for the correct firewall if you have multiple options. Note this is recommended for a proof of concept until the analytics and workflows materialize. Other considerations are to use Azure Firewall Manager.

Home > Azure Sentinel > Azure Firewall >

Firewalls ✗ ⋯
Default Directory

+ New   ⚙ Manage view ⌄   ⟳ Refresh   ⬇ Export to CSV   ⌥ Open query | ⊘ Assign tags | ♡ Feedback

| Filter for any field... | Subscription == **all** | Resource group == **all** ✕ | Location == **all** ✕ | ⁺⛢ Add filter |

Showing 1 to 1 of 1 records.

✓ Name ↑↓	Type ↑↓	Resource group ↑↓
✓ 🔥 firewall1	Firewall	sandbox-lrn-mlc-rg

15. Select the firewall (firewall1 in this view) and then select the Diagnostics
    settings option and then select the + Add diagnostic setting option to add the
    logs and metrics.

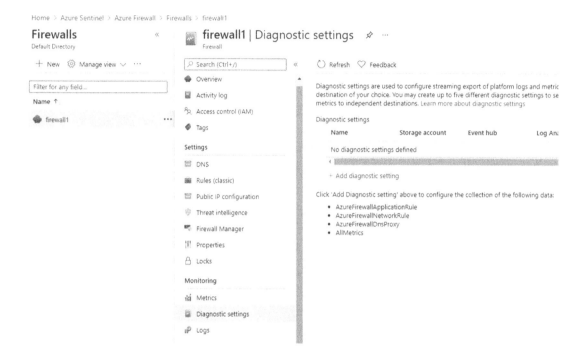

16. Enter the name for the diagnostic setting by using the same production Log
    Analytics workspace, select the Save option, and return to the Sentinel view.

Home > Azure Sentinel > Azure Firewall > Firewalls > firewall1 >

Diagnostic setting   ...

🖫 Save   ✕ Discard   🗑 Delete   ♡ Feedback

A diagnostic setting specifies a list of categories of platform logs and/or metrics that you want to collect from a resource, and one or more destinations that you would stream them to. Normal usage charges for the destination will occur. Learn more about the different log categories and contents of those logs

Diagnostic setting name *   [AzureFirewall-diag   ✓]

Category details   Destination details

   log   ☑ Send to Log Analytics workspace

     ☑ AzureFirewallApplicationRule   Subscription
                                                             [prod-150   ⌄]
     ☑ AzureFirewallNetworkRule   Log Analytics workspace
                                                             [prod-loganalytics-wrksp (southcentralus) ⌄]
     ☑ AzureFirewallDnsProxy

   metric   ☐ Archive to a storage account

     ☑ AllMetrics   ☐ Stream to an event hub

17. Continue to enable the connectors for each of the Microsoft products that are included in your enterprise subscription.

Note   In this chapter, there is a separate exercise to enable Threat Intelligence – TAXII from Microsoft.

You may see some data instantly available, and other data points may take time to collect and start to populate in the Log Analytics workspace.

Log Analytics Storage Options

You created a single Log Analytics workspace to collect data from virtual machines and applications for your production Azure resources. The VMs write log and metric data, so information can be provided on the individual VM bases. The logs from Azure Active Directory and Azure host systems are collected so that now both Azure Monitor and Azure Sentinel continue to process in real time.

In our Sentinel demonstrations, you learn about the functionality and data points. However, a large enterprise may realistically look at much more data. The best recommendation is to use a single Log Analytics workspace. However, if data is in Europe, Germany, or the United Kingdom, multiple workspaces may be needed for compliance support.

One of the reduction of cost considerations is knowing which of the data connector logs incur no additional cost and are included with Azure Sentinel. Select the Settings option on the left-hand side to review the Azure Sentinel pricing page as shown in Figure 4-3.

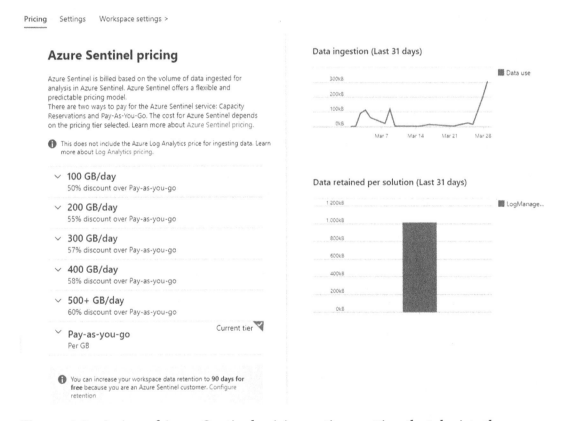

Figure 4-3. *A view of Azure Sentinel pricing options setting that depicts the cost options for multiple hundreds of gigabytes per day collected*

As the Log Analytics workspace continues to improve the quality of data as the velocity increases, the cost savings can be achieved at 100 GB/day increments. You can select a discount for storing more data; however, the timeline is every 30 days. If your

Azure Sentinel deployment reaches more than 300 GB/day, you can select the 57% discount through the pay-as-you-go model as shown in Figure 4-4. However, before you select the Apply button, realize this is a commitment for the next 30 days. If there was an anomalous influx of data for a few days to exceed the current size and then it now falls back down to a lower amount, you cannot select a lower pricing model until day 31.

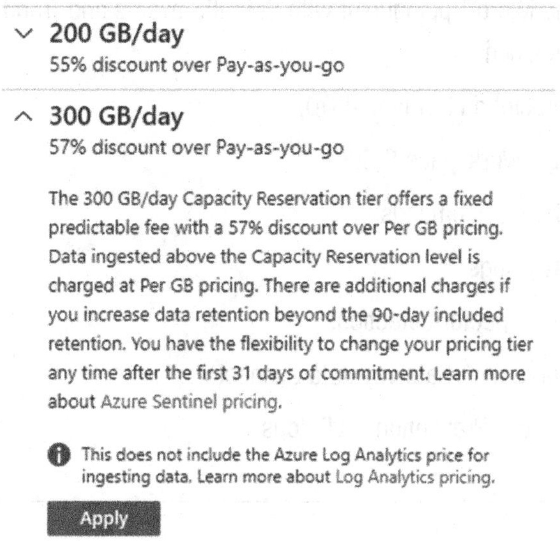

Figure 4-4. *The view of an option to select a 57% discount for data exceeding 300 GB/day*

Industry Leaders' Third-Party Data

There are many announcements for partners and third-party data connecters and the pre-created KQL queries that are released monthly and quarterly.

Table 4-2. *Azure Sentinel announced data connector examples*

Company	Details
Cisco	Four connectors including Cisco Umbrella, Cisco Meraki, Cisco Firepower, Cisco UCS
Salesforce Cloud	38 logs that include audit, files, and more
Trend Micro	Trend Micro TippingPoint with SMS IPS events and Trend Micro XDR workbench
Proofpoint	Proofpoint on Demand (POD)
Google	Google Workspace G Suite
VMware ESXi	vSphere system logs
SonicWall	Firewall logs
ESET	ESET Inspector detections
Imperva	Imperva WAF Gateway data connector
Broadcom Symantec	Data Loss Prevention (DLP) logs

Next, you learn how important the Kusto Query Language (KQL) is in your ability to identify information in logs and metrics provided by data connectors. In addition, you start a journey to enhance your knowledge of KQL to use beyond Azure Sentinel.

Kusto Query Language

Microsoft has invested in the need for Azure security to go beyond just learning the Kusto Query Language (KQL). You need to know how to create queries in greater depth than first realized. The support for KQL is included with Azure Monitor, Azure Security Center, and Azure Sentinel and at the Server OS level.

This section of the chapter starts your KQL learning journey at a beginner level, and in later chapters, advanced topics in the Kusto Query Language are introduced. This, of course, is the introductory module. In the next module, you will begin exploring user analytics. You will uncover interesting statistics about users who access our systems. Next, we will spend time executing queries to perform geographic analysis. You gain insight into how to use KQL to look for clusters of activities based upon their location on a map. In the next module, you can spend time performing diagnostic and root cause analysis. The processes to bring metrics and logs into the Azure Log Analytics workspace can be seen in Figure 4-5. The Log Analytics workspace, sometimes represented by the acronym LAW, is a repository for Azure Monitor, Azure Security Center, Azure resources (i.e., VM metrics and logs), and Azure data plane logs.

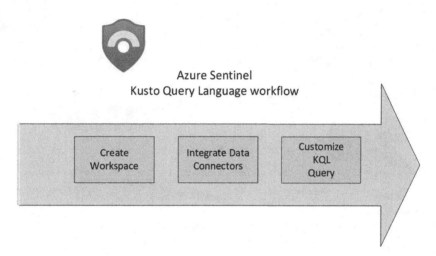

Figure 4-5. *Visual representation of the workflow of Azure data used by the Kusto Query Language*

You will use KQL to look for issues in our systems and try to discover their root cause. The next step will guide you through two exercises on time series analysis. The first of the two exercises will look at how to create a time series and then notice important functions for working with our time series. In the second exercise, you focus first on anomaly detection. How do we analyze our time series to look for anomalous patterns in our data?

Then you can see how to forecast our data using the Kusto language. As awesome as Kusto is, sometimes it needs a little extra boost. The Azure Data Explorer team have provided the ability to search for information in the explorer data using the same Kusto queries used in Azure Sentinel.

Prerequisites require you to have a Microsoft Outlook account or Microsoft free or paid Azure account to be authenticated to the Microsoft Log Analytics demo workspace. The URL to access the free-of-charge demo site is `https://portal.loganalytics.io/demo`, and a shortcut URL is `https://aka.ms/lademo`. The Log Analytics workspace DEMO has prepopulated logs and metrics for running all the KQL examples in this exercise. Chapter 9 provides no-cost log feed and additional-cost log feed.

The interface is easy to use, and the guidance using Figure 4-6 should help you get up to speed and comfortable with the current features. You have limited permissions in this demo site, so you should not worry about deleting data or making changes that cannot be corrected.

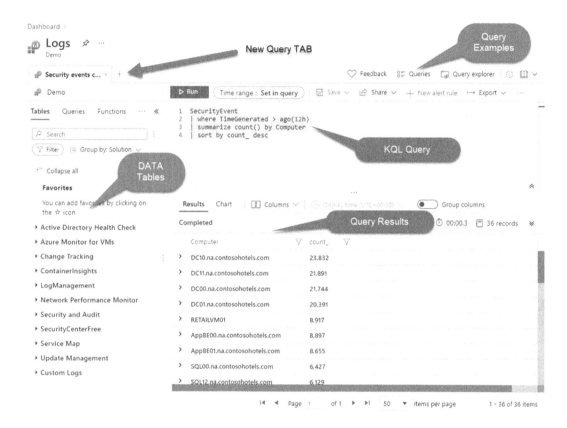

Figure 4-6. *Overview of the Log Analytics query demo site*

Note   Once you are authenticated with an Outlook account, then in your browser, you should access `https://portal.azure.com/#blade/Microsoft_ Azure_Monitoring_Logs/DemoLogsBlade`. Also, the shortcut is `https://aka.ms/lademo`.

The exercise in this chapter starts at a beginner level (level 100) and takes you to an intermediate level (level 200). If these examples are too simplistic for your KQL skill set, I recommend you go through the KQL exercises in Chapters 5, 7, and 9. Before you start the Kusto Query Language exercise, take a few minutes to review some basic foundations.

Note   Microsoft standard-level definitions are

Level 100 Introduction

Level 200 Intermediate

Level 300 Advanced

Level 400 Expert

There are column types in the KQL syntax to help in understating how and why a query provides the results after it runs. This foundational understanding goes a long way to support a method to construct more advanced queries. The data collected by Sentinel and presented is identified by the "column" type. If the data is found in the Log Analytics workspace (LAW), then columns can be added and removed to help filter to the exact results you want. The KQL column type displayed after the query has a format as shown in Table 4-3, and elements used in a KQL query are shown in Table 4-4.

Table 4-3. *KQL column data types used for reference*

Type	Description
Basic	Int, long
	Bool (true or false)
	String using double quotes or single quotes
Time	Datetime: datetime(2021-08-08 21:22:11.1), now(), ago(7d)
Complex	Dynamic: JSON

The next table (Table 4-4) provides an example of the operators used in a query. This book is about Azure Sentinel, and many KQL references would divert the conversation about security. However, more Keyword Query Language references can be found at `https://docs.microsoft.com/en-us/sharepoint/dev/general-development/keyword-query-language-kql-syntax-reference`.

Table 4-4. *Query syntax short example reference*

Syntax/Operator	Property Values
Where	Filters on data and time.
Search	Searches columns for the match of the text.
Take	Limits the number of records, prevents timeouts of large data sets.
Ago	Time relative to the query execution now, for example, ago(7d).
Sort	Sorts results in ascending or descending order.
Count	Number of record times in the table.
Summarize	Groups rows according to the groups of columns ( ).
Render	Results are displayed in a graphical view.

The KQL exercise takes you through the steps to build example queries. After the first few walk-through steps, you are provided examples to copy and paste to review and learn from the results.

LOG ANALYTICS BEGINNING KQL

1. Log into the demo website at `https://aka.ms/LADEMO` using your Microsoft credentials. You should see a Log Analytics workspace to begin to learn the KQL structure.

```
[In this first query, you are going to learn as you type the
individual lines. The entire completed query is]
SecurityEvent
| where TimeGenerated > ago(12h)
| limit 10
```

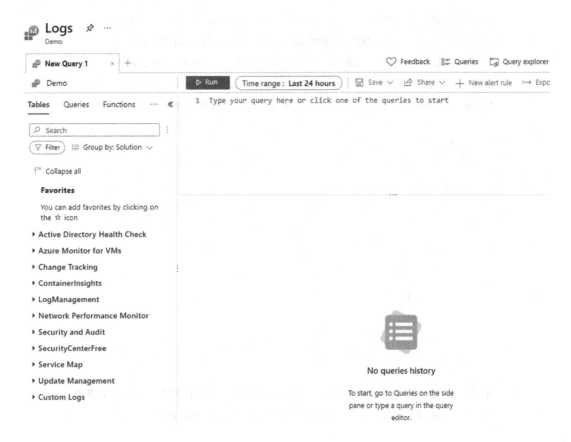

2. Place your mouse cursor to the right of the number 1 in the query editor and start to type the log table "SecurityEvent," and as you type, you see the interface "IntelliSense" code completion support at work to aid you by providing search options.

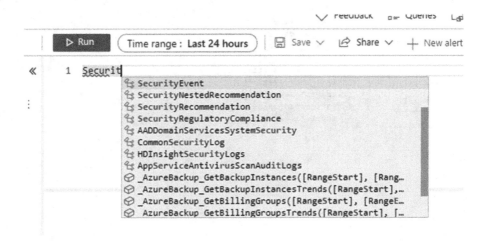

3. After you enter the text "SecurityEvent" and press Enter, a "pipe" symbol is displayed. The pipe symbol is a vertical bar (|), and when used in KQL, it signifies filtering the preceding data (data to the left of the pipe or the line above the pipe) further. Press the return key to add the "where" statement. The "where" statement helps to further focus our data query on a specific timeline.

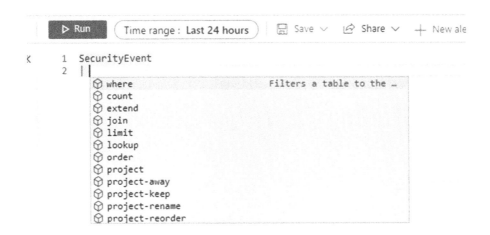

4. While your cursor is on the same line as the "where" statement, start typing the word "TimeGenerated." Notice the options presented as you type.

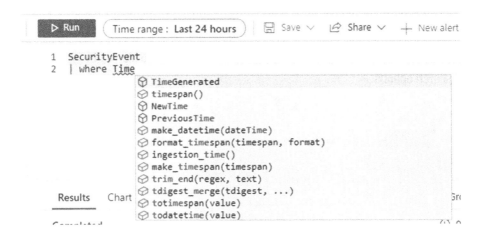

5. We need to define the query timeline by keeping the cursor on the same line, entering the greater than sign ">", and typing the word "ago." Notice the options presented by IntelliSense. What is displayed is "ago(timespan)", and when you press Enter, your query is "ago( )". For this query, we want to limit the time to 12 hours, so move the mouse in between the parentheses and enter 12h. You should have "ago(12h)", and press Enter to go to the next line.

6. When you move to the next line in the query statement, the beginning of the line should have another pipe symbol. You can add it manually using the keyboard. Type the word "limit" and choose the number 10.

7. Now you can choose the option to run the query. The results are displayed at
    the lower pane of the KQL console. Congratulations! You have written your first
    KQL query.

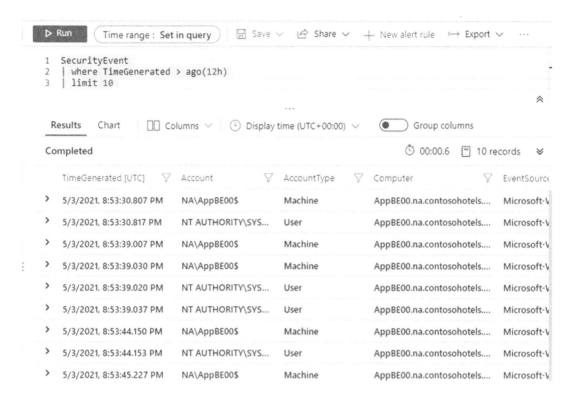

8. With the data connections in place, it is now easier to expand your KQL query
    options. Copy, paste, and run the example syntax in the demo console. List the
    VM performance counter types.

```
Perf
| summarize by ObjectName, CounterName
```

9. Copy, paste, and run the example syntax in the demo console. Show security
    events for failed log-in (event ID 4625).

```
SecurityEvent
| where EventID == 4625
| summarize count() by TargetAccount, Computer, _ResourceId
```

10. Now you can simply copy, paste, and run the example syntax in your Sentinel console. This example is a simplistic KQL search to look for systems in your Azure domain using a wild card asterisk (*) (i.e., Grueneco.com).

```
search in (Event) "Gurene*.com"
```

11. You can also copy, paste, and run the example syntax in your demo console. Simple query to show the metrics generated by the Azure logs collected. Limit to the top 10.

```
AzureMetrics
| top 10 by TimeGenerated
```

12. Copy, paste, and run the example syntax in your Sentinel console. This sample is looking for failed log-ins over the last 24 hours.

```
AADNonInteractiveUserSignInLogs
| where TimeGenerated > ago(1d)
| summarize CountPerIPAddress = count() by IPAddress
| order by CountPerIPAddress desc
| take 10
```

The KQL exercises are designed to be used often by saving them, sharing, and using the basic structure to create your own queries.

As you continue to build your Kusto Query Language skills, the details that can be incorporated would include multiple filtering options. This next example is not something a new KQL user would be expected to create. It is only an example of the type of filters that are possible. You are not expected to create this query after completing the KQL exercise.

Example KUSTO query:

```
union withsource=TableName1 *
| where TimeGenerated > ago(30d)
| summarize Entries = count(), Size = sum(_BilledSize), last_log =
datetime_diff("second",now(), max(TimeGenerated)), estimate = sumif(_
BilledSize, _IsBillable==true) by TableName1, _IsBillable
| project ['Table Name'] = TableName1, ['Table Entries'] = Entries, ['Table
Size'] = Size, ['Size per Entry'] = 1.0 * Size / Entries, ['IsBillable']
= _IsBillable, ['Last Record Received'] = last_log , ['Estimated Table
Price'] = (estimate/(1024*1024*1024)) * 0.0
| order by ['Table Size'] desc
```

When you decide to copy, paste, and run the query inside your Azure Sentinel deployment logs view, the example results is the data table name size and is a billable data point, as shown in Figure 4-7.

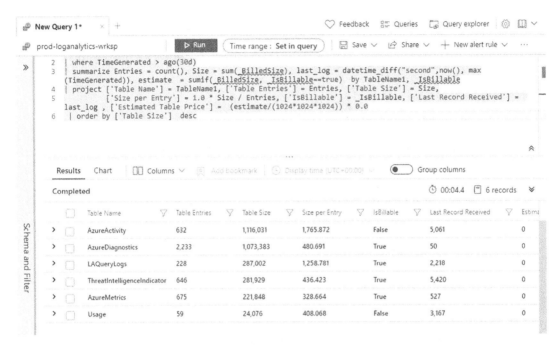

Figure 4-7. *Results in table format of data queries for KQL is billable example*

Threat Intelligence – TAXII Integration

The world of cybersecurity is full of acronyms, and one that is often used without explanation is TAXII, which is an acronym for Trusted Automated Exchange of Intelligence Information (TAXII). It is a notation protocol, a combination of Hypertext and JavaScript Object Notation (JSON), and it is an application layer protocol for the communication of cyber threat information.

Note   Chapter 6 covers TAXII and STIX in detail.

TAXII is a transport protocol used by defenders and research professionals to securely exchange cyber threat intelligence (CTI) over HTTPS (Secure Hypertext Protocol). TAXII enables organizations to share cyber threat intelligence (CTI) by defining an API that aligns with common sharing models. TAXII is specifically designed to support the exchange of threat intelligence (TI) represented in STIX, Structured Threat Information Expression.

STIX is the language protocol used with the TAXII transport protocol. STIX enables organizations to share updated threat intelligence data with one another consistently. By using STIX data and TAXII transport, the researchers have the latest information and understand what computer-based attacks they are most likely to see and anticipate and/or respond to those attacks faster.

With the addition of information with STIX data provided and TAXII transport, together in Azure Sentinel, you can improve timely provision of data to improve capabilities, such as collaborative threat analysis, automated threat exchange, and automated detection and response.

Note   This exercise guides you through a basic configuration of Microsoft threat intelligence using a service called Anomali Limo (a service from anomali.com). This is a product you have access to, and there's no license fee for this STIX data proof of concept.

ENABLE AZURE THREAT INTELLIGENCE DATA CONNECTOR

1. Open a new web browser and enter the URL `https://limo.anomali.com/taxii` and enter the admin name guest and password guest.

Sign in

https://limo.anomali.com

Username	guest
Password	•••••

Sign in   Cancel

2. You should see a response from the server like this example:

{"api_roots": ["https://limo.anomali.com/api/v1/taxii2/feeds/", "https://
limo.anomali.com/api/v1/taxii2/trusted_circles/", "https://limo.anomali.com/
api/v1/taxii2/search_filters/"], "contact": "info@anomali.com", "default":
"https://limo.anomali.com/api/v1/taxii2/feeds/", "description": "TAXII 2.0
Server (guest)", "title": "ThreatStream Taxii 2.0 Server"}

3. Log into Azure Portal. The RBAC privileges recommended for access to Sentinel include Contributor and Security Administrator. Search for Azure Sentinel and go to the Azure Sentinel service.

Note   Additional privileges may be required based on the Azure service or third-party service Sentinel is connecting.

---

4. Select Data connectors from the menu on the left-hand side of your screen. Search for Threat Intelligence – TAXII from Microsoft and select this option.

5. Select Open connector page on the right-hand side of the page and review the prerequisites. This exercise will guide you through using the free access from a Microsoft partner Anomali.

6. Enter the API Root URL: https://limo.anomali.com/api/v1/taxii2/feeds/.

    Configuration in this format for each server and ID is needed.

Instructions   Next steps

Prerequisites

To integrate with Threat intelligence - TAXII (Preview) make sure you have:

✓ **Workspace:** read and write permissions are required.

ⓘ **TAXII Server:** TAXII 2.0 or TAXII 2.1 Server URI and Collection ID are required

---

Configuration

Configure TAXII servers to stream STIX 2.0 or 2.1 threat indicators to Azure Sentinel

You can connect your TAXII servers to Azure Sentinel using the built-in TAXII connector. For detailed configuration instructions, see the full documentation.

Enter the following information and select Add to configure your TAXII server.

Friendly name (for server) *

Emerging_Threats_CC_Server

API root URL *

https://limo.anomali.com/api/v1/taxii2/feeds/

Collection ID *

31

Username

guest

Password

guest

Add

List of configured TAXII servers

7. Notice Friendly name requires no spaces and allows underscores only. Select Add and you should see a validation message.

 TAXII connector added

TAXII connector 'Emerging_Threats_CC_Server' has been added successfully for API Root URL 'https://limo.anomali.com/api/v1/taxii2/feeds/' and Collection ID '31'.

8. Once you run the first collection feeds, you can substitute others that your organization may need for Azure Sentinel data. A short list for this POC includes

- Id: 31 Emerging Threats C&C Server

- Id : 41 CyberCrime

- Id : 107 Phish Tank

- Id : 200 Malware Domain List

9. As you enter the configuration information to the TAXII service to stream the
    STIX data, notice the information received starts to increase.

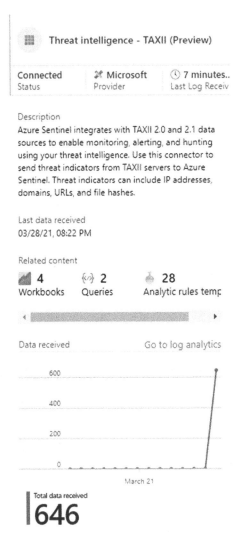

10. That is the end of this exercise.

11.   However, if you are curious to learn more about the code used to update threat intelligence using different "id" markers, after gaining access to Anomali's servers, you can connect with this URL: `https://limo.anomali.com/api/v1/taxii2/feeds/collections/`.

12.   The list in the browser tab is displayed in the following. You may be tempted to ingest all STIX data in this example; however, remember you should be focused on data that helps your business provided by the MITRE organization:

```
{"collections": [{"can_read": true, "can_write": false, "description": "",
"id": "107", "title": "Phish Tank"}, {"can_read": true, "can_write": false,
"description": "", "id": "135", "title": "Abuse.ch Ransomware IPs"}, {"can_
read": true, "can_write": false, "description": "", "id": "136", "title":
"Abuse.ch Ransomware Domains"}, {"can_read": true, "can_write": false,
"description": "", "id": "150", "title": "DShield Scanning IPs"}, {"can_
read": true, "can_write": false, "description": "", "id": "200", "title":
"Malware Domain List - Hotlist"}, {"can_read": true, "can_write": false,
"description": "", "id": "209", "title": "Blutmagie TOR Nodes"}, {"can_read":
true, "can_write": false, "description": "", "id": "31", "title": "Emerging
Threats C&C Server"}, {"can_read": true, "can_write": false, "description":
"", "id": "313", "title": "DT COVID-19"}, {"can_read": true, "can_write":
false, "description": "", "id": "33", "title": "Lehigh Malwaredomains"},
{"can_read": true, "can_write": false, "description": "", "id": "41",
"title": "CyberCrime"}, {"can_read": true, "can_write": false, "description":
"", "id": "68", "title": "Emerging Threats - Compromised"}]}
```

Once you have connected some of the data produced by Microsoft Azure, in the next exercise, you will take a tour through the Azure Sentinel information summary to become familiar with the interface.

Once the threat intelligence data begins to be ingested by Azure Sentinel, you can quickly identify that information is flowing by selecting Threat intelligence (Preview). Figure 4-8 shows some of the data that has been processed by our test Azure Sentinel configuration.

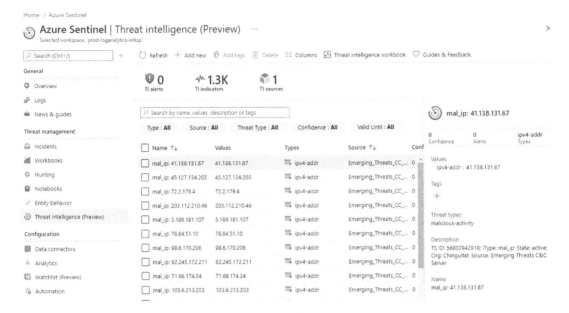

Figure 4-8. *View of Azure Sentinel threat intelligence after enabling STIX data through the TAXII transport exercise*

You may choose to enable other Limo services in your Azure Sentinel data connector service. Please refer to Table 4-5 for an in-depth reference.

Table 4-5. *Azure Sentinel Limo services*

Friendly Name (No Spaces or Special Characters)	Collection ID
Phish Tank	107
AbuseRansomeWareIP	135
AbuseRansomwareDomains	136
DShieldScanIP	150
MalwareDomain	200
TORnodes	209
EmergingThreatsC2	31
MalwareDomains	33
CyberCrime	41
EmergingThreatsCompromised	68

Summary

In this chapter, you had a deep dive into the differences between the Azure data plane and Azure control plane. You learned how to appreciate the Kusto Query Language with some Azure Sentinel–specific data queries.

You learned from a basic example how to develop a process to enable Sentinel data connectors for Microsoft data points and cybersecurity threat indicators using STIX and TAXII. You learned that STIX is the data language used to share attack data through the TAXII transport protocol. Next, you gain greater insight into the use of this foundational knowledge to improve your cybersecurity posture through Azure Sentinel.

CHAPTER 5

Threat Intelligence

This chapter provides needed insight to understand the value of evidence-based information and knowledge about emerging cybersecurity through relational data called threat intelligence (TI). You begin by being introduced from the level of a SOC Manager or Director role. Then quickly going deeper than definitions, you leverage current historical cyber-criminal tactics, techniques, and procedures. The examples in this chapter help guide you to understand TI. You must decide the best way to leverage threat intelligence in Azure Sentinel deployment.

Security controls rely on trustworthy sources that include correlation for accuracy for security analysts. The data is highly valued if from open source organizations or commercial platforms. The context and mechanism of indicators of compromise (IOC) must be timely and support remediation advice. Making decisions about the security controls in place and the appropriate response is part of the security formula to leverage threat intelligence.

In this chapter you learn about

- Threat intelligence (TI)

- Communicating TI using STIX and TAXII

- Options for threat intelligence

- Implementing Microsoft threat intelligence

- Considerations for threat intelligence

Threat Intelligence

There are alignments in Azure Sentinel with industry standards, and you need to be aware of the purposeful coordinated efforts. Just like the security language that has been shared through each chapter, you learn more in this section, which includes indicators of compromise (IOC). An indicator of compromise can be a small anomaly that may only

145

© Marshall Copeland 2021
M. Copeland, *Cloud Defense Strategies with Azure Sentinel*, https://doi.org/10.1007/978-1-4842-7132-2_5

be an individual artifact that is linked to known attack software or cybercriminal family usage. The data points of threat intelligence (TI) or anomalies could be the tip of the iceberg that creates a deep dive into cyber threat intelligence (CTI). As a security analyst, you look at real-time data and relate it to historical data to help the SOC team provide more proactive guidance when you find interesting anomalies and measure those data points as "outliers" from baselines.

The MITRE ATT&CK framework, discussed in greater detail in Chapter 8, provides Microsoft Sentinel a way to better align threat intelligence with the MITRE matrix of tactics and techniques. This supports alignment with attributes alerted through Azure Sentinel threat intelligence data collection. Additionally, the information is shared publicly to identify, define, and catalog cybersecurity threats, which is the mission of the Common Vulnerabilities and Exposures (CVE) program. This program is managed under the MITRE organization, and more details can be found at `https://cve.mitre.org`.

The information collected by the Common Vulnerabilities and Exposures program is meticulously cataloged in the US National Vulnerability Database (NVD). The NVD adds additional data points like severity scores and impact ratings. The National Vulnerability Database is managed by NIST, the National Institute of Standards and Technology. The website can be found at `https://nvd.nist.gov`. You may recall that NIST is responsible for many US government security frameworks like the NIST 800-53 Risk Management Framework, and you can read more at the website: `https://nist.gov`.

Note   I would like to thank all the hardworking team members from the NIST organization. Sharing cybersecurity data feeds would not be possible without their dedication. You, the reader, can use the NVD and all NIST publications free. They are available in the public domain according to Title 17 of the United States Code.

The NVD data feeds that are used from the Common Vulnerabilities and Exposures collection are available for access through XML and JSON standards, and the entire NVD can be downloaded. You can find out more at the website, `https://nvd.nist.gove/vuln/data-feeds`.

Critical sources of threat intelligence include not-for-profit organizations like MITRE, open source intelligence (OSINT), and Malware Information Sharing Platform (MISP). Other commercial platforms like RSA, FireEye, Cisco Secureworks, Microsoft, and Apple allow optional service contracts for support. You should continue to expand security data using many different reports and read research by leaders in the industry like Andy Greenberg, Bruce Schneier, Brian Krebs, Ellen Nakashima, Kim Setter, Mark Russinovich, and others. In addition to creating a habit and reading the cybersecurity threat intelligence reports, provided in Chapter 8, you should read some academic journals from the same perspective such as the *Journal of Strategic Threat Intelligence* (Harvard), *Journal of Cybersecurity* (Oxford), and others.

The cybersecurity data that is collected through both the MITRE organization CVE, and NIST CVD database provided Indicators of Compromise (IOC) that Azure Sentinel uses in discovery from extracting data points from reverse engineering malware and used with the real-time agents and sensors exposure form your cybersecurity platform. Azure Sentinel also searches through all the logs shared through the data connectors, which you learned about in Chapter 1.

Next, take the time and begin to make logical connection that the individual indicators of compromise found in threat intelligence feeds have many recognizable characteristics like

- Domains

- Email address

- File hashes

- IP addresses

- Certificates

You continue to learn about criminal campaigns in reading the Microsoft Security Intelligence Report (SIR), Verizon Data Breach Investigations Report (DBIR), or Red Canary Threat Detection Report in Chapter 8. During the attacking campaigns processes from start-to-finish, you should realize the data attributes of the indicators of compromise are affected with quickly expiring values. The expiration can be seen in the confidence score because once the campaign, malware, and IOC are shared publicly, the attackers are already obscuring the weaponization stage of Cyber Kill Chain.

At this point in your learning processes it may be extremely helpful to have more details of the threat intelligence relationships between attributes of indicators of compromise using a learning example from a real-world cyber-attack. The example used is analyzing how the cyber-attack compromised the supply chain of SolarWinds. This example is for educational purposes only with IOC attributes, applying some of the knowledge about indicators of compromise shared between security providers, which is the focus for the example.

ANALYZING SOLARWINDS CYBER-ATTACK SIDEBAR

The analysis framework is attributed to the Cybersecurity and Infrastructure Security Agency (CISA, `www.cisa.gov/`) (search for SolarWinds) and Center for Internet Security (CIS, `www.cisecurity.org/solarwinds/`).

Modern attacks are much more sophisticated than attacks in the past. One common tactic today is the use of lateral movement. In the SolarWinds attack, a software update process in a network management tool was compromised, and threat actors were able to gain deep access into targeted networks. The attackers were able to easily pivot from one system to another, gaining access and data as they moved.

1. The IT company SolarWinds produced their Orion Platform, a monitoring platform that companies use to analyze computer network bandwidth and high availability of applications among other features.

2. In early December 2020

    a. FireEye disclosed details of an attack by a sophisticated threat actor that left indicators of compromise that support a "nation state–sponsored" attack.

    b. There's coordination with the Federal Bureau of Investigation and Microsoft to validate the analysis and attacker novel techniques. The attacker targeted FireEye "red team" assessment tools.

    c. FireEye developed over 300 countermeasures for their customers and the security community to use to minimize the potential impact of the tools stolen.

    d. The IT company SolarWinds announced a cybersecurity breach, and the cyber-attack compromised the software update channel of the Orion Platform and injected code. The attacker was able to push (introduce) malicious updates into the Orion Platform, affecting more than 18,000 customers.

3. Shared indicators of compromise (IOC) were provided from several sources including Microsoft, FireEye, Volexity, CISA, and other cybersecurity researchers. A short IOC list included

    •   SolarWinds.Orion.Core.BusinessLayer.dll (embedded **Trojan** malware code) versions 2019.4 HF5 to 2020.2.1 released between March 2020 and June 2020: Many DLL hash values

- Additional DLL(s): Many hashes

- TEARDROP (malware): Hash values

- RAINDROP (backdoor malware): Many hashes

- SUNBURST (backdoor malware) (backdoor.sunburst/backdoor.webshell)

- Attributes of network indicators of compromise

  - Asvmcloud.com (Command and Control, C2)

  - Freescanonline.com

  - Databasegalore.com

  - Zupertech.com (many more)

  - 54.193.127.66

  - 139.99.115.25

  - 5.252.177.2 (many more)

4. Malicious code in the SolarWinds Orion product resulted in attackers gaining a foothold in the network (**Delivery** and **Persistence** kill chain stages) and then gaining elevated credential access (**Installation** and **Execution** kill chain stages).

5. Criminal attackers compromised the on-premises admin account and then pivoted to the global admin account (through a trusted SAML token signing certificate) [**pass-through hash attack**]. Through impersonation, they created additional privileged credentials and called APIs to applications.

6. Microsoft has named the SolarWinds attack and all related components as NOBELIUM. Volexity labeled the attackers as Dark Halo. FireEye labeled the nation state attacker and activity of the continued attacks as UNC2452. Sunburst and Sunspot are labels by KPMG and others. Each of these is attributed to or related in some tangible way to the SolarWinds security breach.

Note   The names selected by security analysts or their companies make it "challenging" to identify when two or more companies are performing forensics on the same company. Microsoft Cybersecurity Reference Architecture can be found at https://docs.microsoft.com/en-us/security/cybersecurity-reference-architecture/mcra.

The Microsoft Threat Intelligence Center (MSTIC) refers to the nation state actor as the NOBELIUM campaign of attacks. The SUNBURST backdoor and the TEARDROP malware are both related to the NOBELIUM criminal attack delivery.

You can review and then enable the Azure Sentinel NOBELIUM Rule Templates for blue team hunting for SolarWinds IOCs in your environment.

The indicators of compromise found through the SolarWinds Trojan hidden malware were shared among the cybersecurity research using data attributes identified through using the technology in the next topic.

Communicating Using STIX and TAXII

The security industry realizes that sharing data attributes for current indicators of compromise is time bound. The data is valid for a short period of time, and if a new IOC is identified through a public database like VirusTotal, the criminal enterprises begin changing their malware attack. Your use of Azure Sentinel should include methods to quickly gain TI data that is actionable for your business security. The sooner you gain access to the data, the faster you can implement the layers of security protection against a known malware attack.

This is where understanding and use of STIX (Structured Threat Information Expression) and TAXII (Trusted Automated Exchange of Intelligence Information) are important. A short mnemonic to help you remember the workflow is that STIX is the "passenger" and that TAXII is the "transportation service." The STIX data is the indicators of compromise that make up threat intelligence.

Structured Threat Information Expression is a language and the serialization format that is used as an industry standard for the exchange of cyber threat intelligence (CTI). STIX supports a schema that defines the taxonomy of CTI to share in a consistent and machine-readable manner for faster visibility of attacks. There are many objects that make up the STIX schema, both CORE and META data STIX objects, as shown in Table 5-1.

Table 5-1. *STIX Objects, CORE and META*

STIX Objects						STIX
CORE Objects			**META Objects**			**Bundle Object**
Domain Objects	Cyber-observable Objects	Relationship Objects	Extension Definition Objects	Language Content Objects	Marking Definition Objects	

The creation of cyber threat intelligence includes the many objects of STIX, and this section provides a greater understanding of the STIX construct. Domain Objects are high-level intelligence that represent behaviors that a threat analysts would normally create while gaining insight to the threat landscape. Cyber-observable Objects are facts witnessed about the network or host that is used in relation to the threat landscape. Relationship Objects are the artifacts that relate the Domain Objects to the Cyber-observable Objects.

The STIX META objects provide a format to enhance the CORE objects with details to provide an overall support of descriptions that enrich threat intelligence. The STIX has both CORE and META objects which are wrapped or packaged in a product that is the

STIX Bundle Object (the bundle includes all object data identified). Review Figure 5-1 for a visual representation. The STIX process is used by organizations that produce cyber threat intelligence; they are the "producers."

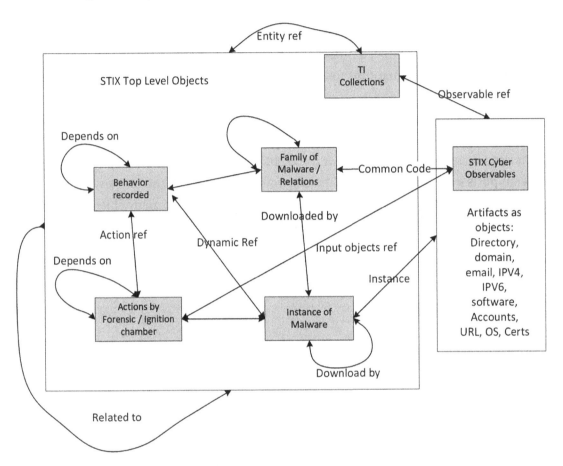

Figure 5-1. *STIX object relationships in a visual graph*

As you start to evaluate the data types and requirements, the amount of detailed information quickly becomes endless and difficult to finalize. As an example, there is a data type for "kill-chain-phase" used to link threat intelligence to a phase of Cyber Kill Chain. If you would like to learn more about a STIX open source organization, use the following URL: `https://docs.oasis-open.org/cti/stix/v2.1/cs02/stix-v2.1-cs02.html`.

Now let's turn our attention to TAXII. Trusted Automated Exchange of Intelligence Information is an application layer protocol that defines a RESTful API. TAXII is the transportation of the STIX data. An easy way to remember the difference between the two acronyms is, STIX is the passenger and TAXII is the, well, taxi service. You followed the Anomali "Limo" exercise using a RESTful API to pull threat intelligence. The TAXII service provides the communication. STIX and TAXII is a common sharing model with the cybersecurity research that defines two primary services, collections and channels. The use of both services provides commonly used sharing of information allowing organizations that produce CTI data to then host the services for consumers. Data channels allow "producers" to push data to many consumers. The two TAXII service types can be seen in Figure 5-2. As a reminder, the TAXII services were specifically designed to support the exchange of cyber threat intelligence that is described using the STIX schema.

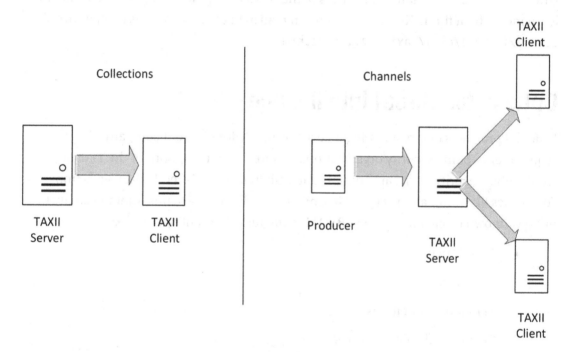

Figure 5-2. *Visual example of typical TAXII collection and channel workflows*

Understanding TAXII requires equal dedication of time and resources when learning how to adopt the STIX methods of security analysts object description. If there is a foundation to help you understand the functions it would begin with the API Root groupings.

The API Root is many groupings of TAXII Collections of different channels of data that are used by the "producers." The API channels include many URL paths of content "types." The different root URL collections may be used by consumers of the STIX data type. (If you recall from the Anomali exercise, there were different TI data types.) Examples of the type of API Root divisions that can be hosted on a single server include

- `https://api.example.com`

- `https://example.com/apiA`

- `https://example.com/apiB`

- `https://example.org/trustgroup1/`

The API Root servers are updated with newly discovered STIX data, and then the URL can be queried by authorized users of the service to "pull" the updated CTI data. To learn more about the TAXII services, you can read at `https://docs.oasis-open.org/cti/taxii/v2.1/cs01/taxii-v2.1-cs01.html`.

Options for Threat Intelligence

Different providers of threat intelligence are available for different company requirements. Some security organizations require 24-hour support for the TI data feeds. Other security teams are comfortable with free or semi-free TI data feeds from companies like Anomali (discussed in Chapter 1). All security teams want the ability to bring your own threat intelligence (BYOTI) to include different options like

- API connection

- TAXII access

- TI manual hunt items

- Customized analytics rules

Some additional options for TI data points include sharing connection feed exposure through an API from the website or a customized database that supports filtering from a Virtual Server, more often a Linux server. There are free solutions and commercial services, and a few are listed here:

- Anomali

- AlienVault

- BlueVoyant

- FireEye

- IBM X-Force

- Palo Alto

- ThreatConnect

This is a short list of the many Azure Sentinel threat intelligence partners that provide free and commercial TI data available to be consumed by Azure Sentinel. The critical features for any threat intelligence feed for use with Azure Sentinel would be the threat hunting rules that are included with the data service. Having only data is not as helpful as data feeds that include pre-created Kusto Query Language (KQL) searches or pre-defined security alerts.

Implementing Microsoft Threat Intelligence

Microsoft provides threat intelligence through access to Intelligent Security Graph, shown in Figure 5-3. Some of the key features include the data for indicators of compromise coming from processing more than 450 billion authentications each day, analyzing 400 billion email messages for malware and phishing attempts, and scanning more than one billion Windows operating systems to collect the IOC data attributes of compromised systems.

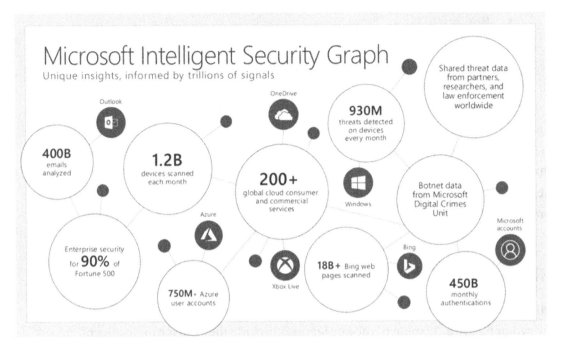

Figure 5-3. *Microsoft Intelligent Security Graph TI data. Courtesy of Microsoft Corporation*

The analytics help to identify newly discovered IOCs, often in seconds, and share that data with all customers and partners using the Microsoft TI data feeds.

Note Microsoft products are created and measured to follow strict privacy compliance standards, and you can read more at the Microsoft Trust Center at `www.microsoft.com/en-us/trust-center`.

Now you can choose to use one or both Azure Sentinel threat intelligence data connectors available. You can see the data connector options shown in Figure 5-4. Remember, in Chapter 1, you learned through a guided exercise to enable the threat intelligence data connector using the free API access from Anomali. If you skipped that exercise, you may want to return and complete it now. The exercise will not be repeated in this chapter. However, another STIX threat indicator feed is Threat Connect Open (TC Open), found at `https://threatconnect.com`. You can use the threat intelligence data connector for any server platform like Palo Alto MineMeld, MSIP, and others.

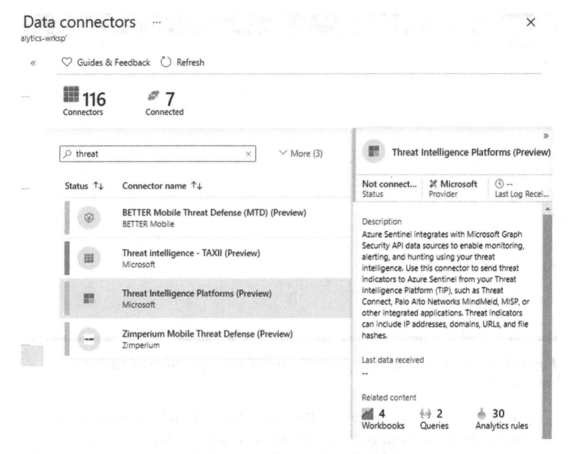

Figure 5-4. *Azure Sentinel Threat Intelligence Platforms data connector*

Please note that even with the current benefits provided by using Azure Sentinel, there are still additional considerations to be aware of for threat intelligence ingestion into Azure Sentinel. You learn about more TI options next.

Other Considerations for Threat Intelligence

Regulatory requirements for compliance with a government agency may include additional threat intelligence validation points. Also some regulatory compliance may require a need to load your own file hashes, IP addresses, URLs/domains, or certifications. You can manually upload up to 15,000 additional indicators with Microsoft Defender for Endpoint, as seen in Figure 5-5.

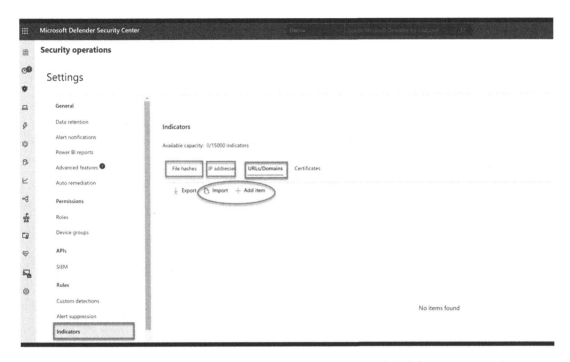

Figure 5-5. *Microsoft Defender for Endpoint TI data upload from an Excel spreadsheet*

If you choose to use TI provided by Microsoft in Azure Defender for Endpoint, you can override the default settings if you have observed variations in the indicators of compromise or if you have specific exclusion requirements. The use of TI from Microsoft Defender for Endpoint is mentioned in a book about Azure Sentinel because of the (out-of-the-box) integration between Defender for Endpoint and Azure Sentinel. A single click of the mouse in the Settings screen and threat intelligence is shared between the two security platforms.

Additionally with Azure Sentinel, you have fusion rules and pull data from on-premises and syslog. With the integration of industry standards supporting STIX and TAXII, as discussed earlier, you may have the need to add additional threat intelligence data. As shown in Figure 5-6, you can add your own threat intelligence indicators directly into TI (Preview).

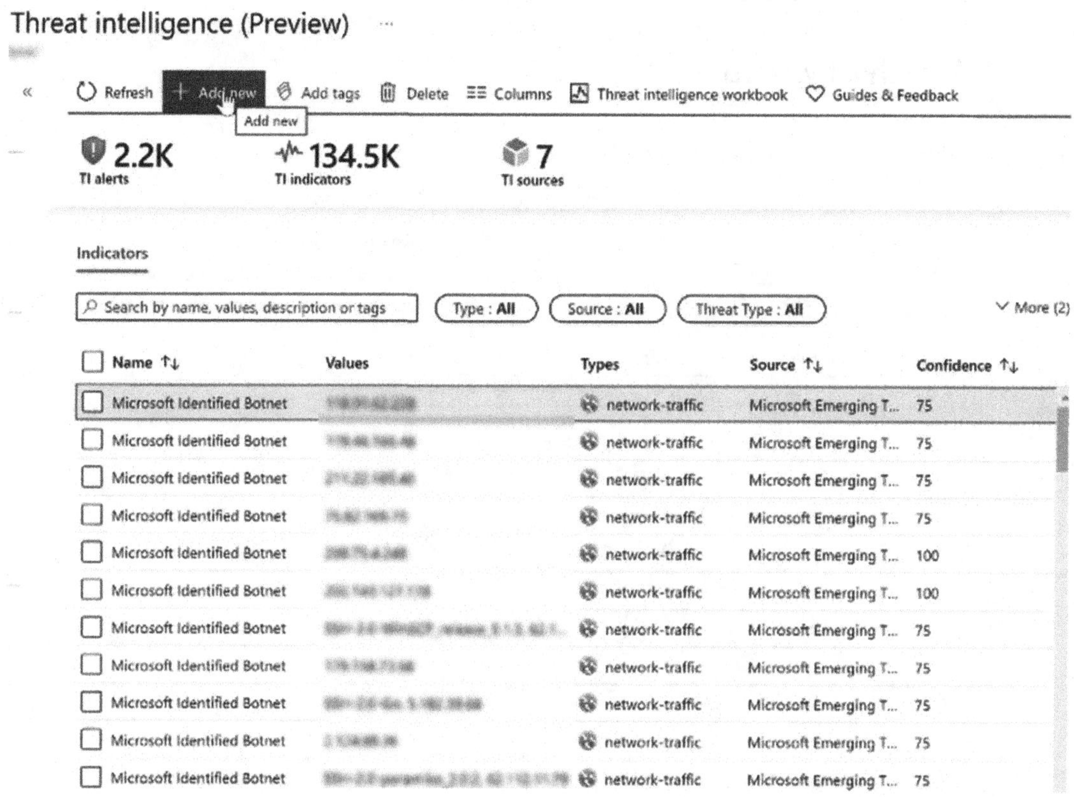

Threat intelligence (Preview) ⋯

Figure 5-6. *View of the Azure Sentinel Threat intelligence (Preview) Add new option*

Azure Sentinel also has a new feature preview called Watchlist. As seen in Figure 5-7, you can add new data items of interest to your security team.

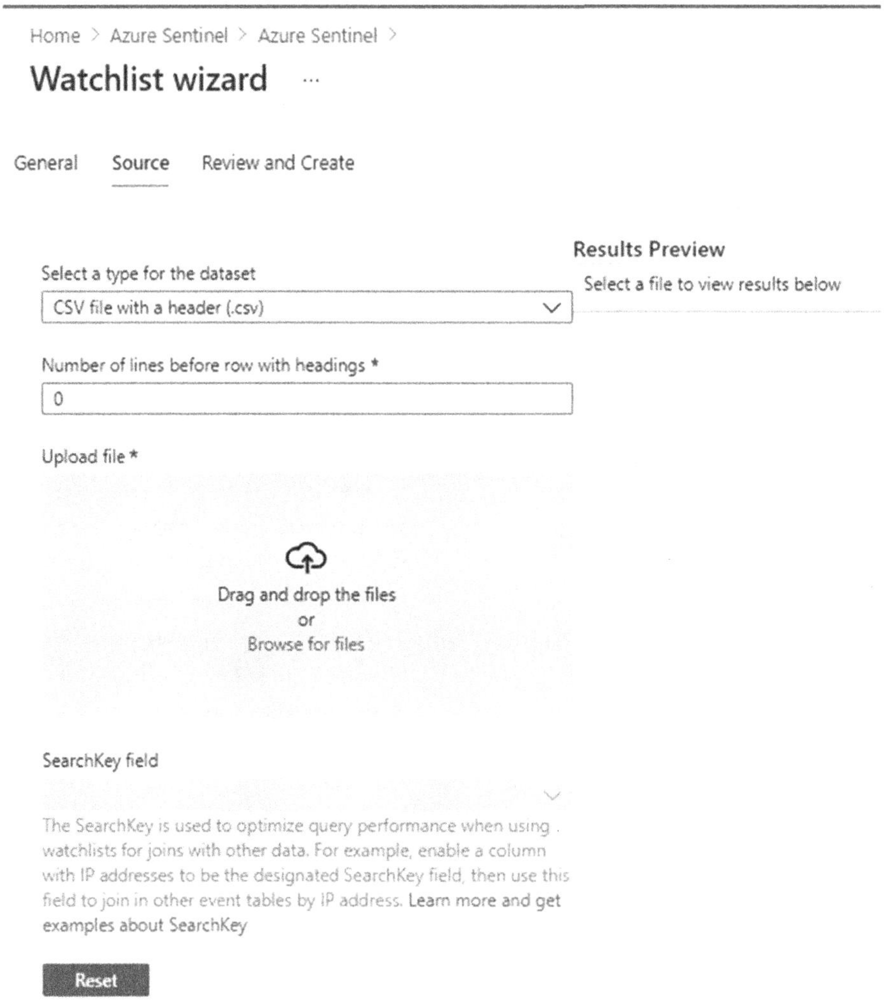

Home > Azure Sentinel > Azure Sentinel >

Watchlist wizard   ...

General   Source   Review and Create

Results Preview

Select a type for the dataset   Select a file to view results below

CSV file with a header (.csv)   ⌄

Number of lines before row with headings *

0

Upload file *

Drag and drop the files
or
Browse for files

SearchKey field

⌄

The SearchKey is used to optimize query performance when using .
watchlists for joins with other data. For example, enable a column
with IP addresses to be the designated SearchKey field, then use this
field to join in other event tables by IP address. Learn more and get
examples about SearchKey

Reset

Figure 5-7. *Azure Sentinel Watchlist view*

You can also manually include threat intelligence data directly into an Azure Sentinel
rule using it directly in the Kusto Query Language. As an example, the THALLIUM rule,
as seen in Figure 5-8, is a data query rule that uses hard-coded IOC built into the rule.

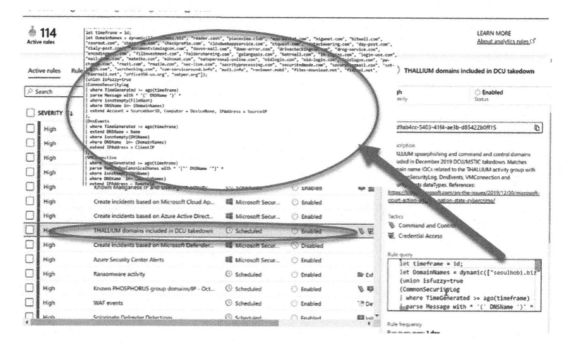

Figure 5-8. *A detailed view of the Azure Sentinel THALLIUM rule with manually hard-coded IOC attributes*

This is an example of TI hunting rules seen hard-coded in KQL. Many of the Rule Templates have this type of threat intelligence embedded in the query allowing you to learn from the template to create customized rules.

Summary

Information in this chapter provided guidance for you to know what threat intelligence is, what attributes are helpful for security controls, and where to read professional security guidance. You learned how STIX is the data set for the indicators of compromise attributes and TAXII is the transmission method. Data options for Azure Sentinel consumption of threat intelligence were provided to help with timely, accurate, and actionable TI data. This information and consideration for threat intelligence is now part of your cybersecurity daily routine.

In the next chapter, you gain architectural guidance on a multi-tenant deployment that includes different Security Operations Centers (SOCs) and global Azure Log Analytics workspace needs for compliance separation.

CHAPTER 6

Multi-tenant Architecture

The Microsoft Azure architecture is complex to design the secure use of resources including hybrid network configuration with revenue-generating applications built on Infrastructure as a Service (IaaS) or Platform as a Services (PaaS). The requirement to include a security architecture may have just increased the overall design time. This chapter is about using security controls needed for Azure Sentinel. You begin with a deep dive into authentication and authorization with Azure Active Directory and Azure Role-Based Access Control. This background is needed when architecting a solution that allows or denies access to Azure security data using the most appropriate security controls.

You should plan to have Azure security data retention so your Security Operations Center analysts can successfully have access to all security data. That data includes events, metrics, logs, and anomalies or "outliers." The security log design would include real-time data with "hot" data access for at least 90 days.

Note The terminology for hot, cold, and cool refers to data access frequency. Hot data requires the fastest and most expensive storage, and it is accessed more frequently. Warm data is accessed less frequently and requires slower and less expensive storage. Cold or cool data is accessed least frequently and can be stored in the most cost-effective data storage archive.

In addition, you need to consider making security data available for up to 6 months. After 6 months, you may need to archive it for years based on security policy and compliance. A consideration for keeping security data searchable for at least 6 months is because of a cyber-attack like that of SolarWinds. Reviewing security events beyond 90 days provided the timeline for the "Trojan" software weaponization kill chain stage.

© Marshall Copeland 2021
M. Copeland, *Cloud Defense Strategies with Azure Sentinel*, https://doi.org/10.1007/978-1-4842-7132-2_6

In this chapter you learn about

- Azure design: single and multi-tenant

- Single-workspace considerations

- Multi-workspace considerations

- Azure security platform

Azure Design: Single and Multi-tenant

Many Azure subscriptions can have a single Azure tenant (one tenant supports multiple Azure subscriptions), which supports individual access for users, systems, applications, certificates, and partners. A single Azure tenant provides a single identity foundation using Azure Active Directory for the security team's AAA (Authentication, Authorization, and Auditing) framework. The framework traditionally supports authentication (verifying a trusted identity) to Azure resources. The complication for the Azure security team and Azure Sentinel that should be understood is auditing. You need to know how authentication and authorization are granted so you can audit and alert when anomalies are discovered. As a point of reference for the single-tenant discussion, see Figure 6-1.

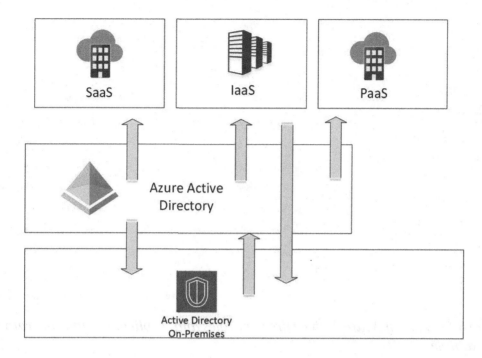

Azure Active Directory support for Multi-Tenant

Figure 6-1. *Azure Active Directory single-tenant logical view*

The types of access may include one or more identities related to users, machines, applications, certificates, and partners. Once access is authenticated, then authorization (permissions to perform work) is provided, in the form of Azure Active Directory (AAD) roles that are different from Azure roles using Role-Based Access Control (RBAC). This is how identity in a single Azure tenant can begin to introduce complications. Let us simplify the workflow by limiting the information to "user" identity.

Begin assigning a single user role from Azure AD. AAD roles can be assigned to a user, and these roles provide various permissions. This discussion will stay at a high level and does not dive deeper to the level of read/write, lists, custom roles, etc. even though that is important. As a few examples, Azure AD roles can be seen in Figure 6-2. Azure AD roles include a title with description on the access the user is provided when assigned with these roles.

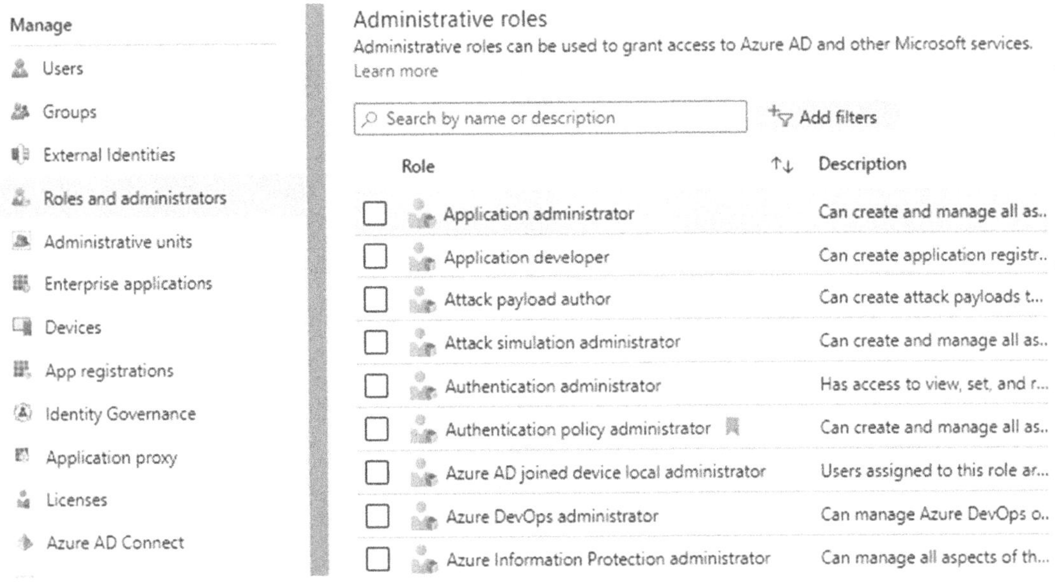

Figure 6-2. View of Azure Active Directory roles and Application administrator role example

The Azure Active Directory workflow includes creating a user's cloud only for identification or sharing a cloud user's identity from another identity provider like Microsoft Active Directory Domain Services (AD DS) or Okta or a partner identity provider platform. Once the user ID is established, an Azure AD role (one or many) can be assigned to that "identity."

Note   You can see a listing and description of the Azure AD built-in roles at `https://docs.microsoft.com/en-us/azure/active-directory/roles/permissions-reference`.

If we use the Application administrator role from Figure 6-2, the privileges granted include "*add, manage, and configure enterprise applications and app registrations and manage on-premises resources using App Proxy.*" This example is a single Azure AD role, and users can be assigned multiple roles (using groups for best practices), but they may not have access to Azure resources in a subscription.

Azure Role-Based Access Control grants access to Azure resources using three basic roles:

- Owner (full access to resources, including delegation)

- Contributor (creates and manages resources, no delegation)

- Reader (views resources)

Assigning Azure AD roles is through the Azure AD console or the API. Assigning Azure RBAC roles is completed at the level of multiple resources or limited resources. Another security data resource that should be considered with the Azure security architecture is Azure policy. Azure policy does not rely on Azure AD or Azure RBAC. Azure policy was designed to focus on actions that can be allowed or denied to an Azure resource based on "business compliance" and not based on "read, write, view" access only. Azure policy data from the Azure control plane should also be included as part of your Azure security architecture.

Access can be granted at the Azure tenant level, Azure subscription level, Azure resource group level, or Azure resource directly. Azure Role-Based Access Control roles are provided through Identity and Access Management (IAM) and can be seen from the Azure console as shown in Figure 6-3.

Name ↑↓	Description ↑↓	Type ↑↓	Category ↑↓	Details
Owner	Grants full access to manage all resources, including the abi...	BuiltInRole	General	View
Contributor	Grants full access to manage all resources, but does not all...	BuiltInRole	General	View
Reader	View all resources, but does not allow you to make any cha...	BuiltInRole	General	View

Figure 6-3. *View of three Azure resource roles from the Azure console view*

Notice, from the column Category in Figure 6-3, "General" for the three examples. However, RBAC has many "BuiltInRoles" that apply to different types of access to different resources. Azure RBAC role categories include

- Analytics

- Compute

- Databases

- Monitor

- Network

- Storage

There is another consideration for "built-in" roles because depending on the Azure service, there may be more specific roles for use by security team members. This is true with Azure Sentinel. It has built-in roles to manage the deployment including

- Azure Sentinel reader

- Azure Sentinel responder

- Azure Sentinel contributor

- Azure Sentinel automation contributor

You can learn more about specific Azure Sentinel roles at `https://docs.microsoft.com/en-us/azure/sentinel/multiple-tenants-service-providers`.

You have learned how a single Azure tenant requires a deep understanding of where access to resources can be granted, Azure AD or Azure RBAC. Now you need to consider the complications if multiple Azure AD tenants are required by the company. A logical reference can be seen in Figure 6-4 to gain a high-level perspective of Azure AD roles and Azure RBAC roles multiplied by two.

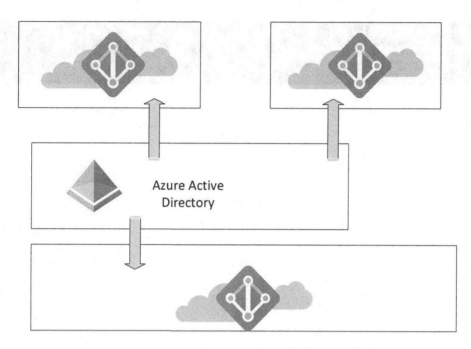

Azure Active Directory Multi Tenant Support

Figure 6-4. *Azure Active Directory multi-tenant logical view*

Additional considerations for an Azure single tenant include the location of data collected, searched, and stored for long-term security compliance. If your business limits remain in the United States, there are many architecture options to consider controlling costs. If the business has a global requirement, data in different Azure geography regions, and a single tenant, the architecture will include the expansion of security logs globally. The business security of a global enterprise requires support for Azure resources through Azure regions and availability of Azure geographic data centers. Refer to Figure 6-5 to gain a high-level view of an Azure geography map.

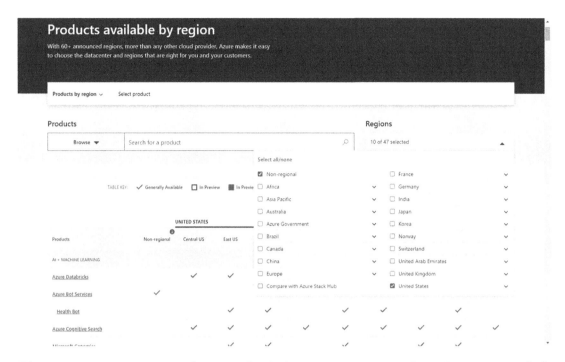

Figure 6-5. *Azure geography map depicting Azure access regions. Image provided by Microsoft Corporation*

Note   Find the most up-to-date Azure geography services by regions when you access `https://azure.microsoft.com/en-us/global-infrastructure/geographies/`.

In Chapter 2 you learned about event data from Azure IaaS and PaaS services. If that discussion is not clear, you may want to review the information and then return to this discussion.

Azure Sentinel leverages the logs from the many Azure resources in a single- or multi-tenant Azure architecture design. Azure metrics, logs, and identity auditing information can increase the complexity of the security architecture when you look at security data sources. Refer to Figure 6-6 for a high-level representation of security data based on an Azure security workflow.

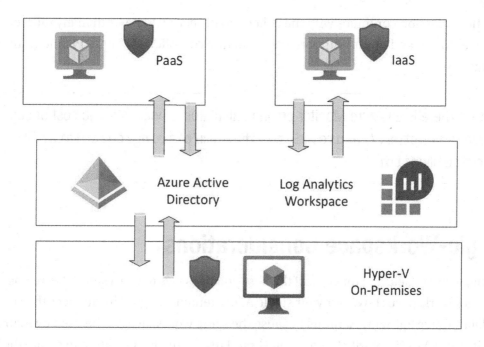

Azure Security Reference data generation

Figure 6-6. *Azure security data generation*

Considerations for the Azure security platform, reviewed later in this chapter, include security data available to other Azure security services and not a proprietary Azure Sentinel data feed. Security Operations Center security data includes

- Identity and access

- Azure subscription and resources

- Network security

- Azure policy

- Vulnerability scans

- Threat detection

- Monitoring of resources

- Workflow automation

The discussion continues with the collection of security data from many different Azure resources and how to support governmental compliance like GDPR and minimize storage costs.

Note   There is an Azure Monitor pricing calculator to help estimate cost of Log Analytics at `https://azure.microsoft.com/pricing/calculator/?service=monitor`.

Single-Workspace Considerations

In Chapter 1 you learned that one of the best practices was to use a single Azure Log Analytics workspace (LAW) for your single Azure tenant design. This reduces the cost for data storage for Azure Sentinel because the same workspace can be used by Azure Monitor and Azure Security Center. You should review the best location to create the Log Analytics workspace for Azure Sentinel and the other Azure security services.

In your Azure Sentinel architecture, have you decided to have a single Security Operations Center (SOC) design, or are you going to have multiple SOC regions to support the "follow the sun" model? If you have a single Log Analytics workspace, you should begin to consider how access from other global locations affects your security design.

Another consideration would be how far the data being retrieved from the Azure resources is. If you use an Azure virtual machine (VM) as an example, that VM should be in the same Azure region as your main data center. Do not complicate the discussion with multiple VMs, but it is another design consideration. What if that VM has multiple locations for customers on the east coast and west coast? You need to calculate the cost to write data from Azure east to Azure west. A few virtual machines may, at first, not appear to be a large, budgeted item. You need to consider how many VMs are used around the world in different Azure regions and the security data stored in a Log Analytics workspace in the United States regions. Notice in Figure 6-7 the charges for data retention.

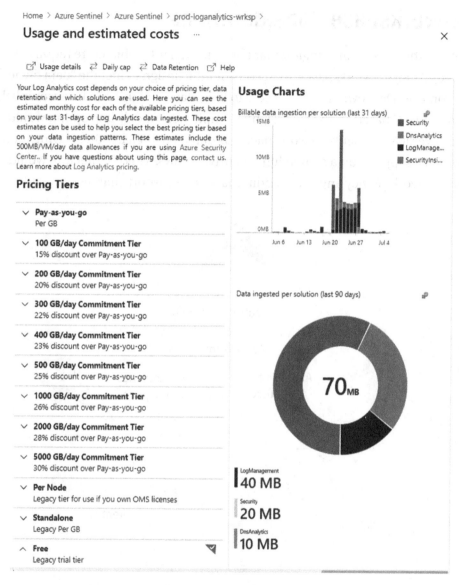

Figure 6-7. *View of Azure Sentinel data ingested per solution*

Azure resources that are directly used by Azure Sentinel include event information, rules created in Azure sentinel, and incidents. A single Log Analytics workspace supports the use of Azure RBAC for data owners. However, currently Azure Sentinel playbooks and workbooks are not stored in the Log Analytics workspace. You need to consider a central location for repositories to enable version control, shared with all SOC team members.

Multi-workspace Considerations

If you decide that your Azure single-tenant or multi-tenant architecture requires two or more Log Analytics workspaces, then consider the design to include "data owner" security controls. Data owners need access to their data, and this can be accomplished using Azure RBAC based on the sovereignty compliance model. One option would be to design several Azure Sentinel workspaces, as depicted in Figure 6-8. Having multiple LAW locations supports data ownership and privacy laws. This architecture would minimize network latency and avoid additional data transport charges.

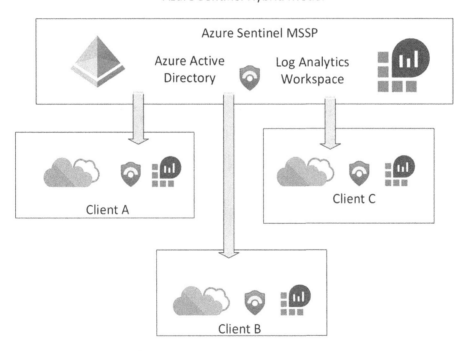

Figure 6-8. *Azure Sentinel hybrid model for workspaces. Provided by Microsoft Corporation*

The Azure security design that includes multi-workspace locations can use fine-grained retention settings through table-level retention. Azure Log Analytics supports

a (pre-defined) scalar data type or a user-defined record (ordered sequence of name/scalar data type pairs).

Data retention in Azure Monitor Log Analytics can now be configured for each data type, rather than only a single retention setting for the entire workspace. This configuration supports the security and business requirements for usage and cost control. This is a way to directly manage usage and costs with Azure Monitor Logs, by operating on the business needs in days, weeks, or months of data retention to proactively monitor ingested data volume and storage growth and identify needed limits to control those costs.

Another consideration would be to limit performance data retention on an Azure Sentinel connected workspace. Performance data is normally considered "cold" after a few days unless you want to store it for data warehouse purposes. You may choose to use blue team hunting using data that includes baselines. Azure Sentinel does not enable (out of the box) a query that runs against the perf table. This would reduce the need to keep this data over the default retention. Azure default is 30 days for normal Log Analytics workspace settings.

To learn more about configuring individually specific data types, select the blue (hyperlinked) text shown in Figure 6-9 for data retention settings. It can change to 90 days with Azure Sentinel connected.

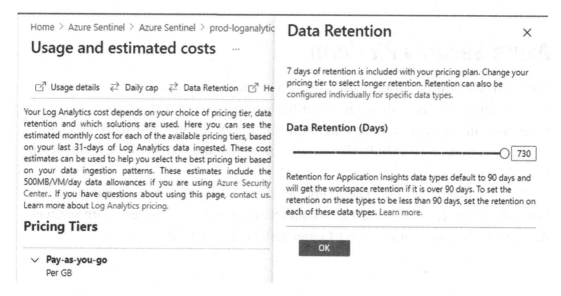

Figure 6-9. Azure Sentinel usage, cost, and data retention settings

The default setting for data retention is 7 days, and the slider, displayed in the screenshot in Figure 6-9, allows data retention to be increased to 730 days. This affects the retention for Application Insights data, which defaults to 90 days.

Azure Lighthouse can help large companies that need to scale out to support multiple Azure Active Directory tenants. The management of Azure Sentinel through Azure Lighthouse provides a single solution for alert detection, threat visibility, malware hunting, and SOC responses. Azure Lighthouse is currently deployed by many Managed Security Service Providers (MSSPs).

Azure Lighthouse requires an onboarding process that each Azure tenant follows to be included with the single management architecture. The details for onboarding can be found at `https://docs.microsoft.com/en-us/azure/lighthouse/how-to/onboard-customer`.

Implementing Azure Lighthouse supports multiple workspaces and cross-tenant queries, workbooks, incident view, and automation.

Note   You can learn more about Azure Lighthouse at `https://docs.microsoft.com/en-us/azure/lighthouse/overview`.

Azure Security Platform

The Microsoft Azure security platform includes all the security solutions you learned about in Chapter 3. Using the Azure security platform, you can better position the security solutions for great understanding and informed architecture decisions. Azure security solutions solve an individual security problem, and you may have a similar type of product in use today.

There is integration of data and alerts between the Microsoft security solutions that benefits the SOC team. You will learn about other integrations between Azure Sentinel, Azure Defender, and Azure Security Center. Refer to Figure 6-10.

Azure Sentinel Integration with Defender for Endpoint
and Azure Security Center

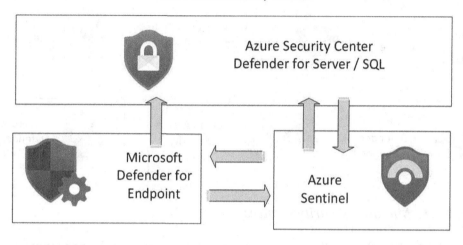

Figure 6-10. *Azure Sentinel integration with Azure Defender and Security Center*

Additionally you learn more about the metrics, events, and other data collected by each security solution and how this security data from many solutions when used in Azure Sentinel incurs no cost. Refer to Figure 6-11 to understand the many Azure security solutions for this discussion.

Azure Sentinel Integration with all Microsoft Security Services

Figure 6-11. *Microsoft security services*

Azure virtual machines allow customization of the metrics and events that are included once the Monitor Log Analytics workspace agent is installed. You can customize the data collected from Azure Portal, as shown in Figure 6-12, Azure ARM templates, or Azure Security Center.

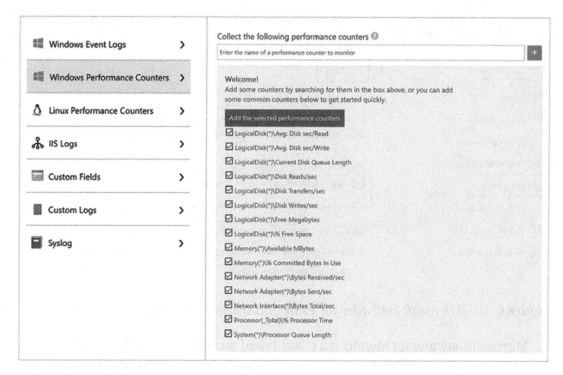

Figure 6-12. *Azure performance counters sent using Azure Portal*

Microsoft Defender for Endpoint is a cloud-delivered endpoint security solution that includes risk-based vulnerability management and assessment, attack surface reduction, behavioral-based and cloud-powered next-generation protection, and endpoint detection and response (EDR). The single integration step for Microsoft Defender for Endpoint can be seen in Figure 6-13.

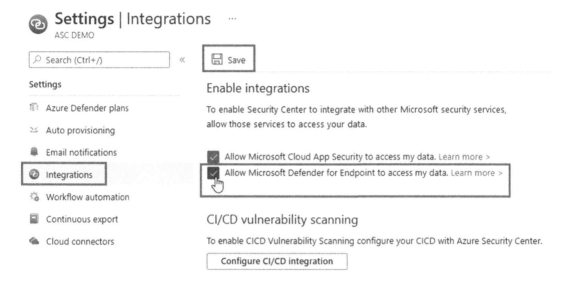

Figure 6-13. *Microsoft Defender for Endpoint Integrations view*

Microsoft Defender for Identity is a cloud-based security solution that leverages your on-premises Active Directory signals to identify, detect, and investigate advanced threats, compromised identities, and malicious insider actions directed by cyber-attacks. It is designed for the security of Microsoft Active Directory Domain Services (AD DS) and on-premises severs. Microsoft Defender for Identity can be integrated with Microsoft Defender for Endpoint as shown in Figure 6-14.

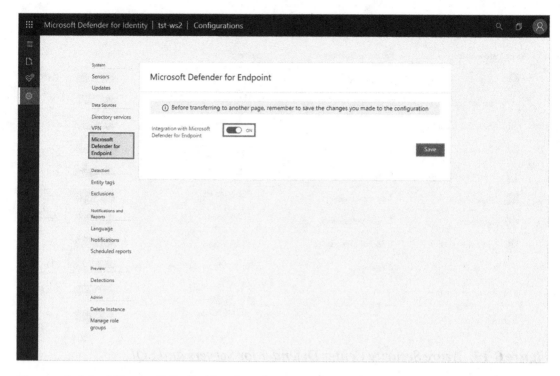

Figure 6-14. *Microsoft Defender for Identity integration*

Azure Security Center includes Defender for Servers and Defender for SQL. Azure Defender for Servers adds threat detection and advanced defenses for your Windows and Linux machines. For Windows, Azure Defender integrates with Azure services to monitor and protect your Azure or on-premises servers.

Defender for SQL is a set of advanced SQL security capabilities, including SQL vulnerability assessment and advanced threat protection. Vulnerability assessment is an easy-to-configure service that can discover, track, and help you remediate potential database vulnerabilities. You should refer to Figure 6-15 for reference and detailed pricing considerations.

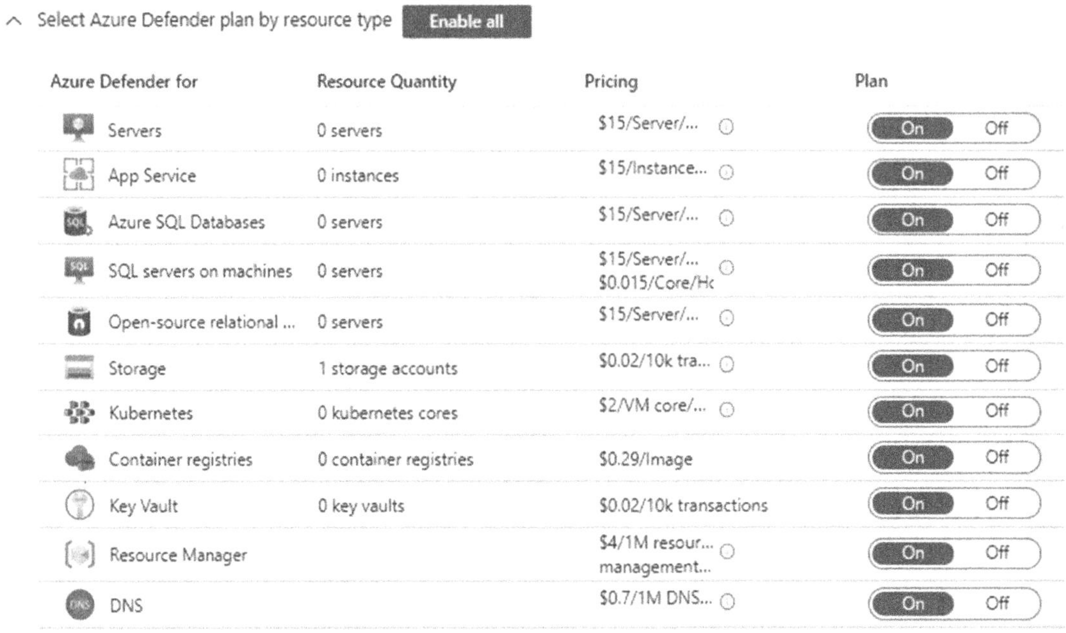

Figure 6-15. *Azure Security Center Defender for Servers and SQL*

Summary

In this chapter you learned how Azure Active Directory (AAD) roles are different than Azure Role-Based Access Control (RBAC) roles. You learned that authentication is provided through Azure Active Directory and that authorization is enabled by AAD or Azure roles using RBAC. Azure Sentinel security design principles using both a single Log Analytics workspace and multiple Log Analytics workspaces were discussed. You now have several considerations in designing a security architecture using one or the other.

In addition you now know about Azure Lighthouse and how it supports a one-to-many management model for Azure Sentinel, which is supported by Managed Security Service Providers (MSSPs) and larger multi-tenant customers. You gained deeper appreciation for the integration of the many Microsoft security services and how that integration provides workflow efficiencies for a Security Operations Center team.

PART III

CHAPTER 7

Kusto Query Language and Threat Hunting

The guidance in this chapter begins by reintroducing you to the data available from Microsoft Azure services both from the Azure data plane and the Azure management plane. Then you immediately have access to an online Azure Sentinel training environment specifically to help you learn the Kusto Query Language and how that translates into the different properties of Azure metrics and logs.

Later in this chapter, the skill levels for threat hunting and clear guidance on how daily work contributes to building your tier 3 hunting skills are discussed (refer to Chapter 3 for tier 1, tier 2, and tier 3 work placement).

In this chapter you learn about

- Where Azure data resides

- Kusto Query Language training options

- Introduction to Kusto Query Language

- Threat hunting with Azure Sentinel

Where Does Azure Data Reside

Knowing how data is found in different Azure services is critical to be able to successfully query for the information needed. In this section, the Azure resources are used to better identify the type of data and where it is stored. For this discussion, the focus for storage of metrics and logs is the Log Analytics workspace.

The Log Analytics workspace (LAW) is an Azure resource and a container that supports the collection of data from multiple Azure resources that can be queried later. You learn about the use of multiple Log Analytics workspaces to support compliance,

185

© Marshall Copeland 2021
M. Copeland, *Cloud Defense Strategies with Azure Sentinel*, https://doi.org/10.1007/978-1-4842-7132-2_7

governance, and least privileged access in Chapter 6. However, as best practice for Azure Sentinel and controlling data storage cost, a single Log Analytics workspace is recommended.

Data stored in a LAW is organized based on monitoring Azure resources, which can be divided into two main areas:

- Application resource monitoring

- Subscription resource monitoring

Application resource monitoring includes the data sent from Azure Application Insights and App Center to the Azure Log Analytics workspace. Subscription resource monitoring includes the data sent from Azure Network Watcher, Azure Security Center, Azure Monitor, Azure Advisor, and Azure Sentinel. The Log Analytics workspace can be divided, as seen Figure 7-1, into a logs workspace and a metrics workspace.

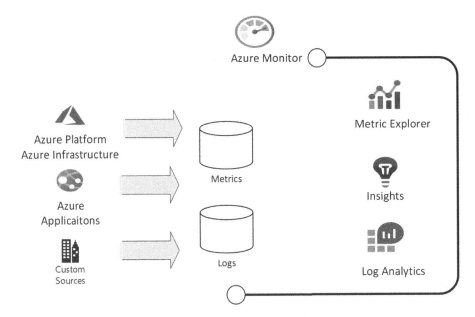

Figure 7-1. *Log Analytics workspace component visual representation*

Azure resource, application, virtual machine agent, and API collector data is stored in the Log Analytics workspace. Data can be reviewed using the Kusto Query Language from Azure Sentinel.

Application logs are collected for use with Application Insights. Azure Application Insights is used to monitor web apps and can monitor availability, performance, usage, and failure.

Azure Monitor can query data about Azure Activity logs, virtual machine metrics like performance counters, and other Azure services. Azure Monitor is the best solution to create automated alerts and responses through the use of Azure Logic Apps.

Azure Network Watcher provides unique utilities to monitor, diagnose, and view metrics used with Azure virtual networks (VNets). Network Watcher is designed to monitor and can make repairs to Azure Infrastructure as a Service (IaaS) resources like VMs, VNets, application gateways, load balancers, and more. Network Watcher today does not support Platform as a Service (PaaS).

Note   Azure resources have different metrics and logs based on the type of Azure service, that is, virtual machine events, diagnostics logs, metrics, etc.

Your business may need to support data retention, and this is discussed in detail in Chapter 6. There are differences in data storage between the different Azure resources that you are using to monitor Azure security. The information in Table 7-1 can provide insight into the individual services.

Table 7-1. Data retention maximum settings

Application Insights	Log Analytics Workspace/ Azure Monitor Logs	Log Analytics Workspace/ Azure Monitor Metrics
Sends raw data to LAW	Up to 730 days	Up to 93 days
Aggregated data up to 90 days Snapshots up to 15 days	Export for long-term retention to storage accounts	VM performance counters from the Log Analytics agent/monitoring agent up to 730 days

You should prepare to learn additional details as you plan for KQL exercises in testing and production to map out the location of data, for both logs and metrics. An example of the type of mapping needed for greater understanding during threat hunting can be seen in Tables 7-2 and 7-3.

Table 7-2. *Example of log and metric data location*

Azure Resource	Log or Log Table
Application Insights	Requests, traces, PageViews, dependencies
Windows OS	Event
Linux	Syslog
Agents	Heartbeat
Metrics	Perf
Custom logs	CustomLogName_Custom Log

Note   You can find the current Azure Monitor Logs table reference and organization at `https://docs.microsoft.com/en-us/azure/azure-monitor/reference/tables/tables-category`.

Table 7-3. *MDI and MDE and Azure Sentinel log location*

	App Insights	Microsoft Defender for Endpoint	Network Watcher	Azure Monitor	Azure Security Center	Azure Sentinel
Web app	X					
Mobile app		X				
Network traffic			X			
Monitor overview				X		
Azure Security focus					X	
End-to-end security view						X

This is data used for cybersecurity logs and metrics with Azure Security Center, Azure Sentinel, and Azure Monitor.

Kusto Query Language Training

There are a few options that are available for you to leverage and come up to speed with your training skills for the Kusto Query Language (KQL). There are some training recommendations, a few at no cost or low cost, that can be found at Pluralsight, at `https://pluralsight.com`.

Now some of the data is dated, but these links have been validated, and there are more than a few options to consider. The blog announcement from Microsoft about a free KQL class can be found at `https://azure.microsoft.com/en-us/updates/free-query-language-course-la-ai/`. This blog post has a link to the Pluralsight page for KQL training. It does state that the training is free, and if that is not the case anymore, you can sign up for a several-day training access to complete the training.

There is another Microsoft support analytics site that you can use for training that has data based on weather. This KQL training demo site can be found at `https://help.kusto.windows.net/Samples`, and note that this is Azure Data Explorer, as shown in Figure 7-2, which is like Log Analytics. Both data access sites support the use of KQL queries.

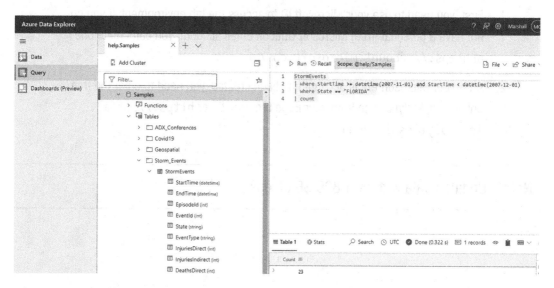

Figure 7-2. *Azure Data Explorer storm database free training site*

Microsoft has created an online training with example KQL queries that allows you to copy and paste into an Azure Data Explorer window. This is another site to help practice your KQL ninja skills. You can follow along with the storm data training examples at `https://docs.microsoft.com/en-us/azure/data-explorer/kusto/query/tutorial?pivots=azuredataexplorer`. The sample queries used in the tutorial have been tested on that database. Specifically, the "StormEvents" table in the sample database, in Figure 7-2, is the key table for information about storms recorded in the United States.

For deeper learning in the world of cybersecurity threat hunting, later in this chapter, you need to practice Kusto Query Language examples. To start your training, you can use the free access from an online Microsoft Log Analytics workspace to the Azure security analytics lab.

Step 0 – Prerequisite: Gain access to the online lab by following the Sentinel analytics lab access exercise.

AZURE SENTINEL ANALYTICS LAB ACCESS

The only prerequisites are to have or create a free personal Microsoft email account and use the Microsoft Edge browser. The email account is only used to authenticate your identity to use the free training site. You can use your Microsoft Azure access from a work account; however, a personal Microsoft email account is recommended.

1. First, you need to use your Microsoft ID to access the lab environment. If you do not have a personal (free) Microsoft Outlook email account, you can create one at `https://account.microsoft.com/`.

2. After your Microsoft email account has been created, you need to enter the free online Log Analytics site from your Edge browser. Enter `https://portal.loganalytics.io/demo`.

Note   Updated data with over 800 GB of logs.

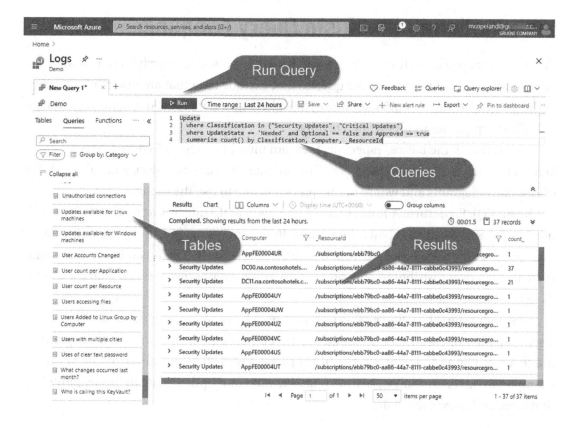

Now you can continue to the basic KQL training in this chapter.

Democratization is a method of delegation of the cloud, to manage the Azure cloud at different levels, tenant, subscription, and resource group. An automation account may be used to create a subscription, not a manual process. This follows the goal to support an ITSM (ServiceNow)-managed service.

Note   A shortcut to one of the Log Analytics training site can be found at
https://aka.ms/lademo.

Introduction to the Kusto Query Language

In this section, you learn how to create queries that are used to search for data and present the results. Also, you create queries that exclude data that are not helpful to see in the results. In many security solutions, this filtering of data is used to remove "security noise" to help you focus on the data results.

You start with the basics, especially for team members new to KQL and Azure Sentinel, which is to see the query "text" in language form. In addition, you gain visibility of workflow diagrams and where in the query console to use the topics.

Basic KQL Structure: A Kusto Query Language (KQL) query is a "read-only" request used for log search and analytics operations. Both processing data and performing data manipulation are accomplished from inside the same query. The Kusto Query Language is created to cover distributed data processing using text queries. It is fast with the ability to support high ingestion rates.

The query starts by using a table or broad search operation, and the data transformation operators are bounded together by the pipe [|] symbol. Multiple queries are separated by a semicolon [;]. The query process is to choose a table (update in this example) to query and subset of rows (classification and update state in this example) in that table and show the results.

Note   Azure Monitor is created from Azure Data Explorer, so the same KQL text requests can be used.

An example of a KQL query can be seen in Figure 7-3, and this visualization can help you to understand the text query components.

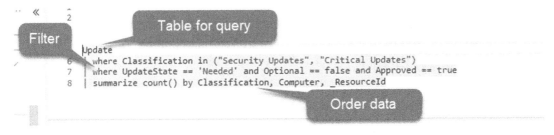

Figure 7-3. *KQL search query example*

A Kusto query is a read-only request to process data and return results. The query schema entities are organized in a similar way like a SQL database does. It has tables, columns, and rows. There is a database that is called "LogManagement". It stores different tables with the likes of "AuditLogs". Refer to Table 7-4.

Table 7-4. *KQL operator listing*

Operator	Description
==	Equals.
!=	Not equals.
=~	Equals, not case sensitive.
has	Search includes specific value, keyword, or match.
!has	Search excludes specific value, keyword, or match (find all except this match).
Contains	Search includes specific value, keyword, or match.
!contains	Search excludes specific value, keyword, or match (find all except this match).
startswith	Search includes something that begins with specific value, keyword, or match.
!startswith	Search excludes something that begins with specific value, keyword, or match (find all except this match).
endswith	Search includes something that ends with specific value, keyword, or match.
!endswith	Search excludes something that begins with specific value, keyword, or match (find all except this match).
matches regex	Search includes specific value, keyword, or match; manipulates data differently than "contains."
in	Search includes multiple values, keywords, or matches.
in	Search includes multiple values, keywords, or matches; not case sensitive.
has_any	Search includes specific value, keyword, or match; manipulates data differently than "contains."

The introduction of query operators helps to see the query workflow with understanding of the mechanics of the operators used. Figure 7-4 is a deeper view to understand the pipeline work.

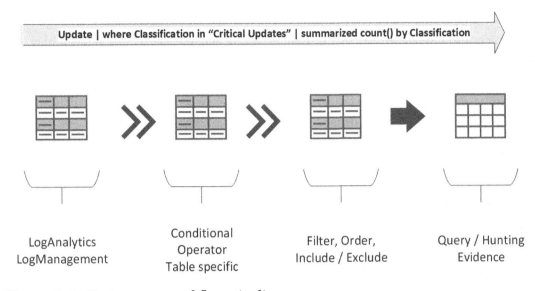

Figure 7-4. *Kusto query workflow pipeline*

Next, you walk through details of the query examples as a simple explanation and not really an exercise. What's important is to begin to understand the use of KQL examples and then start making minimal changes to customize the filters until the evidence is presented. Refer to Figure 7-1 for a KQL query example provided in code as you review the following code for additional guidance. Pay close attention to the pipe symbol [|], as shown in Listing 7-1 because the conditional filter of each line provides that data scope to the next query line.

Listing 7-1. Update query working example

```
Update
| where Classification in ("Security Updates", "Critical Updates")
| where UpdateState == 'Needed' and Optional == false and Approved == true
| summarize count() by Classification, Computer, _ResourceId
```

Again the pipe [|] filter can be understood with the flow code or sudo-code as shown in Listing 7-2.

Listing 7-2. Update query sudo-code example

```
Table to query [filter send]
> | where classification filter is X, Y [filter send]
> | where updatestate equals [filter send]
> | summarize by some order [display]
```

After you have reviewed the code or listing, refer to Figure 7-5 to review the operations used for the results.

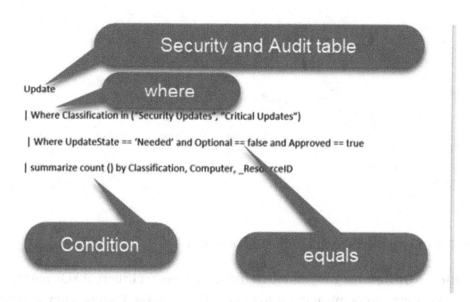

Figure 7-5. *KQL query with operations identified*

There is one more view from the Log Analytics query console to help you understand where the data table pulled the information. Now if you review Figure 7-6, the Log Analytics data table can be seen on the left. This view is an explanation of the location of the query starting place. By declaring the table with the statement "update" KQL would then query that data directly and column data in the table.

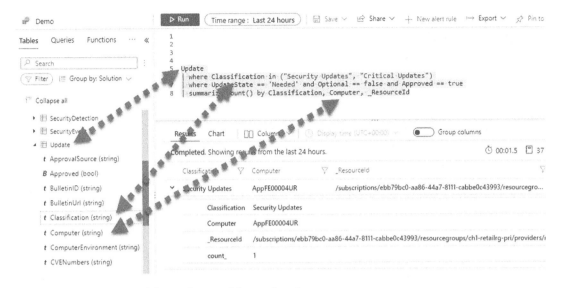

Figure 7-6. *Data table update table and column*

Multiple KQL Results: You want to be the subject matter expert of KQL queries, and the only way to accomplish this is to run the KQL queries. The good news is that the console is designed to help you with example queries. From your browser, log into the demo site and select the simple examples used in the LAW online demo to provide greater learning through the text.

KQL QUERY EXAMPLE EXERCISES

1. For a new query tab, simply click the small plus sign.

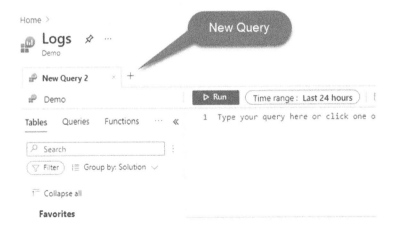

2. Next, scroll to the right of the console and use your mouse to select the Queries option. It presents a view of default queries for testing. Notice that this is the default.

3. This view shows the examples that you should perform. These queries are for you to run, change and run again, and change and run again. Become familiar with the changes that can be made in the KQL text.

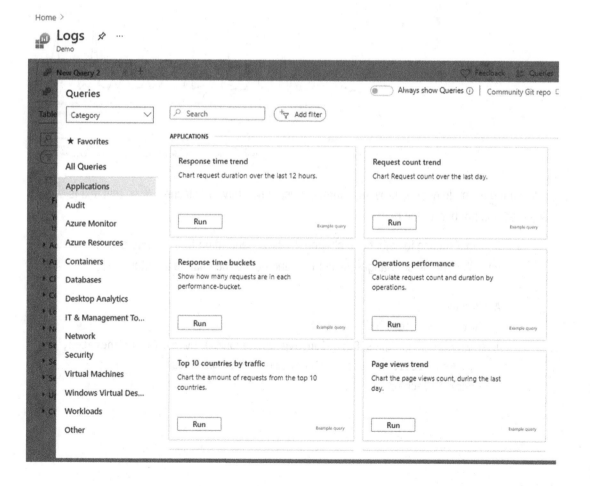

4. Select to "Run" the Response time trend report. The KQL query is entered into your new query tab and displayed.

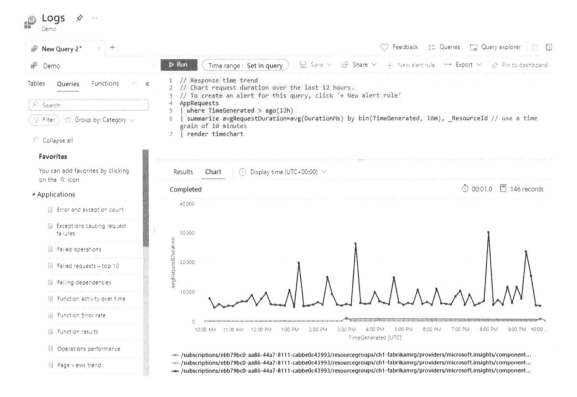

Notice the example queries provide comments using two forward slashes, //, so this text is ignored and not part of the query.

5. Use your mouse to select and change the time generation from 12 hours to 1 hour. With no other changes, select Run and notice the change in output.

```
AppRequests
| where TimeGenerated > ago(1h)
| summarize avgRequestDuration=avg(DurationMs) by bin(TimeGenerated,
10m), _ResourceId // use a time grain of 10 minutes
| render timechart
```

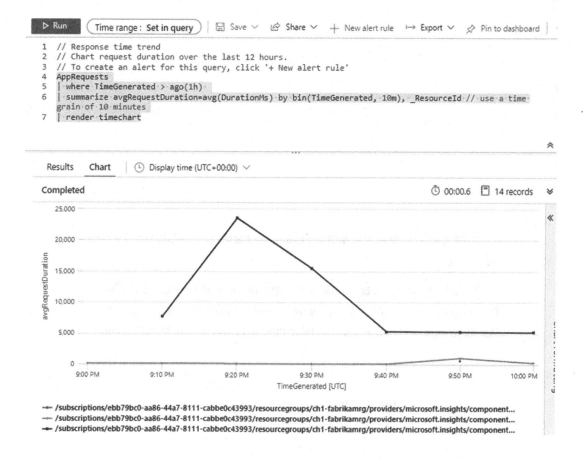

```
1   // Response time trend
2   // Chart request duration over the last 12 hours.
3   // To create an alert for this query, click '+ New alert rule'
4   AppRequests
5   | where TimeGenerated > ago(1h)
6   | summarize avgRequestDuration=avg(DurationMs) by bin(TimeGenerated, 10m), _ResourceId // use a time
    grain of 10 minutes
7   | render timechart
```

6. Notice the condition to render using the time chart. Comment this out using // |
    render timechart and run the query again. The chart can be toggled on and off;
    however, this KQL code example includes this visual option.

7. When you run the query, the view of query examples is closed. Open the
    examples as you did in step 3. Scroll down on the left and select Azure Monitor
    and run the Count heartbeats example query.

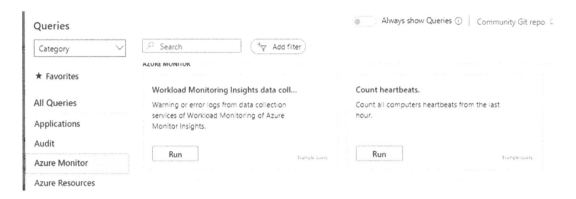

8. From the query console and with the example queries not visible, select a new query tab.

9. On the left side of the query console, change the view by selecting the "Group by Category" option, and notice how the listing of tables changes. Toggle to Resource type, and notice how the table display changes. Toggle to Solution.

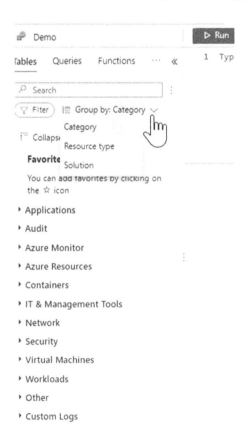

10. Next, let's type a KQL query from scratch inside the query window. Open a new query tab, and place your mouse cursor next to the number 1. Start typing the word update. As you type, notice the KQL IntelliSense begins to show you matches.

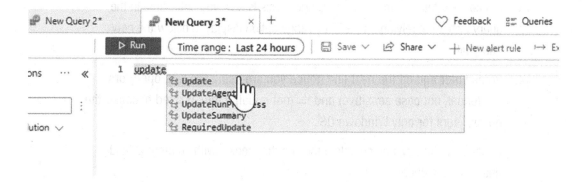

11. Continue to type the entire word and press return or press the Tab key to have the pipe symbol on the next line and notice the IntelliSense options for the new line.

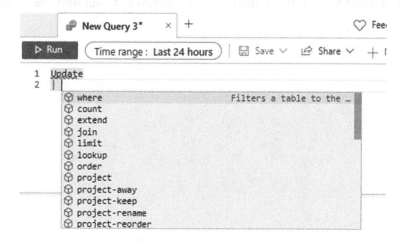

12. Continue to type each of the lines of this KQL query:

```
Update
| where TimeGenerated>ago(24h)
| where UpdateState =~ "Needed" and OSType != "Linux"
| summarize by Computer, Classification, Product, KBID, ResourceId
```

13. Notice the filter for TimeGenerated>ago(). This is how you enter time in the query instead of relying on the Time range option displayed below the new query tab.

14. Press Enter and on the next line notice you are using the KQL operators =~ (equal, not case sensitive) and != (not equal). Linux is used because the query filters for only Windows OS.

15. Press the Enter key, and complete the line that begins with summarize and finally run the query.

Note   If you're still using the LA demo site, there may be data available, and you would see results. If you don't see results, check to see if any KQL query filters are misspelled. If there are no misspelled words, it could indicate there is no data in the "Update" table.

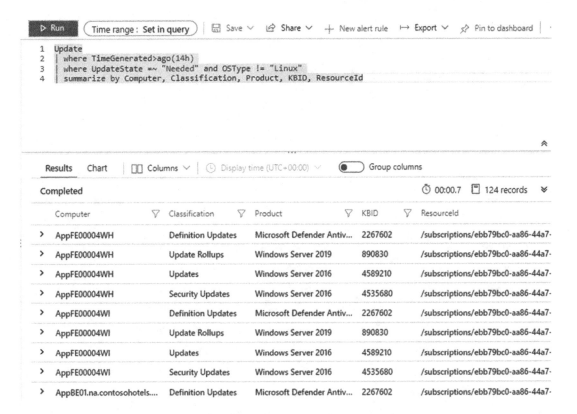

16. As a final point to entering a query by using the KQL filters or query console,
     there are still filtering options to explore. As an example, after the query runs
     and data is displayed, select the Columns filter from the console. Try to toggle
     the resource ID in the Results pane.

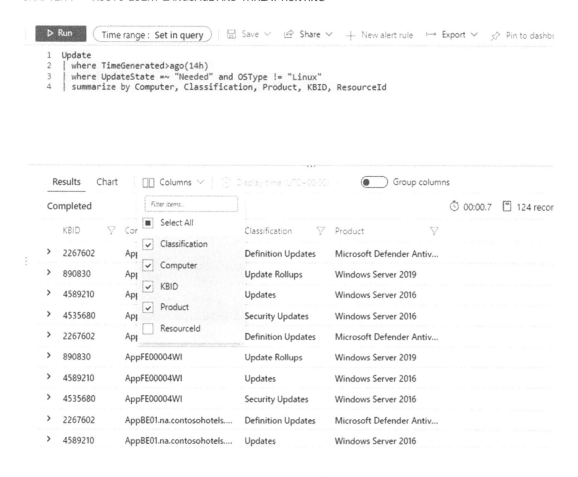

The Kusto Query Language is used in many Azure resources including Azure Monitor, Azure Security Center, and Azure Sentinel and individual resources like the virtual machine console. This is a good start to your KQL learning journey. Remember to schedule time daily to enhance your Kusto query ninja skills.

Note   Kusto.Explorer is a desktop application that can be used to practice your skills. You can download the application and Chrome extensions at `https://docs.microsoft.com/en-us/azure/data-explorer/kusto/tools/kusto-explorer`.

Advanced KQL Exercises: Gain access to the online lab by following the Sentinel analytics lab access exercise. Find more Microsoft community sponsored hunting queries at `https://github.com/Azure/Azure-Sentinel/tree/master/Hunting%20 Queries`.

Threat Hunting with Azure Sentinel

The Security Operations Center is often busy with SOC analysis studying the different computer monitor screens full of data, graphics, and real-time threat intelligence (TI). If you have invested much of your time in either research for cyber threats or one of the thousands of SOC analysts, you realize there is always a need for more data points, more contact data, and more deep security information.

A term used in cybersecurity is "blue team" or "blue team hunting." This color terminology comes from the type of security work each team is traditionally responsible. Red teams are offensive. They are well-trained security professionals with expertise in attacking systems and penetrating network security defenses.

Members of the blue team are defensive. They are equally well-trained security professionals responsible for prevention of the red team attacks. The blue team defends, prevents, and continuously hunts for cyber-attackers.

Red teams simulate attacks against blue teams to test the effectiveness of the network's security. These red and blue team exercises provide a holistic security solution that protects the business using cybersecurity defense technology and processes.

Blue team hunting is being very proactive and looking for security threats. Blue teams use security solutions like Azure Sentinel to filter through the mounds or "haystacks" of data to find that one meaningful "needle." Azure Sentinel supports hunting and searches for security threats, often just anomalies, using its built-in hunting KQL queries that guide you into asking pedantic questions to reveal security threats.

Note   The hunting dashboard is currently in preview. Items relating to this upgrade will be marked with "(Preview)" in the Azure Sentinel portal.

The current Microsoft cybersecurity threat remediation model in Figure 7-7 shows the constant movement of people, processes, and technology.

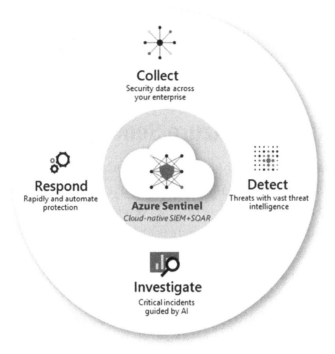

Figure 7-7. *Microsoft Sentinel view of the cybersecurity process. Image courtesy of Microsoft Corporation*

You should begin the hunting process using the built-in queries provided by Azure Sentinel. The main hunting view is accessible from the Azure Sentinel navigation menu as shown in Figure 7-8.

It is a refreshed view with changes to help you focus on threat hunting. The new data view allows quick access to the many ready-made query examples created to start hunting quickly and help you become familiar with the many tables of Azure data and improve your ninja KQL query skills. These hunting queries are developed by Microsoft security researchers and are updated continuously. The console receives new queries and fine-tune existing queries. This is the starting point to look for new alerts and detected anomalies.

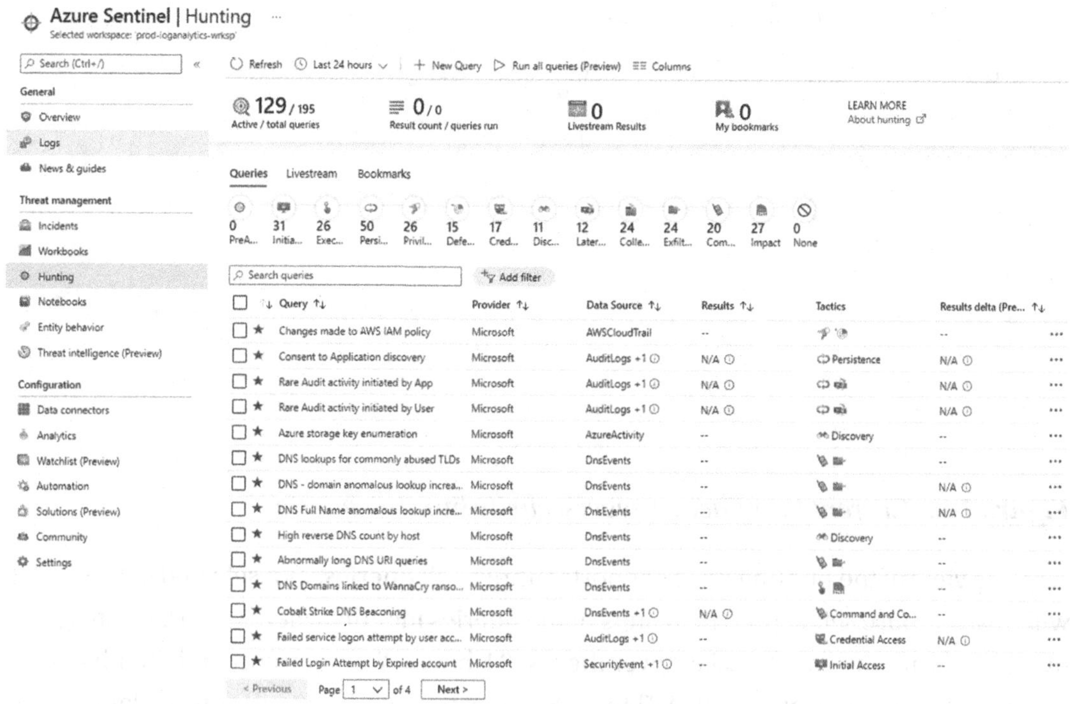

Figure 7-8. *Azure Sentinel hunting view*

The design is streamlined to help find undetected threats more quickly. The prioritization has new ways to identify which hunting results are more relevant to your security business. Along the top right of the screen, shown in Figure 7-9, are the current hunting queries that are aligned with the MITRE ATT&CK framework and Cyber Kill Chain. The queries are built using the Kusto Query Language (KQL) that you learned through exercises earlier in this chapter. It is the same KQL used by the queries in your analytics rules in many Azure services.

○ Refresh   ○ Last 24 hours ∨   + New Query   ▷ Run all queries (Preview)   ☰☰ Columns

◉ **129** / 195	☰ **0** / 0	▦ **0**	▨ **0**	LEARN MORE
Active / total queries	Result count / queries run	Livestream Results	My bookmarks	About hunting ☐

Queries   Livestream   Bookmarks

○	▣	⍨	⌕	⚡	⌐	▦	∿	⬚	▤	▧	◈	▣	⊘
0	31	26	50	26	15	17	11	12	24	24	20	27	0
PreA...	Initia...	Exec...	Persi...	Privil...	Defe...	Cred...	Disc...	Later...	Colle...	Exfilt...	Com...	Impact	None

⌕ Search queries	⚲ Add filter

	↓ Query ↑↓	Provider ↑↓	Data Source ↑↓	Results ↑↓	Tactics	Results delta (Pre... ↑↓	
☐ ★	Changes made to AWS IAM policy	Microsoft	AWSCloudTrail	--	▨ ▧	--	···
☐ ★	Consent to Application discovery	Microsoft	AuditLogs +1 ○	N/A ○	⌕ Persistence	N/A ○	···
☐ ★	Rare Audit activity initiated by App	Microsoft	AuditLogs +1 ○	N/A ○	⌕ ▨	N/A ○	···
☐ ★	Rare Audit activity initiated by User	Microsoft	AuditLogs +1 ○	N/A ○	⌕ ▨	N/A ○	···

Figure 7-9. *Current list of active cybersecurity hunting queries*

This view of the hunting page supports running all queries, or a selected subset, with just a mouse selection. The results of the queries identify where to start hunting by starting with the count, spikes, over the last 24-hours. You then sort and filter by favorites, data source, or MITRE ATT&CK. Some of the queries may not have data because there are no data sources connected. Partner updates are seen in Figure 7-10; Azure Sentinel has been updated and continues to have partner solutions added.

Azure Sentinel | Solutions (Preview) ⋯

Selected workspace: 'prod-loganalytics-wrksp'

🔍 Search (Ctrl+/) «	🔍 Search
General	
🛡 Overview	✅ **Symantec Endpoint Protection (Preview)** Azure Sentinel, Microsoft Corporation Azure Sentinel Solution
🗒 Logs	
📰 News & guides	**Cisco ISE (Preview)** Azure Sentinel, Microsoft Corporation Azure Sentinel Solution
Threat management	
📋 Incidents	**Senserva For Azure Sentinel Plan** Senserva, LLC Use Senserva to Enhanced Security and Compliance Data for Azure Sentinel and Azure Active Directory
📊 Workbooks	
⊙ Hunting	**Proofpoint POD (Preview)** Azure Sentinel, Microsoft Corporation Azure Sentinel Solution
📓 Notebooks	
🖋 Entity behavior	**Cloudflare (Preview)** Azure Sentinel, Microsoft Corporation Azure Sentinel Solution
🕓 Threat intelligence (Preview)	
Configuration	**Check Point Sentinel Solution** Check Point Check Point Software Technologies Logic Apps Connector and Sentinel Playbook templates
▦ Data connectors	
♦ Analytics	**TitaniumCloud File Enrichment** ReversingLabs Azure Application
🖼 Watchlist (Preview)	
🔁 Automation	**vArmour Application Controller and Azure Sentinel** vArmour Networks Integrate application relationship management into Microsoft Sentinel
🅰 Solutions (Preview)	
🌐 Community	**CrowdStrike Falcon Endpoint Protection (Preview)** Azure Sentinel, Microsoft Corporation Azure Sentinel Solution
⚙ Settings	
	Azure Firewall Solution for Azure Sentinel Preview Microsoft Corporation Deploy Azure Firewall content in Azure Sentinel
	Azure Sentinel for Azure SQL

Figure 7-10. *Azure Sentinel Solutions view*

Note   Microsoft continues to introduce new security alliances through Azure
Sentinel Solutions that can be downloaded into your Azure Sentinel deployment.
Read more at `https://techcommunity.microsoft.com/t5/azure-`
`sentinel/introducing-azure-sentinel-solutions/ba-p/2347312`.

Now you can add the steps used or steps you are currently following during the
hunting process through the use of "bookmarks". As you run the built-in queries and
copy and paste examples to customize your own queries, you may come across results
that may look unusual or suspicious. You simply save them in a bookmark and refer back

to them in the future. You can use your bookmarked items to create or enrich an incident for investigation.

Notebooks give you a kind of virtual sandbox environment, complete with its own kernel. You can use notebooks to enhance your hunting and investigations with machine learning, visualization, and data analysis. There are many notebook templates, as shown in Figure 7-11, that you can use to help complete your investigation.

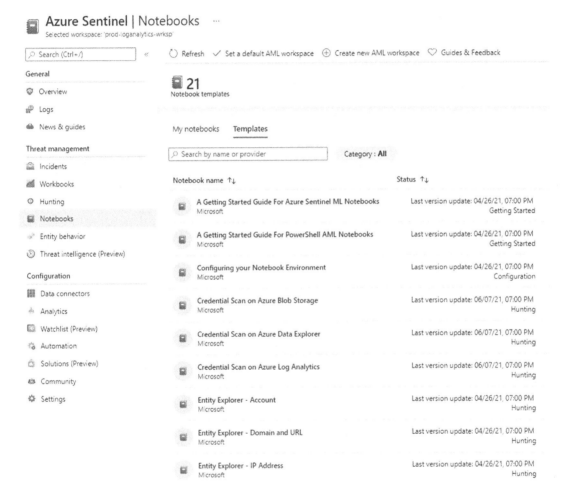

Figure 7-11. *Azure Sentinel notebook templates*

Each notebook is used to encapsulate the raw data and code you run on it. Others can use the same saved notebook to get the results and support your data anomaly investigation. The query data is accessible in Azure Sentinel data tables for you to update different queries.

> **Note**   Microsoft continues to update Azure Sentinel including the new watch list features found at `https://techcommunity.microsoft.com/t5/azure-sentinel/what-s-new-azure-sentinel-update-watchlist-ui-enhancements/ba-p/2451476`.

Summary

In this chapter you were provided detailed information about the location of log data and metric data. You learned the information in Log Analytics workspace is available for many Azure resources and Azure security services. You also begin to create queries using the Kusto Query Language by connecting to the free Microsoft Log Analytics workspace online. Exercises provided details to leverage the Monitor portal and KQL with IntelliSense to customize queries. The last part of the chapter introduced the concept of threat hunting from inside Azure Sentinel.

Next, you are guided through the connection and use of a cybersecurity framework called the MITRE ATT&CK matrix. MITRE is a not-for-profit organization that exposes researched cyber criminals, criminal activity, historical target attacks, and attack malware of choice by malware families and then guides you on how to prepare security defenses to repel cyber-attacks.

CHAPTER 8

Introduction to the MITRE Matrix

You continue to support expanding business into the Azure cloud, and information in this book is used to help customize the layered security approach. In this chapter you gain an insider's view of the MITRE ATT&CK framework. This chapter benefits the CEO, CIO, and CTO with guidance to understand the security risks that affect businesses as network teams adapt to a hybrid cloud model. If you are a C-level executive, you need foundational security insight to understand a hacker's motivation with factual resources for insightful security data and not just scary statistics.

You then need a process to put people into roles and roles into practice using a proven cloud security framework that leverages the addition of cloud secure features found in Azure Security Center. As a CEO, you are too busy to read all chapters, so this chapter is especially crafted to guide you to enable your current security team to rapidly expand with the adoption of a defensive cloud security framework.

Note   MITRE ATT&CK is a registered not-for-profit service.

In this chapter, what you need to know is provided through these main topics:

- MITRE ATT&CK
- CISO summary
- Cybersecurity threats
- Current security facts

© Marshall Copeland 2021
M. Copeland, *Cloud Defense Strategies with Azure Sentinel*, https://doi.org/10.1007/978-1-4842-7132-2_8

MITRE ATT&CK

This topic is one of the most important for any Security Operations Center (SOC) analyst to learn and wield like a cyber "sword." Sometimes there can be misinterpretation when information is not shared effectively or if questions asked are not pedantic and sufficient. The product you will learn is the first ATT&CK framework launched in 2015. ATT&CK stands for Adversarial Tactics, Techniques, and Common Knowledge:

- A: Adversarial, like a nation state or criminal organization

- TT: Tactics and Techniques, methodology used to analyze cyber-attacks

- CK: Common Knowledge, documentation of TT in the form of a matrix

The MITRE Corporation is an American not-for-profit organization that manages federally funded research and development centers supporting US government agencies. The tactics and techniques are identified and categorized, as shown in Figure 8-1.

ID	Name	Description
TA0043	Reconnaissance	The adversary is trying to gather information they can use to plan future operations.
TA0042	Resource Development	The adversary is trying to establish resources they can use to support operations.
TA0001	Initial Access	The adversary is trying to get into your network.
TA0002	Execution	The adversary is trying to run malicious code.
TA0003	Persistence	The adversary is trying to maintain their foothold.
TA0004	Privilege Escalation	The adversary is trying to gain higher-level permissions.
TA0005	Defense Evasion	The adversary is trying to avoid being detected.
TA0006	Credential Access	The adversary is trying to steal account names and passwords.
TA0007	Discovery	The adversary is trying to figure out your environment.
TA0008	Lateral Movement	The adversary is trying to move through your environment.

Figure 8-1. *Numbering and naming of enterprise tactics in the ATT&CK* matrix*

MITRE restructured their research and development operations in the year 2020 to form MITRE Labs. The MITRE Engenuity nonprofit foundation was launched in 2019 to collaborate with the private sector industry and focus on cyber defense. Microsoft is one of the founding members in the MITER foundation's "Center for Threat-Informed Defense" organization.

You should share cybersecurity references because it is important to understand – really understand – painful details, for the company to truly gain value. The MITRE ATT&CK site (`https://attack.mitre.org/`) provides the following:

> *MITRE ATT&CK® is a globally-accessible knowledge base of adversary tactics and techniques based on real-world observations. The ATT&CK knowledge base is used as a foundation for the development of specific threat models and methodologies in the private sector, in government, and in the cybersecurity product and service community.*

When you first connect to the MITRE ATT&CK website, scroll down. There is a view of the matrix presenting the enterprise business information. The enterprise view is the most common. However, there are many different common knowledge matrixes including

- Windows

- MacOS

- Linux

- Cloud

- Network

- Containers

Your time to research information is required to appreciate the overwhelming information provided from this default view of the global defense matrix of cyber-attacks. The matrix aligns criminal attackers and activities through various movements using the Cyber Kill Chain model.

There are several measures used by the kill chain model to help identify of actions taken by cyber-attackers. You should learn the model in greater detail and then start to review the ATT&CK matrix. Do not be confused by some documentation that puts the number of kill chain states at six, seven, eight, or more because learning about forensic data and how malware supports criminal actions is what's important. Security analytics teams learn interworking of malware through "malware detonation" in a controlled sandbox and reverse engineering. You need exposure to different malware families and learn how they infect and how they go undetected to better aid you in categorizing malware actions into each kill chain stage. Often malware actions do not perfectly align with the stages of the model.

Next you are provided a short explanation of the kill chain stages, often interchangeably referred to as actions or movements. Each stage is foundational when speaking the language of security.

Reconnaissance is learning potential weakness in the security layers and using this intelligence in the planning of an attack. You should rethink posting a graphic of the business organization on your website. Org charts provide clear identification of executives for a phishing campaign. It also provides departments that could be used in a social engineering attack to gain access to the network, like an attacker pretending to need a password reset but they lost their laptop. Reconnaissance is not just using tools like Network Mapper (NMAP) run in stealth mode to evade network detection. It is often about the data available by browsing websites, pulling down PDFs, and learning the internal structure of the target organization. With enough information, an attacker can begin to craft one or many possible attack campaigns.

In the weaponization phase, it may have already been completed before the reconnaissance phase is over. Some steps can take place in parallel and do not necessarily need to wait to begin. However, the information gathered may help better crate malware in a specific form that can provide the installation needed to gain access. There are many options to consider like EXE installation hidden in a document, URL, or Office document. Weaponization is placing malicious payload into a delivery method.

Delivery of the payload can be in the form of a phishing campaign where fake emails are emailed directly to company employees who work in the departments identified from the organization chart on the website. Spear phishing could involve clearly crafted emails to company executives. They may not have the time to complete company-mandated phishing training. The phishing campaign could resemble an executive congratulating one of the employees in the organization on a bonus and urging them to open the attached document, only the sender's email address is in use, not the true email address of the executive. Delivery could be from a USB stick that was found in the employee parking lot. Some well-crafted delivery has been using a USB returned to the original store package, as if the USB were never opened.

Exploitation/installation is the compromise movement. You get that sinking feeling you should not have clicked that document or URL. There is installation of malware based on software vulnerability, but most exploitations happen by human vulnerability titled "social engineering." The exploitation action of criminals is sometimes found during discovery or installation after the exploitation action. These two kill chain links are separate but based on attackers' actions sometimes analyzed as the same phase. One example is when an exploit is used by delivery of shell code that in turn pulls down and executes larger-sized code. The shell code is crafted small to evade endpoint software protection and then executes additional malware. The installed malware is crafted to be **persistent**, often called a nation state advanced persistent threat (APT). These forms of malware evade detection and eradication. As one example, some malware cleverly has no installation, no EXE to install, and runs entirely in memory. Also, malware may replicate from machine to machine living off the land. This term means that no additional downloads from hackers' sites are used to create backdoor, rootkit, or credential-harvesting tools. The compromised machine's operating system is the new attacker's toolkit, using OS utilities and other resources from networks. Utilities in place include Bash, PowerShell, and Windows Management Instrumentation (WMI). The tools do not normally create an alert or an anomaly event.

The **Command and Control** (C2) phase of the attack represents the period after exploiting the OS. The term comes from the actions of the malware, after compromising the operating system, or the power companies' industrial controller or the hospital imaging device. The malware sends out a request for additional commands. The cybercriminal sends commands to the compromised system by the malware code, and often the malware transmits stolen data from your company's' network. Data sent could be business plans for the next five years, engineering drawings for the next jet fighter, or username and password to your life savings you just entered when you checked on your 401(k). Many of the C2 actions involve ransomware, using a security key to encrypt data on your hard drive, and network drives, criminals often requesting payment in bitcoins.

Exfiltration removes data from your network. The data that is sent is often the most valuable to the attackers. The attacks steal digital currency, valuable business data, and what you may have identified as the company's "crown jewels." Some compromised computers do not fall into the exfiltration stage or action because data is gathered for a longer-term criminal action. The state of exfiltration can include personal information, usernames, addresses, credit cards, and other information that can be exchanged on the "dark Web."

Now let's return to the subject of the ATT&CK framework and how it can help defend against cyber-attacks. Earlier in this chapter, you were guided to the website `https://attack.mitre.org/`. If you did not go to the site for a view, then do it now and return. There is a relationship between defense using the ATT&CK matrix and the organization of the cybersecurity kill chain. You should review the relationship of both in Figure 8-2, showing framework and kill chain alignment.

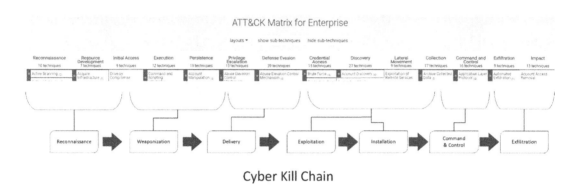

Figure 8-2. *The ATT&CK framework aligned with Cyber Kill Chain*

As you have now realized, the width of the matrix spans your computer monitor from left to write. There is a focused matrix that presents pre-attack information. Pre-attack information describes what techniques are used in preparation for an attack campaign. You can view PRE Matrix by selecting the PRE option on the left menu as shown in Figure 8-3.

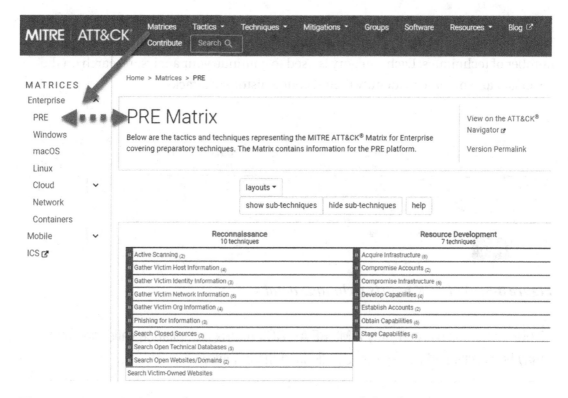

Figure 8-3. *PRE Matrix showing reconnaissance and development motions to gain information before the campaign attack*

A complete listing of the categories can be seen in Figure 8-4. This is only to provide a clear image for this discussion. Refer to this image as you learn the different techniques and attackers.

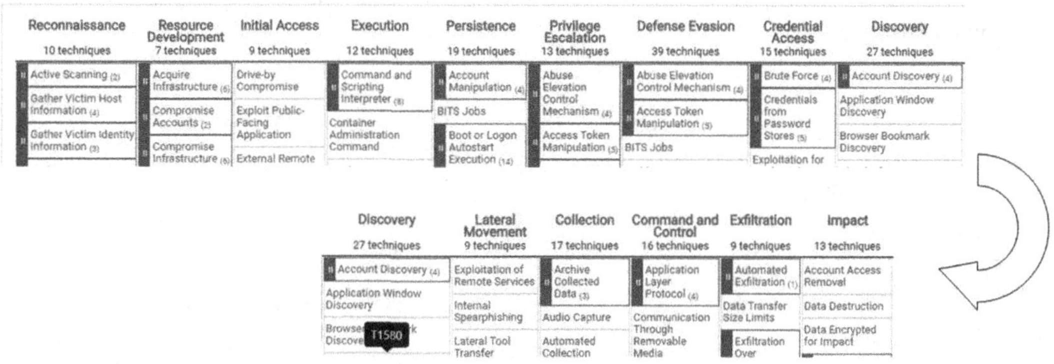

Figure 8-4. *ATT&CK matrix columns view in detail*

As you review this matrix, notice the current number of techniques for each category. To highlight this information, refer to Figure 8-5 for a clear visual understanding of the number of techniques. Each category is used to continue your analyst research on the adversary and prepare to identify their recoded history of attacks.

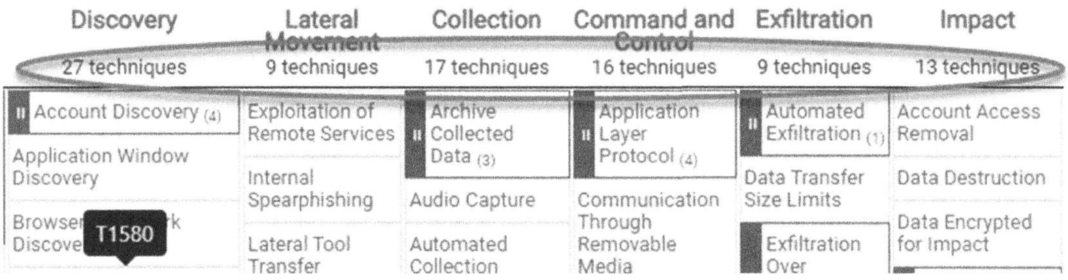

Figure 8-5. *ATT&CK matrix technique details*

Note   There is not currently a MITRE ATT&CK matrix compliance validation that may be proclaimed by security solutions in the industry.

The number of techniques may increase. However, there is a change in the utilization of sub-techniques. If you select the option to review the sub-techniques, as presented in Figure 8-6, additional guidance is provided. There are open requests for security organizations to contribute to the matrix data and improve the value with their data. Remember that Microsoft is one of the founding members. Any new content in Enterprise ATT&CK is added to the current (sub-technique) version. Future contribution of techniques is considered if the behavior might be an appropriate sub-technique of an existing technique.

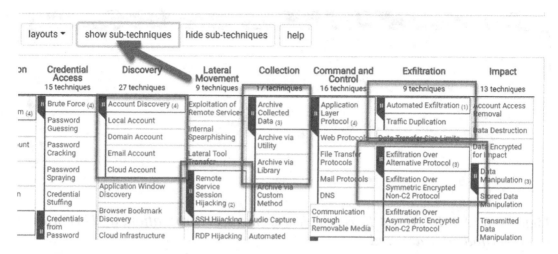

Figure 8-6. *Sub-techniques shown in the matrix view online*

One of the best methods to learn and leverage defense techniques in the ATT&CK matrix is with a working example of using the ATT&CK navigator. Attackers continue to change and obfuscate defense, so their playbook can change in the future. The information provided in the ATT&CK matrix is based on historical data collected and compiled from cybersecurity open source technical organizations. If you are not sure where to get started, you can select either the Groups or Software view, as shown in Figure 8-7.

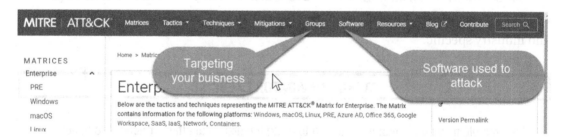

Figure 8-7. *ATT&CK matrix view to search for known groups or software to create defensive measures*

The question may be, from which bad actors do you defend? Use the Groups view to search for attackers that attack similar corporations, like medical or pharmaceutical, shown in Figure 8-8.

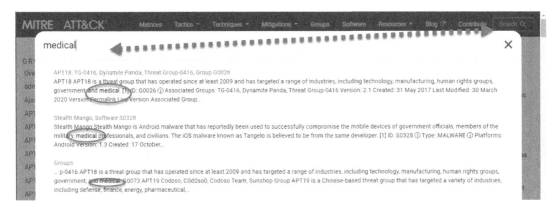

Figure 8-8.   MITRE ATT&CK search view for medical corporations and historical attackers and malware used

Another question may be, how do I defend from attack software? Use the Software search view for attacker software used.

The next exercise walks you through the steps by using an incredibly powerful cybersecurity defensive tool. During the exercise you may be asking

- What is the list of criminal actors that attack your business?

- What are the techniques they use?

- What are the defenses to put in place for repelling?

Use the information after the exercise to understand the global threat landscape. Guidance provides historical criminal actors against companies that are global, regional, and industry specific.

ATT&CK NAVIGATOR EXERCISE

This example may be the first introduction to using the historical attacker actions to better prepare against their attacks. This exercise supports the current workflow, which in the future may change slightly to incorporate new functionality and interface.

This exercise would be used after you searched for and found two groups that attack corporations similar to your business. Who are the attackers, how did they attack, what malware did they use, and how to mitigate the risk?

1. Open your Edge browser to the URL `https://attack.mitre.org/`. From this screen, select the option View on the ATT&CK Navigator, in the top right-hand view.

2. From the new screen, you start on a blank tab, so select Create New Layer.

3. When you select Create New Layer, options are provided for this exercise. You first need to select a version of ATT&CK techniques and a domain: Enterprise, Mobile, or ICS.

4. Use the drop-down arrow next to version to select the latest version. In this example, you use ATT&CK v9.

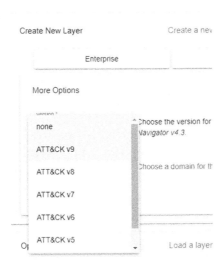

5. Next, select the drop-down arrow next to domain. Select Enterprise and then select Create.

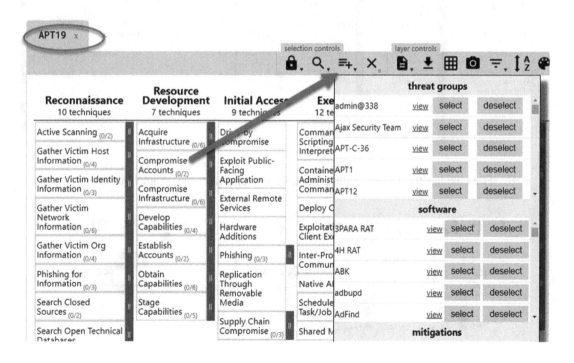

6. Once the new tab is populated, change the default title from LAYER to APT19,
    which stands for Advanced Persistent Threat (group) 19. Across the top menu
    bar of the navigator view, select the plus (+) icon.

7. Scroll down under "threat groups" and select APT19 and click the select button.

    During the review of the APT19 group, you notice that Cobalt Strike is one of the tools used. If you search for Cobalt Strike, you see that another group Chimera uses that tool also.

    When you select the group, notice a few matrix cubes are highlighted behind the pop-up window. Select the plus icon again to toggle the window closed.

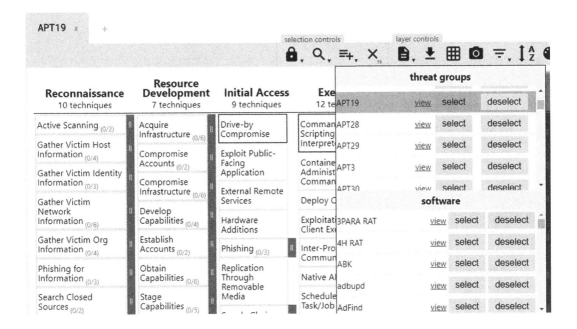

8. From the navigator menu, select the score icon and enter the decimal number 1.

9.   There is a color that is assigned to the highlighted cubes. Select the score icon
     to toggle the menu off. Select the color setup wheel on the navigation menu
     and enter this range: low value = 1 and high value = 3. Select the color setup
     wheel to toggle the window closed.

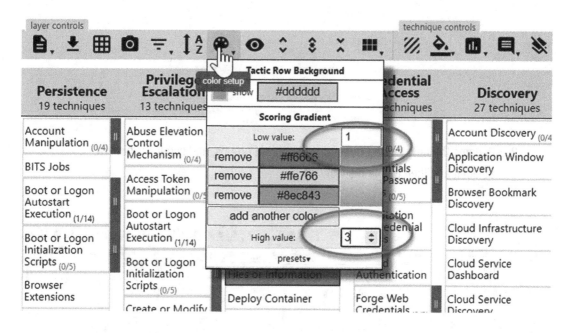

10.   To create a new layer, select the plus sign to open a new tab.

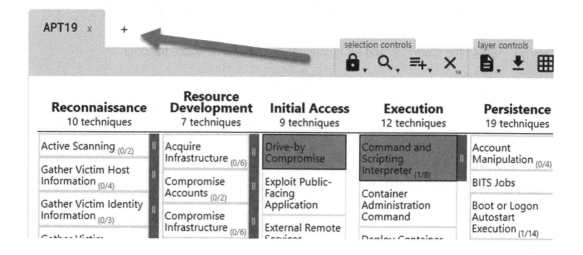

11. Select Create New Layer and repeat steps 3, 4, and 5. This selects the version of the framework and the Enterprise domain. Rename the new tab to APT17.

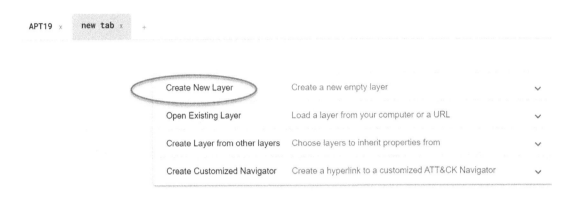

12. Rename the new tab to Chimera, select threat groups, and scroll to Chimera. Select it and then toggle the view off.

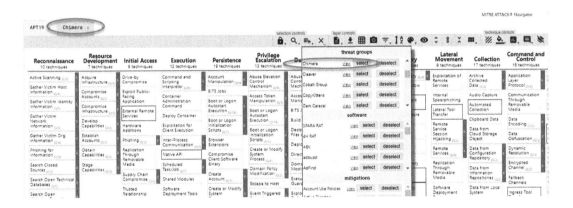

13. Select the score icon and set Chimera to the number 2. Notice the color changes.

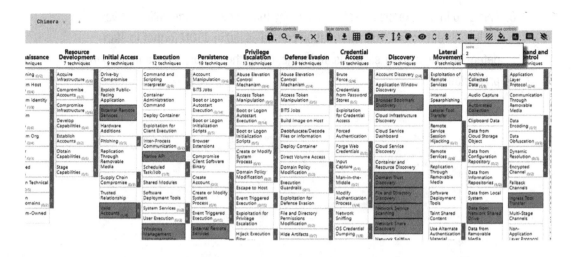

14. There is a color (from step 9) that is assigned to the highlighted cubes. Select the score icon to toggle the menu off. Select the color setup wheel on the navigation menu and enter this range: low value = 1 and high value = 3. Select the color setup wheel to toggle the window closed.

15. Create a new tab. From the options, select Create Layer from other layers. Select the domain as Enterprise ATT&CK v9. Notice the numbers above the tabs for APT19 and Chimera. Enter a+b in the score expression field. Select Create.

16. This step in the exercise creates an overlay that shows commonality between the two threat actors. This information can be saved in JSON format to start defensive exercises or saved as an image, using the camera icon, and used in a presentation.

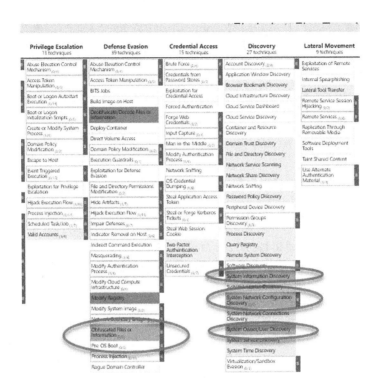

You now have a simple example of how to leverage the MITRE ATT&CK matrix to learn historical facts about threat actors and how to better defend against their criminal behavior. A key point to remember, beginning with your first threat actor up to your tenth threat actor, is that security is a journey. In security work you are never done. You work as a team to become an effective team, sharing what you learn through this journey.

The MITRE work is incredibly insightful and should be leveraged by your security organization. There are other frameworks to be aware of and considered as you prepare for your "murder board" review, and they include the NIST Five Functions (`www.nist.gov/cyberframework/online-learning/five-functions`), Cyber Defense Matrix (`https://cyberdefensematrix.com/`), and others.

> **Note**   You can find out more about preparation for a security murder board review by searching for security analytics interviews and presentations created by Rob Dartnall, Intelligence Director at Security Alliance.

There are additional ways to leverage the historical data once the threat actor or software has been included into the navigator view. As an example in Figure 8-9, right-click Modify Registry and view the options to view the technique in detail. This is another way to build skill set for the defensive measures of the SOC.

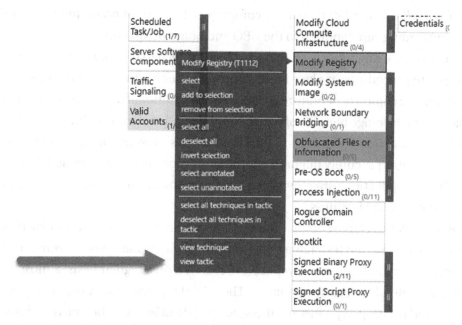

Figure 8-9. *Detailed view of the ATT*CK navigator tool by right-clicking features*

CISO Summary

A Chief Information Security Officer (CISO), SOC Managers, security architect, and security analyst need a jump start into secure cloud by leveraging the same guidance provided by the Azure Security Framework. Later, they continue to expand security with best practices and procedures to integration with their current security processes. For a security team, the on-premises layered security model expands into the cloud, which requires you to fully understand your adversary's determination to breach your cloud infrastructure. You and your team must learn about the increased availability of attacking tools as a service. Many of the current attack tools are created leveraging automated deployment, often within minutes after a Bitcoin purchase, and some come with a Service-Level Agreement (SLA) to be rebuilt if taken down by authorities.

Your business has a board of directors and CEO who provide the high-level requirements for necessary security policy. As cloud security policies are written, they should be reviewed annually and updated to remain current as the business leveraging cloud services changes. Security procedures are created and updated to support the cloud security policies and then followed by guiding security teams with a "how-to" implementation process. These security procedures are later reviewed and audited by third-party auditors to validate security compliance for the company, and the security assessment findings are reported to the CEO and board of directors.

Companies are migrating to the cloud, and they need to migrate securely. They have processes and procedures in place for their on-premises business but business wants to lower or remove capital expenditures (Capex) from traditional on-premises datacenter. Companies can leverage benefits of Azure cloud operational expenditures (OPEX). This is not a discussion on benefits of the cloud. This is a discussion using a common language to support securely migrating to the cloud, specifically a Microsoft Azure secure cloud. Applications are moving, services are moving, and security has to move at the same speed as the business.

Most companies create copious amounts of security data in the form of log files that are transformed into text, tables, and graphs. The information is delivered using many automated methods, so the reports are received on a regular basis, almost never following the intended security guidance. There is a language of security, a language the business needs to properly consume the security data effectively. Business teams need to provide informative presentation that is effective for business decisions, and from a security standpoint, that focuses the business on the right perspective. This is often presented by a CISO, reporting with key performance indicators (KPIs) and key risk indicators (KRIs). Gathering, evaluating, and presenting the correct information for the business KPIs and KRIs is often challenging.

The CISO has the challenging task of building a long-lasting relationship with the business, and they together choose the right KPIs and KRIs after understanding what is important to the organization. One of the major security concerns is selecting information from a database that contains depth and breadth and then sampling the data so that KPIs and KRIs can be well defined. The National Vulnerability Database, a database of all known types of vulnerabilities, provides the ability to search for keywords.

Figure 8-10 provides information like code injection, cross-site forgery, input validation, and many others, tracking utilization over the years.

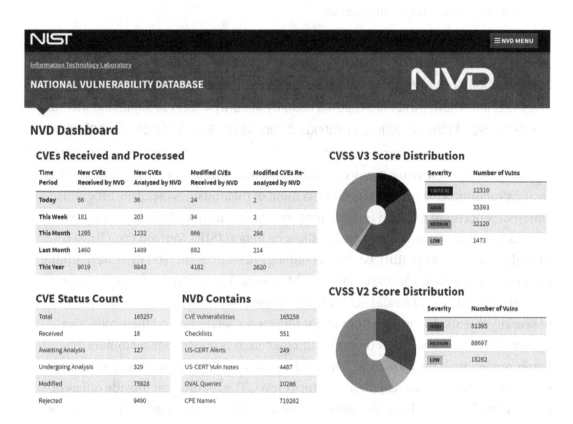

Figure 8-10. *US National Vulnerability Database of vulnerabilities. Original information edited to provide details*

Note   The NVD with all assets and visualizations can be freely accessed from `https://nvd.nist.gov/`, and the specific visualization updates are found at `https://nvd.nist.gov/vuln/visualizations/cwe-over-time`.

The National Vulnerability Database (NVD) is a product of the National Institute of Standards and Technology (NIST) and is a repository of all reported vulnerabilities. The NIST project is sponsored by the Department of Homeland Security's National Cyber Security Division. The information in the database includes security checklists, security-related software flaws, misconfigurations, product names, and impact metrics. All NIST publications are available in the public domain according to Title 17 of the

United States Code, which means companies are able to use the data provided. However, an acknowledgment to the value of NVD would be appreciated. Additional details about NVD are discussed later in this chapter.

Security Tip   Key performance indicators (KPIs) evaluate the success of an organization or business unit as the business continues to achieve business goals. Key risk indicators (KRIs) are metrics used by security teams to signal the increase or decrease of risk exposures in various business units as it affects the enterprise.

Over the past few years, many companies are hiring more security analysts and security architects for continuous improvement of their business security programs. Different reports are released from major corporations with worldwide data insight, such as from the Microsoft Security Intelligence Report (SIR), Verizon Data Breach Investigations Report (DBIR), Global Technology Resources Inc. (GTRI), Cisco Annual Cybersecurity Report, and 2021 Mandiant M-Trends (FireEye) report (`www.fireeye.com/current-threats/annual-threat-report/mtrends.html`), to improve the view of security threats. As the data from major reports are analyzed and their collective information correlated, focus on many different areas is needed for customers to better protect their infrastructure. The security focus is different according to the type of business, location, and capability maturity level. The reports can provide different information based on the respondents, locations, and known historical data, and it is exceedingly difficult for only a single report to provide all the information to understand the global view of cyber breaches. However, common themes or areas that need security focus are past reports and for the next few years include recommendations for companies to invest security resources in many areas including the following:

- Software development security

- Website and application protection

- Endpoint threat detection and response

- Securing the Internet of Things (IoT)

These attacks have continued over many years, and the trend to notice is the short amount of time the company's network is breached, often in minutes or hours, and how long it takes before the attack is discovered, often in weeks and months. You must improve security defenses and shorten time to discovery and remediation of security breaches.

The criminal attacks are proliferating by state actors and non-state actors. Sharing security information is critical to support the correlation of events to quickly identify new or morphed cyber families of malware. The most powerful defense is to share the information, but because of misaligned incentives and mistrust between customers and law enforcement, some security breaches are reluctantly reported.

Companies are losing intellectual property by the terabytes, petabytes, and exabytes yearly to cybercrime, cyber espionage, and cyber terrorism. Future conflicts may include a cyber component beyond what was seen in the 2016 and 2020 US elections. The businesses of today are in a world of competitive global economy built on innovation.

As a CISO, you need to create a cloud security discovery team to provide an update to you and other executives weekly as you prepare to migrate data, servers, and application services to Microsoft Azure. The world and private companies are built by digital technology and need to improve security with best practices and continued due diligence:

- Intelligent security analytics

- Context-aware security analytics

- Big data security analytics

Note   A current total cost of ownership (TCO) calculator can be found at `https://azure.microsoft.com/en-us/pricing/tco/`.

Cybersecurity Threats

Businesses have valuable assets, but one of the most difficult tasks is to assess the value of business assets. If we state the problem another way, what is the value of an asset and the cost to the business if it is compromised? Placing value on a business physical asset is easy, but providing the cost of compromise is often exceedingly difficult especially if the business doesn't understand security impact.

The loss of assets impacts the business directly and indirectly. The direct impact is the cost to keep, maintain, or replace the asset if it stolen or compromised. An example of compromise is the possibility of a ransomware attack. The cost of a security breach is often difficult to calculate. There is no single formula that includes the cost of potential fines, man hours to remediate, and loss of business related to damage to brand. The purpose for viewing data facts is to gain attention based on the impact of the security breach in the NIST NVD Database showing severity (high, medium, low) over time.

The data breaches are visualized live as part of a larger project. However, for our purpose, this information can be used in live presentations to the board to gain insight into the overall effect of security breach.

Editing the visualization with the appropriate data is helpful to remove all the security noise and focus more on the relevant type of business, legal aspect, healthcare aspect, type of attack, leaks, hacks, and poor security to make clear the discussion topic.

The indirect impact to the business is hard to quantify because of the unknowns about how the assets lost affect the business in totality. Business impacts caused by security vulnerabilities require a different perspective and introduce a different severity cost or penalty if you will, based on the impact. It often helps for executives to gain insight into the unknown cost of security vulnerabilities by using a real-world example.

The question most customers have is "why an attacker would want to attack me." Some of the information is provided through a much longer report, the 2021 Verizon Data Breach Investigations Report (DBIR), highlighted later in this chapter. However, Figure 8-11 provides a clear motivation over several years.

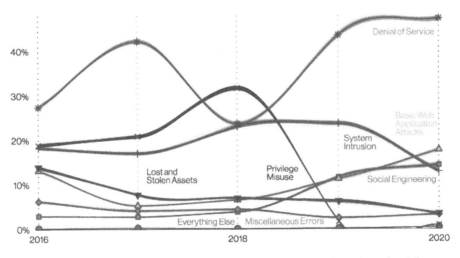

Figure 8-11. *Verizon DBIR showing patterns over time. Reprinted with permission. Verizon 2021 Data Breach Investigations Report*

The criminal attacker or attacker nation is after financial gain. However, your company may not be a financial institution. The dollars requested are often requested in "bit coins" from attackers that use "ransomware." You should read the Microsoft SIR and Verizon DBIR to understand the greater motivations. If time does not allow reading from cover to cover, then the Executive Summary for each is a very informative guide that limits time needed to understand the motivation.

Current Security Facts

Security analysis is the key to remaining agile as the number and impact severity of security breaches continues to increase as announced publicly. You, as a security professional, must stay aware to show support for the board of directors as they significantly increase their focus on cloud information security, hybrid network cybersecurity, and IT risk management. Your security team requires resources that provide a global view of international cyber armies, with in-depth information about their attack vectors, weaponized payloads, and industry-specific targeting that is up to date.

You may recall in the Executive Summary there are several key annual security report publications that should be required reading over time. This list is not all that should be reviewed, but a very good list to start reading and that has been published yearly and biyearly. Infrastructure teams new to security should start with this list with the most current publication, before reading through the previous ones. The value of the current publications is to gain a footing of current cyber-attacks. As you read through the current year, then the year before, and then the year before, notice the commonalities of the criminals and criminal families of malware. What is sometimes seen is the resurgence of previously successful attacks that return with modifications and new signatures. The following list is a starting point for cloud architects who are new to cybersecurity:

- Microsoft Security Intelligence Report (SIR)

- Verizon Data Breach Investigations Report (BDIR)

- IBM sponsored 2021 Ponemon Institute report

- Other security reports:

  - Cisco Annual Cybersecurity Report

  - FireEye M-Trends 2021

Microsoft Security Intelligence Report (SIR)

You need to have good guidance on protecting your Microsoft Azure cloud subscription with solutions that include Azure Security Center. However, an overall view of the cybersecurity landscape with attacks and weaponized payloads is required to "level set" your security research team. Many Microsoft customers were not aware of the SIR, and others have not realized the depth of information, understanding, and guidance provided by this free publication. However, Microsoft does not allow reuse of data graphs, so they do not appear in this section.

Cyber-attacks continue with increased agility and newer sophisticated tool suites with, what can only be interpreted as, very methodical procedures. Some of these criminals are very organized and use cyber tactics that indicate complexity, which is evidence of state-sponsored attacks including cyber espionage and cyber terrorism. Some of the weaknesses in the layered security model include the data provided by end users on social media sites, and many attackers use proven social engineering and zero-day vulnerabilities to break in to corporate networks.

As criminals acquire access to gain considerable knowledge on a corporate network, stealing data and breaching privacy, all for financial gain, once the breach is made public, public trust on the business by the public begins to crumble.

For well-protected enterprise companies using many layers of security, attacks are incredibly expensive, costing organizations millions per incident. The total impact or damage to a company's brand is difficult to quantify.

The information in security reports helps identify the many different types of attempts to exploit a security vulnerability. This information identifies the need to stay informed around more than just vulnerabilities for the operation system, but all applications used on business systems. Additionally, the use of "Exploit Kits", which may have the ability to try different exploit methods rather than a single exploit type.

Thousands of cybersecurity attacks were reported in 2020 and 2021. There are other annual security reports, introduced in this chapter, and if a common thread can be derived from the different reports, it can be interpreted with two data points. The two most interesting data points are

- Hackers breached networks in minutes.

- IT security teams took over 100 days to discover breaches.

Microsoft SIR information comes from the many different operating systems that are being used in the world, including online services. Information in the Microsoft SIR identifies the individual threat types, with "Trojans" being the most common.

One of the many reasons to read the Microsoft SIR is the learning provided to a security team and best practices you can use as standards. A compliant system is connected to the Microsoft network. A user's computer must be running the latest version of the Defender or Defender for Servers. Antimalware signatures must be no more than six days old, and real-time protection must be enabled.

As the attackers' techniques seem to be evolving at a faster pace than in the past years and become more sophisticated, the layered security approach needs to be updated and become smarter, to provide valuable security guidance to large enterprises. If you ask an IT director, they will most likely tell you they do want and need a full-fledged advanced threat protection solution that identifies attacks as fast as possible with wide-ranging intelligence and built-in actionable remediation and requires less maintenance. Azure Security Center is clearly positioned as a cloud service as discussed in Chapter 3 that provides automated responses that in many applications alert on the threat potential and remediate. Automating security alerts is a critical component because even professional developers can provide attackers an unexpected advantage.

Why It Is Important

The Microsoft Security Intelligence Report (SIR) focuses on software vulnerabilities, software vulnerability exploits, malware, and unwanted software. Past reports and related resources are available for download at `www.microsoft.com/sir`. The Microsoft Security Intelligence Report has been released twice a year since 2006.

The Microsoft Security Intelligence Report, used in this example, focuses on the first and second quarters of 2020, with trend data for the last several quarters presented on a quarterly basis. The reports are updated each year with three different options to freely review and share:

- Entire SIR

- SIR key findings

- SIR regional threats

Criminal attackers can trick an end user, through a phishing email, to install software that looks to the end user a cloud storage folder. The software replaces the user's cloud storage synchronization token with the attacker's cloud storage token, and then the attacker receives a copy of each file stored in the cloud folder. This type of attack is called a "man in the middle." However, since it is for cloud storage, the company Imperva coined the phrase "man in the cloud attack."

Where to Download

The free Microsoft Security Intelligence Report (SIR) download page provides the latest SIR, key findings, and regional threats. Also you can download previous editions. You are required to enter company and personal information, so read the terms on sharing of data in the "Acceptable use" section before completing the form. The download URL is `www.microsoft.com/en-us/security/business/security-intelligence-report`.

2021 Verizon Data Breach Investigations Report (DBIR) Update

Over the past 15 years, Verizon has been releasing the DBIR, and the 2021 edition was recently released to be publicly downloaded. As a security professional, you need to understand cyber criminals that threaten the security of your business. Reading security reports helps provide you timely information like the information provided by the DBIR.

The 2021 DBIR effectively exposes a world view of cybersecurity with "5,250 confirmed breaches" over time. This information is necessary to bring to any board of directors meetings and executive briefings to present narratives and slides that can tell the "security" story to help the business make clear connections between cybersecurity and business objectives. Figure 8-12 provides highlights of patterns of breaches.

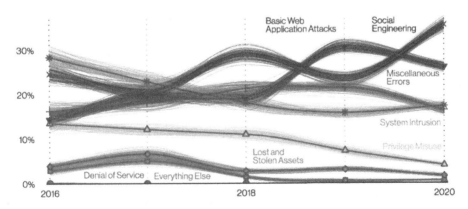

Figure 8-12. *Verizon 2021 DBIR patterns of breaches over time. Reprinted with permission. Verizon 2021 Data Breach Investigations Report*

In the 2021 report, you will learn the latest data concerning

- What business sector has the biggest cybersecurity threats, with updated information on mitigation of the threat

- The "who" in attacks and more importantly the entry point that needs to be reviewed in your own business

- Motivations of the bad actors

In the Executive Briefing section, there is more data that identifies hacking, malware, and social engineering efforts to penetrate the layers of network security.

The Verizon 2021 Data Breach Investigations Report provides great insight into the attackers' motives, patterns, and attack methods based on the reported incidents.

Security Tip   You can download the 2021 DBIR at `www.verizon.com/business/resources/reports/dbir/`.

The Verizon DBIR uses the Vocabulary for Event Recording and Incident Sharing (VERIS). VERIS is a framework to record and share customer-reported security events and incidents that lead to breaches and could be used by any company using a predictable naming standard for repeatability. VERIS compartmentalizes data collection to categorize the cyber action taken, the attack method (like a relationship to known malware family if any), and the asset targeted. The overall DBIR process also captures timeline, victim demographics, discovery method, impact data, and much more.

Social engineering and spam like phishing emails are a challenge to prevent. However, using the definition of "spear phishing," a phishing email targeted at the CEO or CIO can be a bigger challenge to stop. Spear phishing with a vulnerability targeted at C-level executives is a high value target for cyber criminals. Data collected and provided in the report reveals insight into social engineering breaches stealing credentials. Figure 8-13 provides data around how successful a weaponized email was when it was identified.

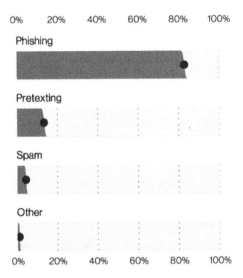

Figure 8-13. *DBIR top social engineering vulnerabilities. Reprinted with permission. Verizon 2021 Data Breach Investigations Report*

Phishing emails allow attackers to drop malware, and the categories of criminal software are shown n Figure 8-14.

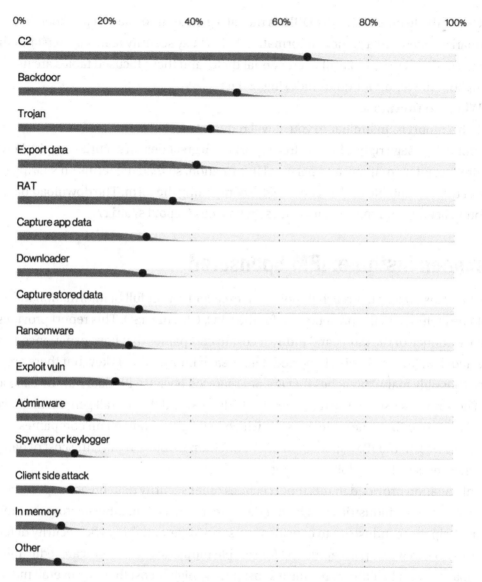

Figure 8-14. *Malware varieties in social engineering incidents. Reprinted with permission. Verizon 2021 Data Breach Investigations Report*

Why It Is Important

The Verizon Data Breach Investigations Report provides details that every security professional should read and use as a reference. You should use the data to educate users, executives, and other IT and security professionals, possibly through "lunch-N-learn" events. You are busy, your team members are busy, and most of the daily information is "noise" the security professional should attempt to overcome.

One of the features from the DBIR is the "at a glance" information provided in a summarized view. "At a glance" information helps busy security teams understand the relevance of a security topic, like "credential theft," and these focused tables are used throughout the report for quick indexing of data.

Where to Download

If this report is unfamiliar to you, it will require entering contact information and accepting the usage rights, but the free report has a great deal of security insight. You are required to enter company and personal information, so read the terms on sharing of data in the "Acceptable use" section before completing the form. The download page can be found at `www.verizon.com/business/resources/reports/dbir/`.

Ponemon Institute: IBM Sponsored

The 2021 Cost of a Data Breach Report is an excellent report full of information that could be included in the presentation for the CEO, CIO, or CISO. This report provides global evidence of the direct and indirect cost to companies that have experienced and reported data breach details. Reported data breach information is key, but there are some (possibly many) breaches that are not reported because PII data may be exposed.

The amounts used in the report are in US dollars, and the overall general message is that the cost of breaches is increasing, which has a global impact on companies and countries. In the IBM-sponsored 2021 Ponemon Institute report, the cost of data breaches reflects the US dollar amount.

Information provided in this report echoes other security data breach reports, and the fact that some industries had higher data breach costs than others across the globe should help those industries to consider investing "differently" in cybersecurity defenses. Figure 8-15 shows the per-capita cost for sample industries like healthcare, education, and finance, with healthcare having a substantially higher cost than the overall mean of $158.

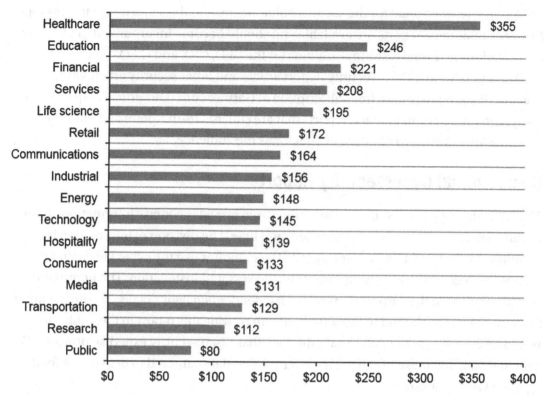

Figure 8-15. *Per-capita cost by industry. Reprinted with permission. Benchmark research sponsored by IBM. Independently conducted by Ponemon Institute LLC*

Why It Is Important

Security analyses look for credible security information to help provide evidence of potential cyber-attacks based on industry, country, impact cost, and root cause. The information from reports like that from Ponemon Institute is needed to gain a view of the cybersecurity issues from both a global and an industry perspective.

Where to Download

There are many reports provided by IBM. They have a great deal of insight for novice and seasoned security professionals. You are required to enter company and personal information, so read the terms on sharing of data in the "Acceptable use" section before completing the form. The download page can be found at www.ibm.com/security/data-breach.

Other Annual Security Reports

Time is never an asset for the security "blue" team, and the same is true for this topic. However, additional reports are available and should become incorporated in the daily conversations and weekly summarizations for the CEO, CIO, and CISO.

The Cisco Annual Cybersecurity Report article and other security articles are available if you sign up for a free subscription at Gartner.com. This article helps security analyst prepare information and reports that are concise, to-the-point and attention grabbing for a CISO, CIO or board of director as the audience.

Cisco Annual Cybersecurity Report

The 2021 Annual Cybersecurity Report from Cisco provides concise information about the attacks and attackers: who, why, when, and how. The division of information is identified by Certified Ethical Hacking (CEH) techniques like the cyber kill chain or phases like reconnaissance, weaponization, delivery and installation. The information provides insight in the corporations through defender behavior details. The information from Cisco is valuable, and without their offer to provide this report to the public, it would be exceedingly difficult to gain the view that Cisco security expertise provides. You should read it and make use of the information and data gathered to help you defend against cyber-attackers.

Where to Download

You are required to enter company and personal information, so read the terms on sharing of data in the "Acceptable use" section before completing the form. Download page can be found at `www.cisco.com/c/en/us/products/security/cybersecurity-reports.html`.

FireEye M-Trends 2021 Annual Security Report

The information in the FireEye report is a continuation of the companies' collaboration, leveraging data provided through customer use of the main product, the FireEye Malware Protection System. The FireEye company still uses the Mandiant name in the yearly report after the acquisition of Mandiant in 2013. Information in the report include trends that define, landscape based on Mandiant's investigation over 2021 breaches and cyber-attacks. It is better to quote the features in the report. The bottom line is the quoted bullet points show the global breath of data in the Mandiant report and you would gain a great deal of insight from the free report.

Where to Download

You are required to enter company and personal information, so read the terms on sharing of data in the "Acceptable use" section before completing the form. Download page can be found at `www.fireeye.com/current-threats/annual-threat-report/mtrends.html`.

Secure Cloud Steps

You need a solid security strategy that is in depth, using the right tools and people to respond appropriately to the threats today and in the future. These are the high-level steps needed to guide you and your security team to a secure cloud. The fundamental foundation about cloud technology from Microsoft Azure services is the speed of change. These steps should be expanded on and incorporated into your company's best practices and guidelines as you move forward.

You need to follow a security framework that extends into the cloud. Federal and state government agencies are able to leverage the National Institute of Standards and Technology (NIST). Several companies leverage the free NIST information provided through the guidance for cloud computing, governance and cyber-security recommendations. You should download and start to review the following guides in Table 8-1.

Table 8-1. *Cybersecurity guide URL listing*

Publication	Download URL
NIST Cloud Computing Reference Architecture Special Publication 500-292	`www.nist.gov/publications/nist-cloud-computing-reference-architecture`
Cybersecurity Framework	`www.nist.gov/programs-projects/cybersecurity-framework`
NIST Special Publication 800-53 Risk Management Framework	`https://nvd.nist.gov/800-53`
Shared Responsibility of Azure Cloud	`https://gallery.technet.microsoft.com/Shared-Responsibilities-81d0ff91`

The NIST Cloud Computing Reference Architecture is a good starting place and should be required reading for any of the security team. In addition, there are Microsoft Azure-specific downloads that should be considered as well. The Cloud Platform

Integration Framework, from 2014, is a first attempt to help customers, organizations, partners, and integrators design and deploy cloud-targeted workloads. The download URL is `https://gallery.technet.microsoft.com/Cloud-Platform-Integration-d37ccd32`.

Additional security frameworks are discussed in Chapter 2. There is a Microsoft-supported free ebook, *2021 Trends in Cybersecurity: A Quick Guide to the Most Important Insights in Security*. The URL for download is `https://info.microsoft.com/SecurityIntelligenceReportDataInsights_Registration.html?ls=Website&lsd=security`.

Azure Cloud Networking, Encryption, and Data Storage

Microsoft Azure virtual networks (VNets) extend your on-premises network into the Microsoft Azure cloud through IPsec-based site-to-site VPN technology or a high-speed Azure ExpressRoute dedicated Wide Area Network (WAN) connection.

The Microsoft Azure networking white paper provides the infrastructure necessary to connect your virtual machines from one VNet to another, as well as bridge between the cloud and your on-premises data center. The document can be downloaded from the URL `http://download.microsoft.com/download/C/A/3/CA3FC5C0-ECE0-4F87-BF4B-D74064A00846/AzureNetworkSecurity_v2_Oct2014.pdf`.

Other than a Virtual Private Network (VPN) connection, ExpressRoute can be used as a private connection from your on-premises network to Microsoft Azure. Read more at the following URL: `https://azure.microsoft.com/en-us/services/expressroute/`.

Identity Multi-factor Authentication (MFA)

One of the changes moving into the cloud is the need for claims-based identity. Microsoft Azure provides support for open authentication solutions like

- OAuth 2.0

- OpenID

Enabling Multi-factor Authentication is a "best practice" for both Azure cloud connectivity and on-premises directory services. Ensuring the user identification is supported for applications, and cloud administration is a security best practice. The need for integration of on premises identity and cloud identity is often the first step

for federation. Read more about using Azure AD connect from the following URL:
`www.microsoft.com/en-us/download/details.aspx?id=47594`

Learn more about claims-based identity in Azure at `www.microsoft.com/en-us/download/details.aspx?id=45909`.

Software Is a Key Vulnerability

Not the only reason but often the main reason for application security flaws is the pressure that application development teams have to time to market new software. This financial pressure forces many developers to overlook or disregard the security aspect in the Software Development Lifecycle (SDLC) process.

According to Gartner Security, the application layer currently contains 90% of all vulnerabilities.

OWASP, Security Development Lifecycle (SDLC)

While there are many different tools, utilities, suites of tools, and techniques for exploiting application vulnerabilities, there is the Open Web Application Security Project (OWASP) Top 10 List, which is free to use and is a list of common vulnerabilities when it comes to web and application development. Top 10 represents a global consensus for the most critical web application security flaws. However, there are thousands of recorded security flaws. The 2021 Top 10 List has been released (based on 2017 current before changes) but early versions of the list are published as "candidates". `https://owasp.org/www-project-top-ten/`

The Top 5 of the Top 10 are

- A1: Injection

- A2: Broken Authentication

- A2: Sensitive Data Exposure

- A4: XML External Entities

- A5: Broken Access Control

Buffer overflows, insecure storage of sensitive data, improper cryptographic algorithms, hardcoded passwords, and backdoor applications are only a sample set of application layer flaw classes. Figure 8-16 provides the Top 10 List for 2017, not 2021. That is still a work in progress.

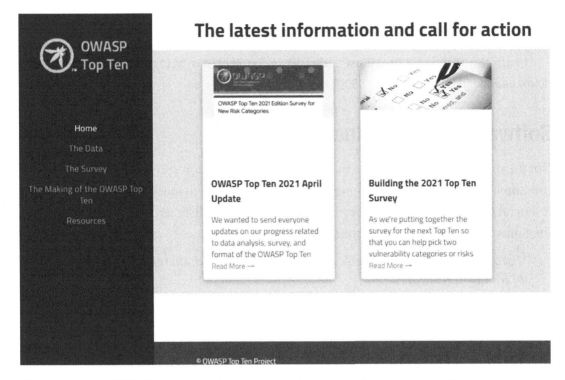

Figure 8-16. *OWASP Top 10 List to support web application security*

You should consider joining the Open Web Application Security Project (OWASP) by going to the following URL: `www.owasptopten.org/`.

Finding Cloud Blind Spots Improves Your Network Security Knowledge

"Microsoft Azure Security Response in the Cloud" is a white paper that helps you understand just how Microsoft investigates, manages, and responds to security incidents within Azure. The URL for download is `https://gallery.technet.microsoft.com/ Azure-Security-Response-in-dd18c678`.

Sometimes customers may not realize the Azure security response Microsoft provides. There is a white paper that helps you understand how Azure investigates, manages, and responds to security incidents. The Azure security incident management program is a critical responsibility for Microsoft and represents an investment for any customer using Microsoft cloud services. The URL for download is `http://aka.ms/ SecurityResponsepaper`.

NVD Use with ITIL/Change Management Patching

The National Vulnerability Database (NVD) provides updated vulnerabilities. The NVD is the US government repository of standards-based vulnerabilities.

You need common understanding of the NVD system, which uses the Common Vulnerability Scoring System (CVSS). CVSS provides an open framework for communicating the characteristics and impacts of IT vulnerabilities. How the individual security vulnerabilities are categorized is by using a list of Common Vulnerabilities and Exposures (CVEs). The CVEs help to quantify the risk of vulnerabilities, calculated from a set of algorithms based on metrics including complexity and availability of a remedy for the vulnerability. Figure 8-17 depicts a site used to understand CVE.

Figure 8-17. *CVE 2021 website to leverage a download list*

Common Vulnerabilities and Exposures is the standard for information security vulnerability. Use the API options for data feed to gain access to content as soon as it is updated.

Security Tip   There are several discussion lists at the NIST NVD website. You can subscribe or update your subscription at `https://nvd.nist.gov/general/email-list`.

Security Responsibility Model

Customers have specific responsibilities to put controls in place, and a Microsoft Azure service has specific responsibility to put controls in place. The security discovery must clearly identify core security of Azure cloud services. The method of investigation is to provide security needs for cloud services your business may use. There are three types of services customers consider when migrating to the cloud: Infrastructure as a Service (IaaS), Platform as a Service (PaaS), and Software as a Service (SaaS). The security requirements are compared to traditional on-premises services including a traditional data center.

Call into question a description of on-premises private clouds identified by the cloud security team. It is a true statement that solutions like Microsoft Azure Stack provides a private cloud solution on-site. However, some teams may confuse virtualization as a private cloud deployment

Microsoft Azure cloud specifically has meet security certifications for regulatory compliance requirements and industry specific requirements, beyond the short list here. You, as a Microsoft Azure customer have access to independently verified cloud services including:

- ISO 27001

- ISO 27018

- SOC 1, 2, 3 Type 2

- CSA STAR 1

Greater details are not included in the executive summary however, father in this chapter, additional information is provided for the specific features and controls the individual management systems. Additionally, the industry specific cloud services are verified include:

- HIPAA BAA

- PCI DSS Level 1

- FERPA

- CDSA

The security certifications are expanded based on US Government requirements and specific to regional or country specific. The first challenge, you may have, if you don't know if your business requires an of these compliance requirements listed, you should align corporate needs for compliance by investing in a security team member or contractor with experience with security audits to help identify company requirements and to validate Azure security attestation.

The problems for a company with security out of compliance may be attributed by growth of Shadow IT. Shadow IT should be addressed quickly with executive security policy and firm enforcement to prevent future security issues. Shadow IT can be described as agile information-technology systems like cloud solutions, created from inside organizations that did not necessary request business approval. When you consider the Azure cloud solutions provide a world-wide datacenter at the cost of a credit card, Shadow IT enables faster prototypes, sometimes referred to as science projects, that may become business critical or revenue generating. Solutions constructed by well-meaning teams almost always do not meet the organization's requirements for control, confidentiality, integrity, availability, and security.

Why it is important

The database provides the Official Common Platform Enumeration (CPE) Dictionary and is a structured naming scheme for information technology systems, software, and packages. The name standard is based on generic syntax for Uniform Resource Identifiers (URI). CPE includes:

- Formal name format

- Method for checking names against a system

- Description format for binding text & tests to the name

The CPE Dictionary hosted and maintained at NIST may be used by nongovernmental organizations, and any company may use the information for work or training.

Summary

In this chapter you were introduced to the historical data of known threat actors and malware tools using the MITRE ATT&CK matrix. In many areas of the Security Operations Center, this information is used by security analysts to prepare for internal red team testing or blue team defense. Additionally, analysts use this data and other data from Microsoft threat intelligence to prepare reports and share with the security team.

The company executives are busy and you learned ways to present relevant security information from reports that help make your security point and provide funding for Azure Sentinel. The need to understand attacker's motivation shown through the metrics, provide the finical or tactical gain of adversaries.

In the next chapter, you begin to put all of this learning together and continue to learn Azure Sentinel through daily operations.

CHAPTER 9

Azure Sentinel Operations

With Azure Sentinel, a cloud-native SIEM service, many of the traditional areas demanding updates are no longer part of the required services. This includes routing maintenance for hardware, updates, patching, and more. Those resources could be migrated to other roles to support the overall success of the Security Operations Center (SOC). This is one of the legs of the triangle for people, processes, and technology.

The most important service updates for you to focus on include the updating of skills for people and refinement of processes in your SOC. There are different levels of experiences, and this chapter guides you on some of the efficiencies that support the maturity of the Security Operations Team mission.

In this chapter you learn

- Modern SOC structure

- Workbooks

- Playbooks

- Notebooks

- Log management

Modern Security Operations Center Structure

There are different sizes of organizations from small and medium businesses with a handful of SOC team members to exceptionally large enterprises with 24/7 support in multiple locations. One of the critical components is for the SOC team to work together and allow Azure Sentinel to provide the built-in Artificial Intelligence (AI) to resolve alerts. This is part of the Security Orchestration, Automation, and Response (SOAR) built into Azure Sentinel and other Microsoft Defender platforms. Azure Sentinel SOAR is a tier 0 support, and then skilled security experts are engaged. Review Figure 9-1 to have a better perspective of work streams supported by a tier 1 SOC analyst.

© Marshall Copeland 2021
M. Copeland, *Cloud Defense Strategies with Azure Sentinel*, https://doi.org/10.1007/978-1-4842-7132-2_9

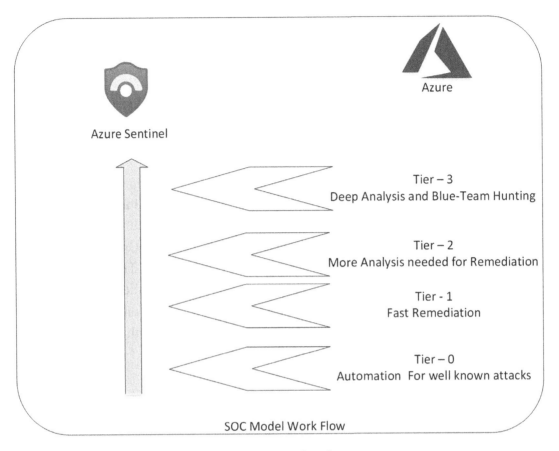

Figure 9-1. Microsoft modern SOC support level

SOC efficiencies can be measured with metrics that help improve overall efficiencies of Security Operations Center teams. Security engineers and security architects work together to enable the appropriate data connectors for acquiring volumes of data that are useful and cover the entire business with Azure Sentinel. As you recall from Chapter 2, there are additional Microsoft cloud services that are also part of the SOC portals and tools. One of the main tools that is used is Microsoft Defender for Endpoint with its integration into Azure Sentinel.

As a security engineer or security architect, one of the GitHub locations for you to review monthly for update is found at `https://github.com/Azure/Azure-Sentinel`. It is this top parent location where all other code repositories are located. Topics include (short list)

- Dashboards

- Detections

- Hunting queries

- Notebooks

- Playbooks

- Workbooks

An area that the SOC team should review as supported by Microsoft and Microsoft partners is **Azure Sentinel** Solutions. Azure Sentinel Solutions provide a partner supported extension workflow using the Azure Market Place deployment process directly into your Azure Sentinel work stream. Similar to other Microsoft partner marketplace solutions it is a single-step deployment to enhance SOC scenarios in Azure Sentinel. Each solution from the individual provider or partner is launched outside of Azure Sentinel workflow and the Azure Portal. The challenge may be in understanding and knowing where to gain support for each solution as each is governed by the Azure Market place licensing contracts separately from your Azure resource services contract. Refer to Figure 9-2.

Figure 9-2. *Support options when you enable Azure Sentinel Solutions*

This partner support is not included as Microsoft support with your Azure Support plans so notice the options with enablement and Microsoft Partner Center for Solutions' authoring and publishing. The solution link is included in the parent GitHub location but should be called out because of the strength of this offering. You can find them directly at Azure-Sentinel/Solutions at master · Azure/Azure-Sentinel · GitHub.

As a SOC manager, you may find that much of the detailed security integration creates security alerts in Azure Sentinel, and the individual management can be performed to include Defender for Endpoint, Servers, or SQL. You can triage the security alerts in the appropriate portal and resolve them. There is no immediate need to recreate automation with Azure Logic Apps in Azure Sentinel.

Microsoft provides a simple Kusto query to quickly review operator data:

```
SecurityIncident
| summarize arg_max(LastModifiedTime, *) by IncidentNumber
```

However, as you continue to ingest data, tune, and filter alerts, you would like to use the guidance provided by the Microsoft Azure team. One of the first frameworks you should consider in an Azure Sentinel test environment would be the Security Operations Center Process Framework. It was originally created as a larger collaboration with Microsoft with a focus on supporting customers new to Azure Sentinel and how to best evolve a modern SOC team.

Note   The SOC Process Framework is a community-created workbook and an excellent source to begin best practices and organize a workflow in Azure Sentinel. This workbook is optional to deploy.

ENABLE THE SOC PROCESS FRAMEWORK

You can read more information from the Sentinel community blog post at

https://techcommunity.microsoft.com/t5/azure-sentinel/what-s-new-azure-sentinel-soc-process-framework-workbook/ba-p/2339315.

1. From the Azure Sentinel portal, select the Workbooks view.

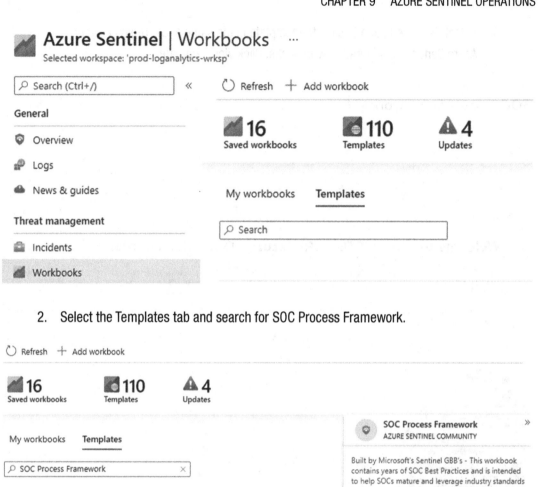

2. Select the Templates tab and search for SOC Process Framework.

3. Select the Save option to save the template in the same Azure region as your Azure Sentinel configuration workbooks. Click View template.

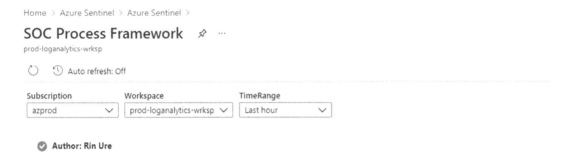

4. Now you can add the subscription name and Log Analytics workspace to use, and select a time range. Click the save icon at the top of the screen.

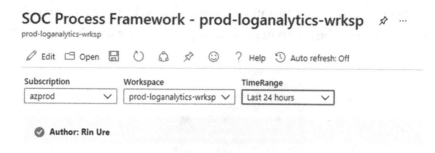

SOC Process Framework - prod-loganalytics-wrksp 📌 ⋯
prod-loganalytics-wrksp

✎ Edit   ⬜ Open   💾   ↻   ⌂   📌   ☺   ? Help   🕐 Auto refresh: Off

Subscription	Workspace	TimeRange
azprod ⌄	prod-loganalytics-wrksp ⌄	Last 24 hours ⌄

✓ Author: Rin Ure

5.   Optionally you can select to edit the workbook and press Ctrl+F from your keyboard to find and replace [CUSTOMER] with the Security Operations Center name. Remember to select DONE EDITING when you have updated the name.

6.   Begin to explore the different areas used to organize your new Security Operations Center by entering data. Start with the first menu option, SOC Main, and continue from there.

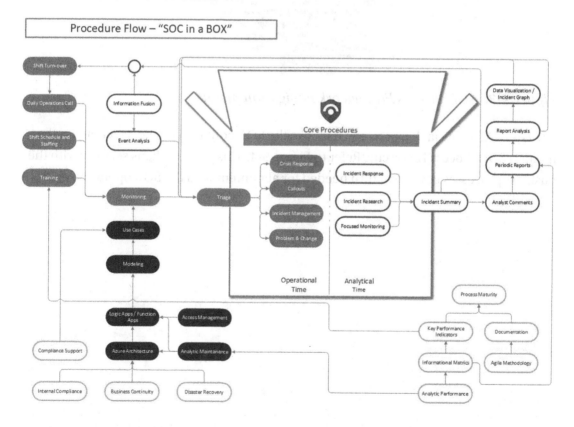

Procedure Flow – "SOC in a BOX"

This workbook requires exploration by the SOC manager and the entire team to collaborate and edit for customization.

As you start to work through the information provided by the Azure SOC Process Framework, you navigate the different areas of support as provided in Figure 9-3.

Figure 9-3. SOC Process Framework navigation menu

The SOC team can begin to edit data like the SOC contact list. The next item on the menu is SOC Process Hierarchy. Refer to Figure 9-4. This section aligns security with the business processes that are in turn needed for alignment with the SOC operation goals.

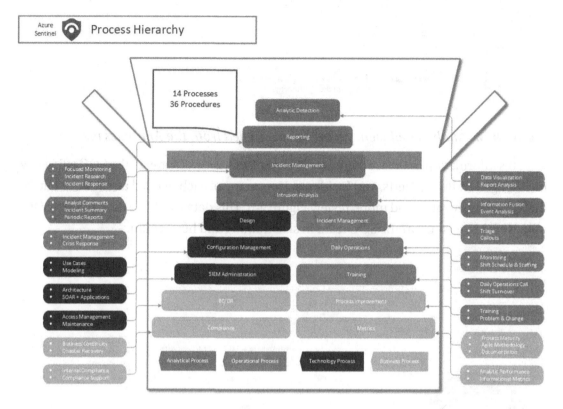

Figure 9-4. *Security process hierarchy*

Workbooks

Azure Sentinel workbooks allow security analysts and security engineers to view data about security in their Azure Sentinel environments. The data is presented in a graphical format and can be queried and reviewed, and the workbooks support editing for customization.

Begin by identifying workbooks to support the SOC goals and missions. One good place to start is using information identified in the built-in workbook. It supports the business drivers for additional security analyst positions based on the workload. An example can be seen in Figure 9-5 in the operations efficiency workbook template that is enabled in the top of the console from the Analytics view.

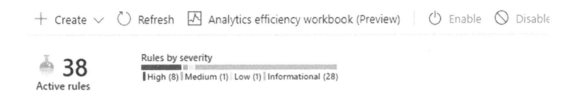

Figure 9-5. *Analytics efficiency workbook enabled from the Analytics view*

This information in the workbook provides a quick view of some of the SOC efficiency including Alert Rules, Alerts, and Incidents. How many of each needed attention, what is the Alert closure rates, and more, review Figure 9-6. This data would be used to help SOC managers better support the SOC team in skill training and head count.

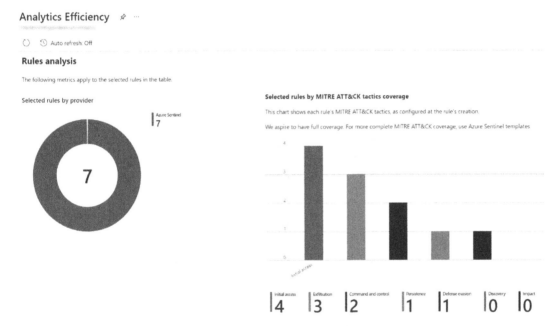

Figure 9-6. *Azure Sentinel SOC efficiency workbook*

SOC team members monitor and resolve alerts according to an incident response (IR) plan. Your team should work through tabletop exercises during a controlled test. The tabletop exercise is a great way to prepare to resolve alerts before there is a production security incident.

Note   One starting place is to review the NIST guidance to test and train, from `https://nvlpubs.nist.gov/nistpubs/Legacy/SP/nistspecialpublication800-84.pdf`.

The SOC team should start to create some automatic workflow responses, such as validating there are no Azure service health issues, from the site `https://status.azure.com/en-us/status`.

Review data connectors for new previews. An example is shown in Figure 9-7, by selecting Data connectors and filtering on Microsoft. Updates and changes are enabled through Microsoft partner releases and as other data connectors are released like the Azure Information Protection data connector.

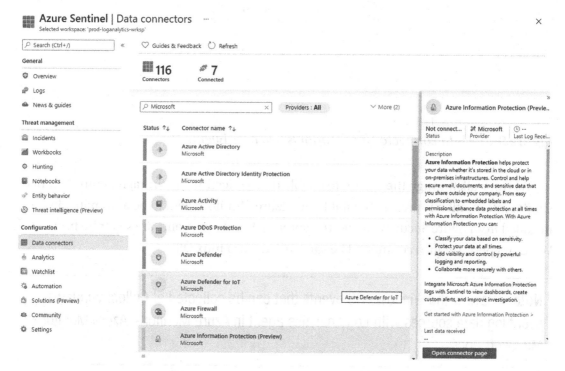

Figure 9-7. *Microsoft data connectors in preview for review*

As Microsoft receives feedback from customers on feature requests to benefit their businesses, you begin to see additional data connectors. Another example is the Windows Security Events data connector shown in Figure 9-8. If your SOC has fewer resources, then take time to open the connector page and read the prerequisites. This connector requires Azure Arc to be installed to collect data from non-Azure VMs.

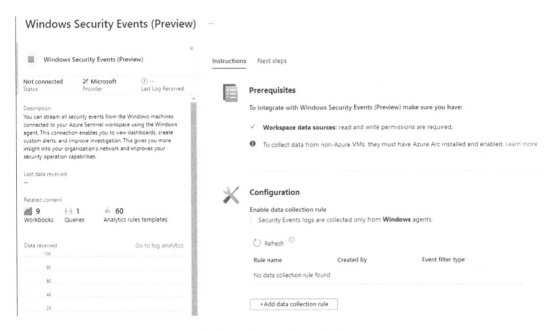

Figure 9-8. *Data connector for Windows Security Events*

As you walk through the wizard to enable data collection on virtual machines, notice similar information is present to enable the Azure Monitor agent to be automatically installed from Azure Security Center (Chapter 3). Windows events are separate from Windows performance counters. The same is true for Linux OS.

Note   Review the Windows OS events that can be collected at Collect Windows event log data sources with Log Analytics agent in Azure Monitor – Azure Monitor | Microsoft Docs.

An additional task is for SOC engineers to review, validate, and then update the current Sentinel workbooks that are in use. As seen in Figure 9-9, there are four updates for Microsoft workbooks. Again, this is another process to evaluate the changes and validate they do not disrupt production workflow.

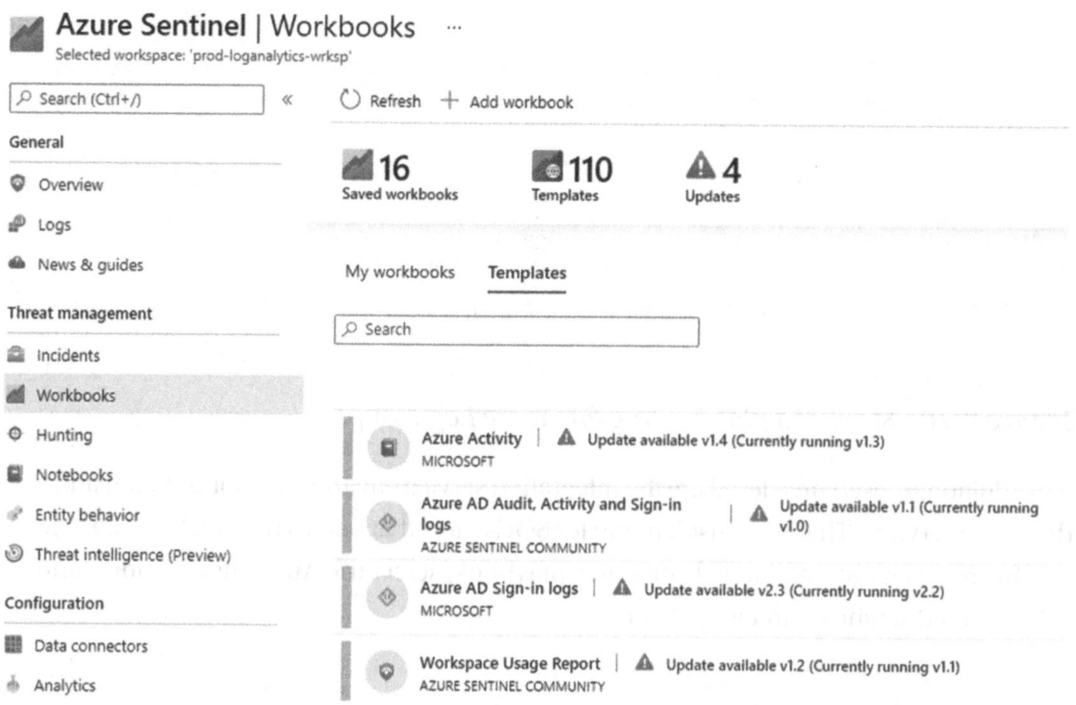

Figure 9-9. *Workbook updates to add new benefits to the SOC*

Playbooks

Azure Sentinel playbooks are very often associated with automation rules to make collections of procedures more useful when they are run with Azure Sentinel. These automated playbooks are used to quickly respond to an alert or incident that was not resolved with the built-in SOAR components. A playbook can be configured to run automatically when specific alerts or incidents are generated. Playbooks require another Azure automation service called Azure Logic Apps.

An example of playbook use would be to prevent actions of a compromised user's credentials from accessing and exfiltrating data to a remote command and control (C2) network outside of your organization. To create a playbook, you need to know more about Azure Log Apps. There is a cost associated with running Logic Apps, and you can choose between a standard plan and consumption plan, as shown in Figure 9-10.

Standard Plan

The Logic Apps Standard plan supports local development on Windows, Linux and Mac, offers a new layout engine that supports complex workflows, and enables custom connector extensions. Leverage the containerized runtime to run Logic Apps locally, in the cloud, or on premises with virtual network capabilities.

	Price (per hour)
vCPU	$0.192
Memory	$0.0137

Figure 9-10. *Standard plan pricing for Azure Logic Apps*

Additional costs considered are the integration service environment for isolation and dedicated services. This is a consideration for SOC teams that need a high scale of activity.

To create an automation rule or a new playbook, select the Automation option and select Create, as shown in Figure 9-11.

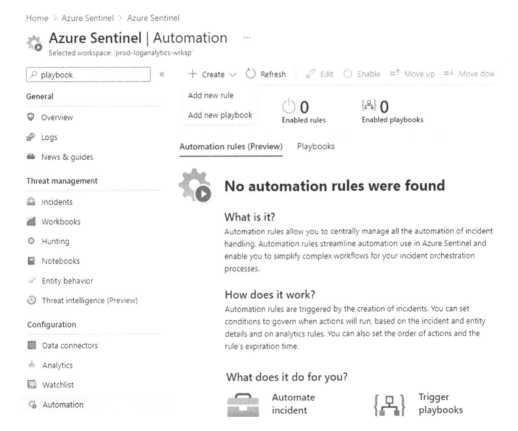

Figure 9-11. *Create a new playbook or automation rule*

The process will have you create an Azure logic app that will be used to enable the automation, as shown in Figure 9-12.

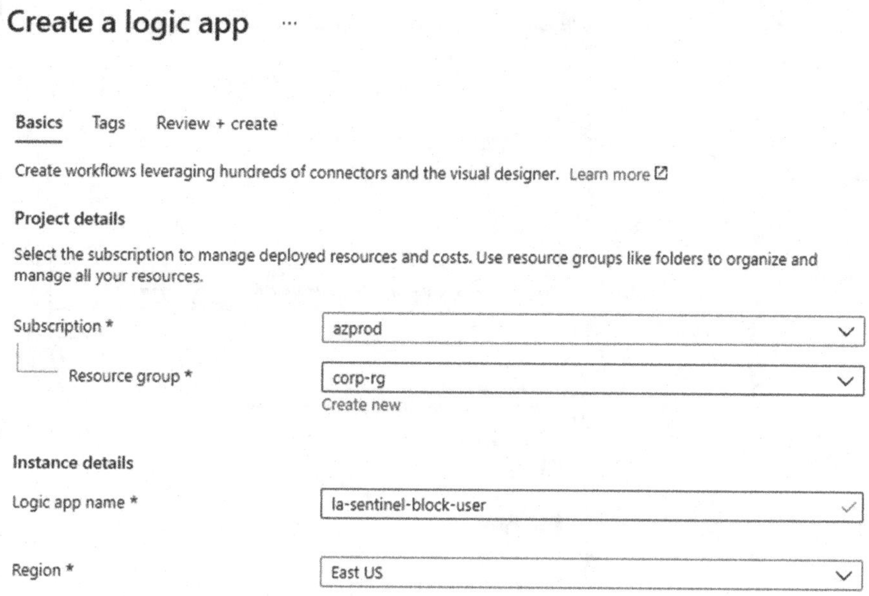

Figure 9-12. *Create a logic app for use in Azure playbook automation*

Once you create the logic app, the incident trigger workflow is provided in the Azure Logic Apps designer console as shown in Figure 9-13.

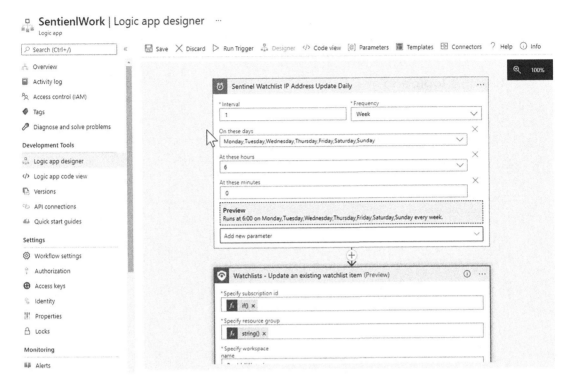

Figure 9-13. *Logic Apps designer decision tree example*

Before you create a playbook from scratch, review the repository at Azure-Sentinel/
Playbooks at master · Azure/Azure-Sentinel · GitHub. This is a listing of Azure playbooks
that can be imported and customized for your Azure Sentinel environment. Refer to
Figure 9-14.

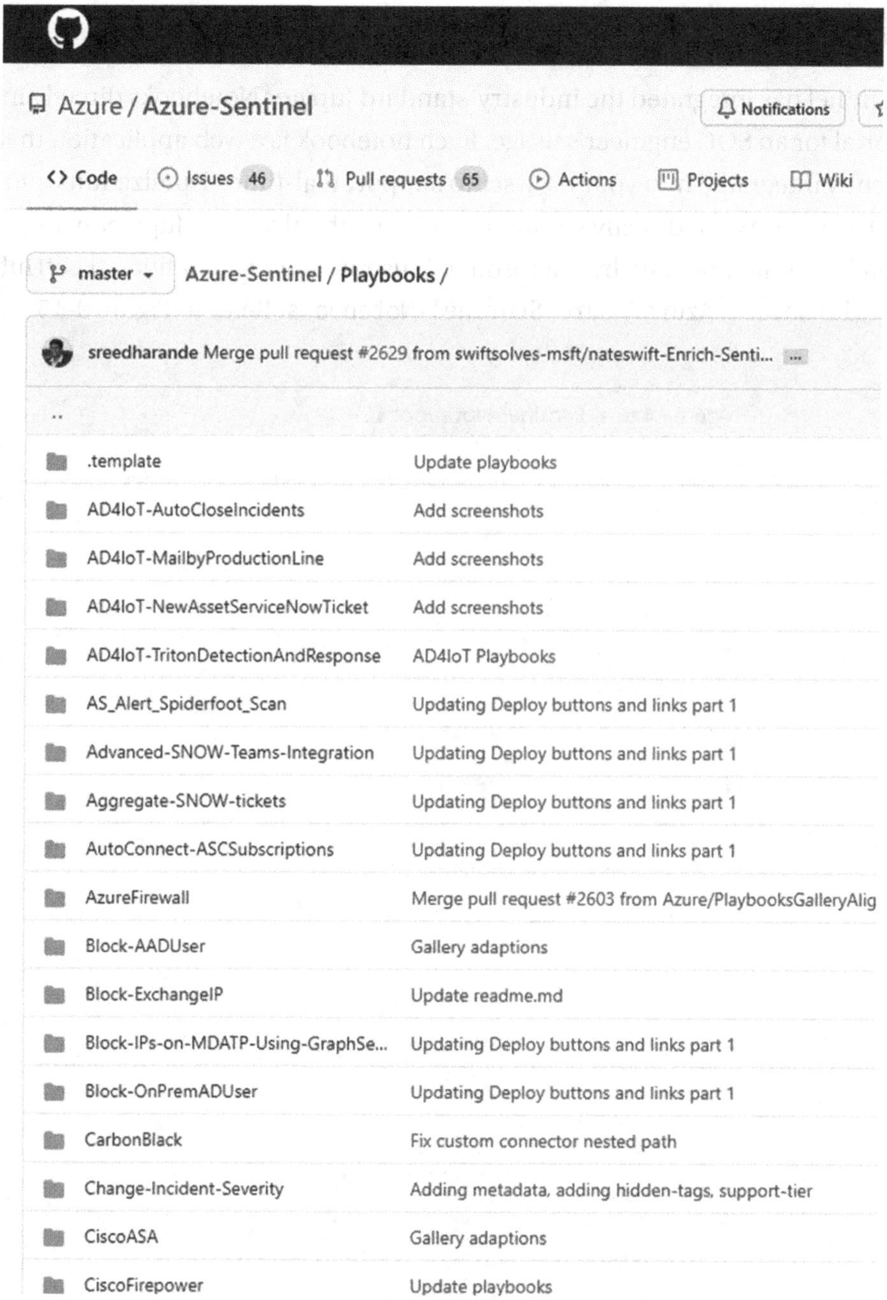

Figure 9-14. *GitHub repository of Azure Sentinel playbooks for consideration*

Notebooks

Azure Sentinel has integrated the industry-standard Jupyter Notebooks directly into Azure Portal for an SOC engineer's usage. Each notebook is a web application that is conveniently integrated into your browser to support real-time visualizations and code queries. The queries run directly within the browser, thanks to the Jupyter backend. A few notebooks are provided by Microsoft to illustrate their capabilities at GitHub: `https://github.com/Azure/Azure-Sentinel-Notebooks`. Refer to Figure 9-15.

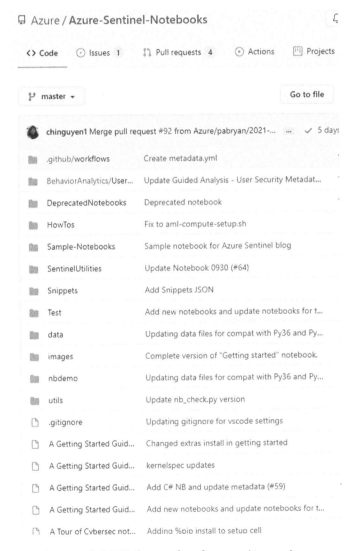

Figure 9-15. *Azure Sentinel GitHub notebook repository view*

Notebooks have two security benefit elements to be aware of:

- A browser-based interface, where you enter and run queries and code and where the results of the executions are displayed

- A kernel that is responsible for parsing and executing the code itself

Each Azure Sentinel notebook that uses "kernel" runs on an Azure virtual machine (VM). Several licensing options exist to leverage more powerful virtual machines if your notebooks include complex machine learning models. The Azure Sentinel notebooks use many popular Python libraries such as pandas, matplotlib, and other modules, including AI modules. There are many other Python packages to choose from, supporting SOC security areas like

- Visualizations

- Analysis

- Data processing

- Statistics

- Machine learning

Additionally, Microsoft has released open source Jupyter security tools in a package named msticpy. This package is already included in the current notebooks. Msticpy tools are designed exclusively to support the SOC team when creating notebooks for hunting and anomaly investigation. For more information, see the MSTIC Jupyter and Python Security Tools documentation at https://msticpy.readthedocs.io/en/latest/.

Log Management

There is no reason to bring all of the security log data and logging information into Azure Sentinel, only the logs that are needed for managing an overall view of security health from Azure Sentinel. Security Operations Center engineers should routinely validate the quality of data and the amount of data and provide cost validation through saved Kusto Query Language queries that should be exercised when required. If you are managing your security endpoint with Microsoft Azure Defender for Endpoint, use that solution and integrate it with Azure Sentinel. The same is true for other non-Microsoft endpoint solutions. If your team is resolving endpoint alerts in that product, you can easily integrate the data with Azure Sentinel for a complete view. Copying all data for Azure Sentinel is not necessary and should be filtered based on security requirements.

As a simple reminder, the use of Azure Sentinel with the Log Analytics workspace has no additional cost for the first 31 days. However, charges related to Log Analytics and automation (Logic Apps) do apply during any trial period. Usage beyond the first 31 days is charged per workload and can be estimated using the following URL: `https://azure.microsoft.com/pricing/details/azure-sentinel`. Refer to Table 9-1.

Table 9-1. *Azure Sentinel data type and cost*

Data Type	No Additional Cost or Additional Cost
AzureActivity	No Additional Cost
SecurityAlert	No Additional Cost
OfficeActivity (SharePoint, Exchange, Teams)	No Additional Cost
SecurityAlert (Azure Defender, IoT, ASC)	No Additional Cost
Microsoft Defender for Endpoint, SecurityAlert (MDATP)	No Additional Cost
Microsoft Defender for Identity, SecurityAlert (AATP)	No Additional Cost
Microsoft Cloud App Security, SecurityAlert (MCAS)	No Additional Cost
MCASShadowITReporting	Yes, Additional Cost

Note   Data storage in the Log Analytics workspace can reduce cost. However, it is important for the SOC data team to understand the data size for ingestion before adding it.

There are additional data sources that are used to ingest data. As you learned in this chapter, even if there is not an additional cost to the ingestion, there is the cost of storage. You should use these tables to best identify data to be saved for 90 days in the Log Analytics workspace or moved to long-term storage. Refer to Table 9-2.

Table 9-2. *Microsoft 365 Defender data type and cost*

Data Type	No Additional Cost or Additional Cost
SecurityIncident	No Additional Cost
SecurityAlert	No Additional Cost
DeviceEvents	Yes, Additional Cost
DeviceFileEvents	Yes, Additional Cost
DeviceInfo	Yes, Additional Cost
DeviceLogonEvents	Yes, Additional Cost
DeviceNetworkInfo	Yes, Additional Cost
DeviceProcessEvents	Yes, Additional Cost
DeviceRegistryEvents	Yes, Additional Cost
DeviceFileCertificationInfo	Yes, Additional Cost

Note   You should review the Azure Monitor Log Analytics pricing at `https://azure.microsoft.com/pricing/details/log-analytics/`.

Logging metrics and data have been discussed throughout the book, specifically in Chapters 2 and 4. You can refer to Figure 9-16 for a reminder of logs and their value for the SOC team.

Microsoft Azure Security LOG Reference

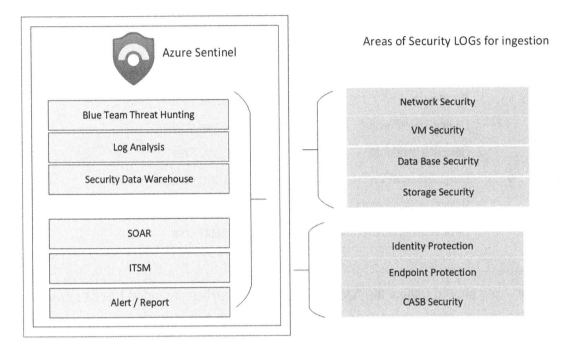

Figure 9-16. *Azure Sentinel log logical view*

Using the Kusto Query Language is a quick approach to managing log data ingestion and log costs overall. These logs are provided by Microsoft and the Azure Sentinel community. You should create weekly procedures to run these queries manually to gain understanding of data in the Azure Sentinel workspace.

Review the "AzureActivity" table with a filter for "security insights" to reveal nonspecific actions completed. In the Azure Sentinel platform, select the Logs view, then type the query into the New Query tab, and select Run, as shown in Figure 9-17. You would complete the same sequence to run each query provided in this section.

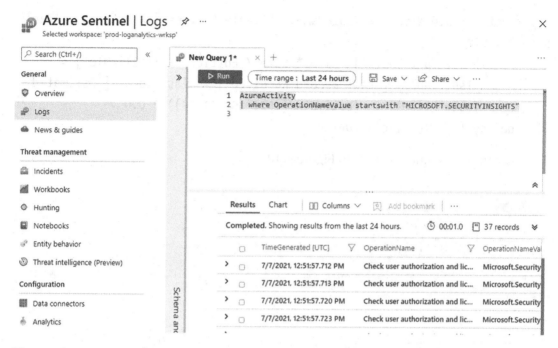

Figure 9-17. *Azure log query to display AzureActivity table data performed from the Logs view*

```
AzureActivity
| where OperationNameValue startswith "MICROSOFT.SECURITYINSIGHTS"
```

The next example requires you to enable the Log Analytics workspace in the diagnostics settings.

```
LAQueryLogs
| where TimeGenerated > ago(7d)
| summarize events_count=count() by bin(TimeGenerated, 1d)
```

The next example is used to display log data and list the billable cost that each entry provides. This query also displays the current size of data for each table. Figure 9-18 shows the following query run in a small test environment:

```
union withsource=TableName1 *
| where TimeGenerated > ago(30d)
| summarize Entries = count(), Size = sum(_BilledSize), last_log =
datetime_diff("second",now(), max(TimeGenerated)), estimate  =
sumif(_BilledSize, _IsBillable==true)  by TableName1, _IsBillable
```

```
| project ['Table Name'] = TableName1, ['Table Entries'] = Entries, ['Table
Size'] = Size,
          ['Size per Entry'] = 1.0 * Size / Entries, ['IsBillable'] =
          _IsBillable, ['Last Record Received'] = last_log , ['Estimated
          Table Price'] =  (estimate/(1024*1024*1024)) * 0.0
| order by ['Table Size']  desc
```

You can see the query results in Figure 9-18.

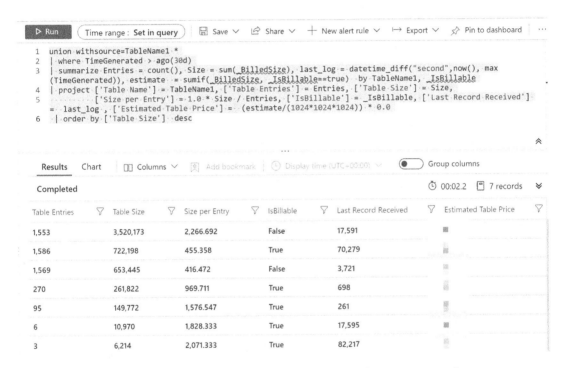

Figure 9-18. *Azure Sentinel query results on billable data types and amounts*

You may want to query Azure Sentinel tables directly, and having the information provided in Table 9-3 would support any custom query efforts.

Table 9-3. *Azure Sentinel commonly used security tables*

Sentinel Table Name	Sentinel Table Description
AzureActivity	Entries from the Azure Activity log, displaying subscription-level or management group–level events.
AzureDiagnostics	Stores resource logs for Azure services; resource logs describe the internal operation of the Azure resource.
AuditLogs	Audit log for Azure Active Directory. This is related to the AAA security compliance reviewed in Chapter 6.
CommonSecurityLog	Syslog messages using the Common Event Format (CEF).
McasShadowItReporting	Microsoft Cloud App Security logs, the integration between Defender solutions.
OfficeActivity	Office 365 tenants that are collected by Azure Sentinel data connectors like Exchange, SharePoint, and Microsoft Teams.
SecurityEvent	Security events from an agent installed on Windows machines from Azure Security Center (ASC) or Azure Sentinel direct logs.
SigninLogs	Azure Activity Directory sign-in.
Syslog	Events on Linux computers using the Log Analytics agent; the agent extension must be installed.
Event	Sysmon events collected from a Windows host.
WindowsFirewall	Windows Firewall events.

Summary

This final chapter is part of the Azure Sentinel journey to improve on your Security Operations Center deployment and processes. In this chapter you were introduced to the processes for improving a modern SOC structure. You continued to understand the value of Azure Sentinel SOAR (automation) using workbooks, playbooks, and notebooks for Azure Sentinel.

You now realize that Azure Sentinel log management is a process that has cost for both ingesting the data and storing the data. The long-term storage should be a consideration if the data is to be queried with KQL or stored for compliance. Log management requires planning and understanding of the security data needed for your Azure Sentinel deployment.

Index

A

Active Directory Domain
 Services (AD DS), 81, 166
Advanced persistent threat (APT), 217
Advanced Threat Protection (ATP), 91
Adversarial Tactics, Techniques, and
 Common Knowledge (ATT&CK)
 framework, 9
Application Insights, 80
Application Programing
 Interface (API), 102
Artificial Intelligence (AI), 4, 255
Authentication, Authorization, and
 Auditing (AAA), 164
Azure Active Directory
 (AAD), 7, 61, 165, 182
Azure Defender services, 81
Azure Diagnostics, 80
Azure Logic Apps, 82
Azure Monitor
 data sources, 49, 50, 52–54
 enable metrics, 45–48
 guest OS data, 42–44
Azure Monitor service, 80
Azure Resource Manager (ARM), 20, 108
Azure Security Center, 81
Azure security services
 cloud native services, 57, 59, 60
 identity, 61
 log analytics, 40, 41

Microsoft Defender, Endpoint, 61, 63,
 64, 68–71
Microsoft Defender, identity, 71, 73–75
monitor, 42
security center, 55, 56
Azure Sentinel, 83
 agile deployment, 8
 AI, 255
 benefits, 4
 CI/CD pipeline, 7
 cloud service, 4
 data ingestion
  data connectors, 27
  enable data connectors, 28–30, 32,
   34–36, 38
 definition, 255
 design/cost preparation
  cyber kill chain stages, 10
  Log Analytics, 8
  MITRE ATT&CK, 11, 12
  sentinel data storage cost, 12, 14
  SIEM, 14, 16
  soft areas, 9
 integration, 5, 6
 LOC management, 273, 274, 276–278
 logs, 17, 19
 metrics, 19–21, 24, 26
 Microsoft solutions, 7
 notebooks, 272, 273
 PaaS, 3

© Marshall Copeland 2021
M. Copeland, *Cloud Defense Strategies with Azure Sentinel*, https://doi.org/10.1007/978-1-4842-7132-2

Azure Sentinel (*cont.*)
 playbooks, 267, 268, 270, 271
 SMEs, 4, 5
 SOC, 256, 258, 260, 262, 263
 solutions, 257
 workbooks, 263–267
Azure Sentinel console, 79

B

Big data projects, 113
Bring your own threat intelligence
 (BYOTI), 154

C

Capital expenditures (Capex), 232
Certified Ethical Hacking (CEH), 246
Chief Information Security Officer (CISO)
 attacks, 235
 definition, 231
 KPIs, 232
 KRIs, 232
 SLA, 232
 vulnerability, 233
Cloud service providers (CSPs), 77
Cloud workload protection (CWP), 82
Command and Control (C2) phase, 217
Common Event Format (CEF), 7, 102
Common Vulnerabilities and Exposures
 (CVE), 146, 251
Common Vulnerability Scoring System
 (CVSS), 251
Control plane, 107, 109, 110
Cyber Kill Chain model, 215
Cyber-observable Objects, 151
Cybersecurity threats
 cloud architecture, 237

cloud networking/encryption/data
 storage, 248
data breaches, 236
DBIR, 236, 240–244
MFA, 248, 249
network security, 250
NVD, 251, 252
Ponemon institute, IBM sponsored,
 244–246
SDLC, 249, 250
security analysis, 237
security responsibility model, 252, 253
SIR, 238, 239
URL, 247
Cyber threat intelligence (CTI), 136, 146, 151

D

Data Breach Investigations Report (DBIR),
 102, 147, 234, 236
Data connector, 126
Data logs, 112
Data plane, 107, 110
Data veracity, 113
Democratization, 79

E, F

Enterprise Agreement (EA), 71
Extended Detection and Response (XDR),
 78, 87, 90, 91

G, H

General Data Protection Regulation
 (GDPR), 26
Global Technology
 Resources Inc. (GTRI), 234

I, J

Identity and Access
Management (IAM), 167
Indicators of compromise (IOC), 89, 145
Infrastructure as a Service (IaaS), 6, 81,
163, 187, 252
Intelligent Security Graph, 156

K

Key performance indicators (KPIs), 232, 234
Key risk indicators (KRIs), 232, 234
Kusto query language (KQL), 49, 80, 107,
126, 127, 155
Azure resources, 186
column data types, 129
data retention, 187
example, 192
LAW, 185, 186
log analytics, 211
log/metric data, 188
operator, 193
results, 196
sentinel analytics access, 190, 191
skills, 135
structure, 192
training, 189
update query, 194, 195, 198, 199, 201,
202, 204
workflow pipeline, 194

L

Limo services, 142
Log Analytics, query demo site, 128
Log Analytics workspace, 123, 124
Log Analytics workspace (LAW), 80, 88,
123, 124, 172, 185

M

Malware Information Sharing Platform
(MISP), 146
Managed Security Service Providers
(MSSPs), 182
Microsoft 365 Defender, 91, 92, 99
Microsoft 365 security center, 100
Microsoft Defender, 158
Microsoft Defender for Endpoint (MDE), 89
Microsoft Defender for Identity (MDI), 81
Microsoft Defender security, 99
Microsoft Monitoring Agent (MMA), 60
Microsoft Threat Intelligence Center
(MSTIC), 150
MITRE ATT&CK framework
attackers/malwares, 222
C2 phase, 217
columns view, 219
definition, 214
delivery phase, 216
exfiltration, 217
exploitation/installation, 217
kill chain model, 215, 218
matrix, 214, 215, 254
measures, 221
navigation, 222, 225–227, 229–231
reconnaissance, 216
technique, 220, 221
weaponization, 216
msticpy, 273
Multi-factor Authentication (MFA), 249
Multi-tenant architecture
AAD, 169
AD DS, 165, 166
Azure design, 171
security operations center, 171
sentinel leverages, 170

Multi-tenant architecture (*cont.*)
 Azure security platform
  endpoint integrations view, 180
  identity integration, 181
  performance counters, 179
  servers/SQL, 182
  services, 178
  SOC team, 176
 multi-workspace, 174–176
 RBAC, 167
 sentinel, 168
 single-workspace, 172, 173
 users, 164

N

National Institute of Standards and
  Technology (NIST), 233, 247
National Vulnerability Database (NVD),
  146, 233, 251
Network Mapper (NMAP), 216

O

One-to-many management model, 182
Open source intelligence (OSINT), 146
Open Web Application Security Project
  (OWASP), 249, 250
Operating system (OS), 4, 40, 80
Operational expenditures (OPEX), 232

P

Platform as a Service (PaaS), 3, 163, 252
Proof of concept (POC), 14

Q

Query syntax, 130

R

Read Only locks, 109
Role-Based Access Control (RBAC),
  61, 108, 165, 182

S

Security Information and Event
  Management (SIEM) service,
  4, 14, 77, 79
Security Intelligence Report (SIR), 102,
  147, 234, 238, 239
Security Operations Center (SOC),
  15, 17, 78, 79, 83, 90, 108, 111,
  172, 214, 255
 terminology, 86
 workflow/skill levels, 87
Security Operations Centers (SOCs), 9
Security operations (SecOps), 42
Security Orchestration, Automation, and
  Response (SOAR), 3, 82, 255
Security subject matter experts (SMEs), 86
Sentinel threat intelligence data, 156
Sentinel Threat Intelligence
  Platforms, 157
Service-Level Agreement
  (SLA), 232
Software as a Service (SaaS), 252
Software-defined network (SDN), 3
Software Development
  Lifecycle (SDLC), 249
Storage account, 111
Structured Threat Information Expression
  (STIX), 151, 152
Subject matter expert (SME), 5, 40
System Center Operations Manager
  (SCOM), 80

T

Technical threat indicators (TTIs), 10
THALLIUM rule, 161
Threat Connect Open (TC Open), 156
Threat hunting
    cybersecurity, 205, 206
    notebook template, sentinel, 210
    queries, 208
    sentinel solution view, 209
    sentinel view, 207
    SOC, 205
Threat intelligence (TI), 81, 90, 137, 145, 146
Trusted Automated Exchange of
      Intelligence Information (TAXII),
      136, 151, 153

U

User and Entity Behavior Analytics
    (UEBA), 102

V

Virtual machine (VM), 4, 55, 80, 108
Virtual networks (VNets), 108, 248

W, X, Y, Z

Watchlist, 159
Wide Area Network (WAN), 248
Windows Azure
      Diagnostics (WAD), 42